# AN INTRODUCTION TO ZEN THOUGHT

© 1993 by George Richard Yool

ISBN-13: 978-1495269868

ISBN-10: 1495269868

# CONTENTS

## CHAPTER I— Introduction to Zen Thought.........1
Words in Zen ...................2
Dharma..........................6
Paths of Zen ...................7
Buddha-mind and nature .8
Scholasticism.................9
Religion or Philosophy...11

## CHAPTER II— Buddhism ...............................................13
Origins of Buddhism ......13
The Four Noble Truths ..15
The Eightfold Path .........17
Satori, Nirvana, Enlightenment ..........20
After Gautama ...............22
The School of Zen .........25
Harmony and Nature .....28
Faith..............................29

## CHAPTER III— The Evolution of Zen .................31
Bodhidharma .................32
Cultural and Historical Influences.................36
Popular Zen ...................38
The Schools of Zen .......40
The Form of Zen............46

## CHAPTER IV— Yoga Tradition ...........................49
Principles of Yoga..........50
Jnana Yoga ...................51
Bhakti Yoga ...................52
Karma Yoga...................53
Raja Yoga......................55
Yoga and Zen ................57
Eight Elements of Yoga .59

## CHAPTER V— Taoism and the Arts ...................65
Introduction....................65
Evolving Eastern Thought66
The Tao Te Ching..........69
The Tao ........................71
Do in Zen ......................74
Power in Taoism and Zen ..................................75
The Ego ........................77

## CHAPTER VI— Confucianism...........................81
Confucius the Man.........82
The Classics and Teachings ...................................83
Confucianism and Buddhism .................86
Compassion (Ren).........93

## CHAPTER VII— Meditation .................................95
Introduction....................95
Nutrition in Zen ...............96
Meditation and Nutrition.97
Posture ..........................99
Concentration and
    Breathing................101
Zazen...........................104
Koans .........................106
Other Forms of
    Contemplation ........109

## CHAPTER VIII— Schools and Teaching Zen...113
Dokusan ......................120
Dharma Talk ...............122
The Zen Sesshin .........124
Teisho.........................124

## CHAPTER IX— The Far Side of Zen ..................127
The Far Side...............127
Humility.......................128
Humor in Zen..............131
Western Humor ..........132
Zen Humor..................135
Iconoclasm .................139
Profound Icons ...........141
Iconoclasm of Scriptures 142

## CHAPTER X— Science Encounters Zen..........145
Holograms ..................145
Dimensional Physics ...146
Zen .............................149
Chaos and Order.........155

## CHAPTER XI— The Future of Zen .....................157

## Appendix A—Chronologies .................................163
Japan..........................163
China ..........................164
Buddhism....................164
Important Persons .......165

## Alphabetical List of Persons ............................167

## Table of Religions Based on Vedism Key .......169

## Appendix B—Meditation .................................171
Purpose ......................171
Discipline .....................171
Concentration ..............171
Content.........................174
Frequently Asked Questions
.............................176

## Appendix C—Postures......................................179
General Rules..............179
Bound Angle Pose.......179
Burmese ......................179
Lotus Posture (*Padma-asana*) Instruction...179

## Glossary of Zen and Buddhism........................181
A ....181
B ....182
C ....184
D ....184
E ....185
F.....186
G ....186
H ....187
I ......187
J .....187
K ....188
L .....189
M....189
N ....191
O ....191
P ....191
R ....192
S ....192
T.....194
U ....195
V ....196
W ...196
Y ....196
Z.....196

## References ........................................................199

# General Introduction

From my experience, general audiences do not read introductions, prologues, and forewords. It is usually the experienced researcher, or a professor that is using the book for a class that reads these materials. For this reason, I will direct this introduction to the professionals who are most likely to read it. I have structured the first chapter of this book to contain matter that often goes into an introduction. It also contains important terminology, making it a necessary chapter to the rest of the book. I did this intentionally so that the laymen would read it. A book is useless if the audience does not first know how to use it.

If you are reading this, then you must be serious about the subject matter of this book. As such, you should be made aware of other materials that would compliment your understanding of this book. It seems traditional for professors to expect students to purchase extra materials that are expensive. What I am suggesting will not do much damage to anyone's pocketbook. It is necessary though that the extra materials be read with the appropriate chapters, if they are to help bring more breadth and depth to these topics. These materials are extra. They are not absolutely essential to this book. All essential information is adequately provided in the text. In the following list the title and author of each book I recommend is listed with the appropriate chapter. These books are also listed in the references section of this book.

Tao Te Ching, by Lao Tse. Chapter 5, Taoism.
The Analects of Confucius. Chapter 6, Confucianism.
The Art of Peace, by Morihei Ueshiba. Chapter 7, Meditation.
Zen in the Art of Archery, by Eugen Herrigel. Chapter 8, Schools and Teaching Zen.
Any collection of The Far Side comics by Gary Larson, and other materials on humor. Chapter 9, The Far Side of Zen.
Zen Mind, Beginner's Mind, by Shunryu Suzuki. Chapter 11, The Future of Zen.

These books all have two things in common, they are all very short, and relatively inexpensive. I suggest not to get editions that are heavily laden with interpretations and scholasticism. Those are both expensive, and misguiding. It is better for each individual to interpret for him or her self. Other interpretations will only serve to prejudice and separate the reader from his or her self. That is counterproductive to Zen practice. You will find most of these in pocketbook size (4.5" by 3"). They all read quickly, and most are easily read in one sitting.

The primary intention of this book is to introduce the audience to Zen thought. This means that the focus is on concept, not trivial terminology. This book does use a lot of terminology though. Where the terminology is not common, it is defined. The relevant terminology is also defined in the glossary, so that the reader does not have to search through the text for

# An Introduction to Zen Thought

the definitions. With Sanskrit and Pali words I try to provide an English equivalent every time they appear. There are some exceptions though, such as nirvana. Most of the equivalents provided are not accurate to the definition, but are instead intended to remind the audience of the formal definition, which was too long to repeat with every use.

Japan is more intensively examined than China, for reasons that will be obvious as this book unfolds. I try to provide the Japanese equivalent for every Chinese word, and less faithfully the Chinese equivalent for every Japanese word. I do not supply many such equivalencies between Sanskrit and Pali words. Instead I try to maintain the common form of each term, as it appears throughout other works on Zen. Again, this is not intended to be a rigorous study. To provide a rigorous study for a book like this would completely remove the possibility of providing a conceptual understanding. It is not the words here that should be studied, it is the spirit of what is being said.

When you examine the table of contents you may wonder what you are getting into. The table of contents seems to reflect religious studies of Asian cultures. It is important to report the facts, and that is my biggest concern. To say Zen just appeared out of nowhere, with the arrival of Bodhidharma, would be inaccurate. Each of the ideologies are discussed in terms of their influence on the development and ideology of Zen. This requires that some background information is given, so that each perspective can be understood correctly. In the foreground you will find that each of these ideologies fits somewhere into the Four Noble Truths, Eightfold Path, or into the cultural environment.

Since environment is very important to the development of any culture, philosophy, or religion the historical and cultural environment are central themes. Since this book is not a rigorous study, many names and events are never covered in the text. The reader may also find some of the historical information hard to follow. Visualization is a gift that not many people have. To satisfy this problem, Appendix A has chronology tables. These tables are provided to help the reader understand time and geography relationships with events and important persons. With so many topics, the reader is bound to get a little confused, if not terribly lost. Neither of these are productive situations that I hope are resolved with the tables. The chronology tables include: Japanese history, Chinese history, important persons, religions that descended from Vedism, and schools of Buddhism.

As much as possible, the topics are presented with examples. These examples I have tried to draw from common Western experiences. Many examples are provided that are Zen stories. I try to avoid interpreting these stories, or making them difficult to understand. Rather than copy the stories from translations, I usually paraphrase so that the reader can find the concepts easier, and with less reading. Background is often necessary in order to understand many of these stories. For this reason it is necessary to make adjustments so that a modern Western audience can

# An Introduction to Zen Thought

relate. I say modern because many of these stories are at least a century old.

**Using This Book in the Classroom**

This book has been written for two audiences. First, this book was written for general audiences. To fulfill this goal, short sentences and common words have been used, and all important information is provided to make this complete. Second, this was written for universities. The topic matter in this text is conceptual. Technical terms and other specific information are also given. To be most effective in a classroom setting, I suggest that this should be an upper division class. The students should have a background in world religions and philosophies, especially the religions, philosophies, and history of Asia. The more background the better. This is not to say that the background is necessary though. The background will make grasping the concepts easier, and enable the students to participate in classroom discussion intelligently. Any book used for a class should only be a starting point. The classroom discussion should add to the book, not just repeat what the book said. Professors who repeat the textbook often wonder why their students do not attend class. Why bother if all you have to do is read the book?

There is another side to the issue of texts and lectures. The book sets the stage for class discussion. Generally, topics that are discussed in class should be in the book. Topics that are tested on should be covered both in the book, and in the lecture. With a complicated topic like this, it is also essential that the students can freely communicate with the professor. Many of these concepts lose students quickly, especially in lectures. The advantage of the written word is that it can be reviewed many times until it is understood. Lectures are gone before they are finished. If a student gets lost early in the lecture, the rest of the lecture is worthless. Thus it is important that the students all understand each concept before the next one is covered.

This book has been divided into eleven chapters. I suggest lecturing on the first chapter, so that the students can read the second chapter and be prepared for class discussion. In this way the students can be prepared for each topic area of the class. As I already indicated, the first chapter is introductory material. This makes the reading of the first chapter optional in a classroom setting. The number of chapters is convenient for dividing lectures for five week and ten week semesters. As for dividing this over an eighteen-week semester, that would have to be done at the professor's discretion. Personally, I would expand on chapters 4, 5, 7, and 8. The last two chapters are optional. It is very common that a text cannot be completed within the semester. Naturally each professor will perceive his or her own priorities in lecturing. It is choices like this that make the teacher's role important. That was not an option available in the writing of this book.

For both the researcher and the teacher, the glossary in this book can be useful. It is a good starting point for much Buddhist terminology. I did

# An Introduction to Zen Thought

not cover all the possible terminology, but there is a total of 226 entries in the glossary. Teachers should review the glossary for terms important to the lecture that are not in the regular text. In this way, the teacher can provide a means by which the students can get the most from a lecture. It also gives the teacher a starting point for lecture topics that are not in the text, but are still in the book. Students can use the glossary to help understand lectures and other materials used in their research. The glossary is filled with information that is in the text, and even more information that is not in the text. Many of these terms are very relevant to the chapters in this book, and would make good topics for in class discussions. The glossary can also be used for assignments and testing, making it a versatile tool for both education and research. I strongly encourage students, teachers, and laymen to read through the glossary. Yes glossaries are boring. They are boring because they are raw information. As raw information the entries are not intended to be a means or an end, nor do they provide the whole picture. Experience is still more accurate and factual than any amount of words.

### **Additional Comments**

What I feel is not what is important. What you feel is. Zen is not a topic that is meant to be intellectually understood. Zen is like poetry. As one comedian said, grading students on their perceptions of images in poetry is like grading them on their sexual activities. As the author of this book, it was my duty to report the facts. The way you perceive these facts must be your own. You must make your own decisions. My intentions were two fold: first, to convey a conceptual framework for the understanding of Zen; second, to put aside any misconceptions about Zen. When the reader has finished this book they will no longer think of Zen as mystical or magical.

It is important that I make a note here about satori, enlightenment, and nirvana. I define these as being different in this text. You will find other authors treating these terms as synonymous. My descriptions and differentiations between these words are my own interpretations, from my own experiences. You will find upon close examination of other literature, that these interpretations can be applied. The other literature may not create these distinctions because they do not wish to complicate their books. The reason I make this distinction is that I do not want the reader to be misled. Solving a koan does not necessarily result in complete enlightenment, in nirvana. Solving the koan does not mean that the individual has become awakened to their Buddha nature either. This is why I provide distinctions between satori, enlightenment and nirvana.

Zen is a difficult subject to write about. Most books on Zen are intellectual research, experience, or compilations of the teachings of a master. This book is all of these and none. The reader should understand that I lived Zen before I studied it. The reason I studied Zen was so that I could convey my experiences for the benefit of others. I do not, however, specifically address my experiences in Zen practice. I do provide

# An Introduction to Zen Thought

experiences from privately teaching Zen though. The reason for this is that each person must find his or her own path. To report on my own path would be misleading.

The research put into this is mostly for support and specific historical information. The support is usually stories, taken from Zen and Buddhist literature. Quotes are also used to provide the audience with specific concepts that I could not improve on. These include quotes from the Tao Te Ching and the Analects of Confucius.

Read this book in contemplation. Do not bother memorizing. No amount of knowledge can provide the spirit of a teaching. You must look at every topic and apply it to yourself. When you intuitively understand a topic, then you have captured the spirit of that topic. Finally, one last piece of advice: this book does not have all the answers, and nor will you find your own path here. No book can provide these things. No book is perfectly accurate either. This is why the spirit is more important than the words. For every subject for which there is a choice of paths, I illustrate parts of the continuum of choices. There is no way to describe every part of a continuum, because there are an infinite number of points. My reasoning is simple. I cannot show you your path. No one can do that. To make up for this handicap, I show you the questions and the spectra of possibilities. It is then your duty to expand on my elaborations, in order to find what works best for you.

# CHAPTER I—
## Introduction to Zen Thought

Zen is a branch of Buddhist philosophy that focuses on meditation. This book is intended to guide you through the terminology and thoughts associated with Zen. Neither this book nor any other will provide you with a road map to enlightenment. This chapter is here to give you, the reader, a general introduction to Zen. Naturally that means this chapter will cover a number of terms essential in the study of Zen and Buddhism. Though this book discusses the relationships of Zen to other influences, Buddhism is still considered the original source of Zen. It is from the Mahayana School of Buddhism, in China, that Zen finds its historical roots. For this reason, the central theme of this chapter, and subsequently this entire book, is the posture assumed by Buddhism in Zen. Thus every ideology introduced will be examined from the perspective of Buddhist themes, and specific influences or complements made by those ideologies to Zen.

First, the reader should be aware of the word Zen. This name comes to us through its popular form found in Japan, and is literally translated as meditation. The Zen thought this book identifies is general, not adhering to a particular school of Zen. The reason for this is that Zen has assumed different postures in different cultures. The culture that Zen is most prominent in, at the time of this writing, is the Japanese culture. Japan is not the point of origin of Zen. Zen came to Japan through China and Korea. Other countries also adopted Zen. The only traditions that will be reported here are those found in Japan and China (where Zen is called Ch'an), and to a limited extent the West. This is not meant to deny or disparage the quality or traditions of Zen in other countries. On the contrary, I advise seeking out information on these traditions. You must remember that any tradition can easily fill volumes of books. It is not the purpose of this book to contain all that is Zen thought. No book, or any amount of books can accomplish this. This book is not intended to be a rigorous study of Zen thought either. Zen is not intended to be intellectually interpreted. It is also not the purpose of this book to persuade you to live Zen.

This book is a scientific approach to Zen. For this reason this book will cover several broad topics to help illustrate Zen thought. This book will not make you think Zen. Only you can do that. By writing this book I admit that I am diminishing the value of Zen thought. For this reason I constantly emphasize living Zen, because Zen is beyond words. Trying to describe Zen thought is like trying to describe childbirth to a class of men. The men just cannot experience it, so they cannot understand the complete image. Thus this book only represents a superficial image of Zen thought. This is so that the readers can recognize what is and is not Zen, and not be filled with misleading prejudices. It is my hope that this book will remove

# An Introduction to Zen Thought

thoughts of Zen mysticism, and educate the readers about the value systems and thought patterns of our Oriental cousins. Perhaps, we will go as far as to assimilate this pattern, which has proved effective for people of the oldest civilizations on our planet. We will also see how countries like Japan can pull themselves up from the bottom, and become a world power in a matter of decades. Something they are doing must be right.

Western society has not been devoid of Zennists until the twentieth century. Though D.T. Suzuki brought the word Zen some Buddhist scriptures, and Zen teachings to the West, Zen had long since lived here. No ideology can take root in infertile ground. There must be something there first for an ideology to build on. Western philosophers, even dating back to the Greeks, displayed some Zen characteristics. The basic philosophies of our civilizations have had much in common with Zen. True philosophy is Gnostic. Gnostic means knowledge that is so pure that it cannot be explained or proven wrong, because it is real fact transcending time and space. By laying the ideologies on a table and comparing them line for line, we will find them filled with Gnostic facts that they all have in common.

## **Words in Zen**

Where we see a divergence is in the word. Western civilizations are very interested in the written word. Ironically, Western philosophers have recognized the problem with using words, but continue to use them anyway. In the West we see huge volumes written on religion and philosophy. In China, the philosophical and religious scriptures do come close to the volume in the West. Along the boarder of East and West we find India. In India are some of the longest books ever written, such as the Mahabharata and the Bhagavad-Gita. There are also some seven-thousand volumes to the Buddhist Dharma. This is misleading though. In the middle we find the biggest texts, and at the same time the biggest denouncement of written and spoken words. Buddha Gautama once said that "The original Dharma of all dharmas (is) in no-dharma" (Hyers, p. 60). What he meant by this, is that the true Dharma cannot be put into words. After Gautama died his teachings were transmitted by word of mouth, until they were eventually written down. It is ironic that this sentence, and others like it, survived the transcription. Why? Because Buddha denounced both his own words and his actions as not being real, factual. What he said was truth, which is what people believe not what really is. The spirit of Buddha's teachings are fact, are reality.

This book on the surface violates one of the principles of Zen. This principle is that Zen cannot be put into words. This book is not an attempt to put Zen into words. This book is intended to provide you with a conceptual understanding of Zen. The path to enlightenment is one that the individual must travel alone. A master is intended more as a guide than a teacher. As a guide the master will not tell you the way, but will assure the traveler when he or she has reached their destination. More importantly, the master is there to tell the student when he or she has not reached their destination. The relationship between student and master is personal, such that no book can hope to imitate the quality and experience.

Through the centuries Zen has been criticized for ignoring scriptures, and even defacing and destroying "sacred" texts and icons. Zen has also been criticized for its quality of decentralization. In the West we may call this a cult, since Zen has no leader. The criticism argues that anyone can up and call themselves a master. Where the criticism fails, is that true masters do not call themselves master. Some of the greatest Zen sages would not even associate themselves with a monastery, let alone be called master. Being called master is degrading to the true master. Thus those who live Zen should be able to distinguish between a true master and a fraud. It is the common people who are the victims of the frauds. For this reason, the criticism is unfair, because every ideology has its frauds who abuse the common people. This is not to say Zen is above criticism. If anything, Zen is Zen's worst critic. This will be discussed in the chapter, "Humor in Zen."

The words that are defined in this book, and the historical figures discussed, are intended only to provide the names which will appear in the study of Zen, and will help understand Zen thought. In reality they are a facade, and are unnecessary in the journey to enlightenment. I lived Zen for over twenty years before I studied the words and history. The only reason I studied these was to understand how I could teach Zen to Western people who were not brought up with Zen. Why are words not necessary? Let me answer this question in this manner:

When flying across the country do you say over every city, "What is the name of that city? What is its elevation? How many people live there? What are their names, ages, occupations, and addresses? Until I know these things I will fly no further."? When boarding the aircraft must you know how the plane works in order to be a passenger? Must you understand the principles of aviation in order to reach your destination? There is also the proverb of the Poisoned Arrow:

A man was pierced by a poisoned arrow, and a surgeon was summoned to pull it out and treat the wound. What would happen if the man objected, saying, "Wait a little. Before you pull it out, I want to know who shot this arrow. Was it a man or a woman? Was it someone of noble birth, or was it a peasant? What was the bow made of? Was it a big bow, or a small bow that shot the arrow? Was it made of wood or bamboo? What was the bow-string made of? Was it made of fiber, or of gut? Was the arrow made of rattan or reed? What feathers were used? Before you extract the arrow I want to know all about these things" (Teaching of Buddha, pp. 296-298). Obviously the first duty should be to remove the poisoned arrow, or the poison will circulate and kill the man.

This book does have a justification though. The material in this book is what is referred to as pre-knowledge. Pre-knowledge is not knowledge, and nor is it essential to gaining knowledge. Zen does not seek knowledge. Knowledge in Zen is not data believed to be true—it is facts. Seeking something is another action that is discouraged in Zen. With pre-knowledge though, knowledge and ability are easier to come by. Just remember that this text is neither a means nor an end. You must discard your knowledge of the materials in this book if you wish to pursue a life of Zen. If you do not plan to do this, then retaining these materials may prove useful.

The terminology and explanations serve a purpose as pre-knowledge. The general purpose of this text is to create a foundation for knowledge, a conceptual framework. From this we can displace misconceptions about Zen and zennists (Zen practitioners). Anyone lettered in education knows that pre-knowledge is essential to the learning process. Pre-knowledge, to reiterate the point, is not knowledge. In Zen the knowledge is experience and intuition, Gnostic facts. For this reason, Zen knowledge is wordless, but the pre-knowledge can be words. The pre-knowledge can also be experience. The pre-knowledge gained through experience is the strongest pre-knowledge, and is the easiest to build on. Unfortunately we cannot seek experience, but instead we stumble upon it and capture it. Experience is numinous. No amount of words can provide a numinous experience.

I must warn the readers to be cautious in their use of the terminology in this book. Many masters will react unpleasantly at the mention of nirvana, Buddha, or any of the other terms discussed here. The reason is that the student must escape the bounds of words. Words limit us to preconceived ideas (a priori assumptions). Neither logic nor rationalism can explain Zen. Words serve no function in Zen. What is gotten through Zen practice is what is called Gnostic knowledge and numinous experience. This is knowledge that is so pure that it cannot be explained or described, especially to someone who has not experienced it. As I said before, childbirth is Gnostic. It is also numinous. My reaction to the student who dwells on words and seeks enlightenment is thus:

Ask any bird, "What is aviation? What does airspeed mean? Which way is north?" The bird does not know. Your words are empty and meaningless to it. But: Does not the bird practice the art of aviation? Does not the bird have to deal with airspeed daily? Does not the bird intentionally fly north to reach a destination? Does the bird need these words to perform these functions?

A pilot needs no special knowledge of terms to fly. A pilot needs skill. In a life or death situation, being caught on a word means death. In a life or death situation putting the words and speculation aside for skilled action means life. In a life or death situation neither words nor skill may make a difference, but skill will enhance chance where words will reduce chance.

# An Introduction to Zen Thought

Words are a means of communicating; skills are a means of doing. Words provide an empty, abstract, and meaningless end. Skills, when used, provide definite results.

In Western society we have found ourselves more and more dependant on words. We read words. We speak words. We think words. When we escape these three traps we can better understand ourselves and everything around us. I can say or write that something tastes sweet. Does this really say what it tastes like? No. If I say it tastes like sugar this word recalls our perception of the taste of sugar. If I say it tastes like honey, then what kind of honey?

No matter how specific and concrete our words are, each of us has a different perception of those words. We see Western philosophers struggling with this problem throughout history. For example, Plato argued the meaning of "just" in the classic The Republic. He illustrated that this one abstract word is unsuitable for its purpose, showing that there is a continuum. Many philosophers have likewise found difficulty, and have worked hard to create syllogistic and dialectic arguments to help define a feeling, situation, or word. Like Plato, they eventually find that there is no correct way. Those who feel they have found the answer to these continuum problems, have come with preconceived ideas, and have done nothing but try to prove their ideas. Their solutions are not fact, though they may be truth to them and their adherents.

To further this argument, Nagasena was asked what nirvana looked like. He responded: "Is there such a thing as wind? . . . Please show me the color and configuration of wind, or as thin, thick, long, or short" (Smith, p. 113). Another master would only hold up one finger in response, and others have also resorted to meaningless responses. You can no more define Zen than you can describe the smell of a rose to someone that has never smelled one. Even describing the smell of a rose to someone who has smelled one, we are inclined to say it smelled like a rose. This abstraction has no meaning what-so-ever.

Another problem with connotations (personal definitions of words) is the learning process. From the moment our brain develops and begins to think we are learning. This learning is commonly referred to as conditioning. If every time a child ate chocolate or any other sweet the child was beaten, that child would be conditioned to hate chocolate and sweets. Most of us have pleasant thoughts, where this child would not. This is extreme though. Our connotations are based on our personal experiences. Since no two people share the same experiences throughout life, no two people will perceive a word exactly the same. George Berkeley (1685-1753) concluded that reality is what we imagine it to be. His argument holds that perceptions through our senses are imagined, creations of our minds. I would contend that Berkeley's argument is not just about the unreality of reality, but also is an attack on our categorization of our perceptions into words.

Each word is a category. These categories are defined by what we perceive to be our experiences. The definitions of categories create little boxes in our minds. When we see something we faithfully seek out the appropriate box and put it in. If I were to say I see a tree, you would go to your box, and pull up an image of a tree. Is the tree you are imagining the tree I am thinking about? No. The probability of this is to small to mention. By creating these categories we are limiting ourselves to the labels and images we have stored in these boxes in our minds. These images are not reality; they are what we believe the words to mean. Thus Berkeley's argument can be expanded on, to include the unreality of words.

What we are taken to is thought released from words. Our thought normally relies entirely on personal imagery. Yes, this is the way most animals think, combined with other perceptions made through conditioning. People do not like to think of themselves as animals though. Both humans and animals have another frame of thought that is discouraged by Zen. This thought pattern is dualism. In other words, thoughts are divided between things that make us feel good, and things that make us feel bad, again categories/boxes. Holding on to these concepts is also misleading, and clouds our thought process. Our thoughts are made more complex than other animals, because of our capacity for imagination and forethought. In Zen our thought must be released from thought. Dualism, language, and fantasy are all obstacles in Zen. With pure thought we can have pure consciousness.

Pure consciousness is essential to Zen. With a pure consciousness we perceive reality. The reason for this is that we are not trying to categorize, and are not trying to interpret. To either categorize or interpret we would have to have preconceived ideas. Thus the zennist approaches every situation with a clear mind, and allows the world to write upon that mind. If the zennist did not do this, then the zennist would have a cluttered mind, and would begin to judge. Jesus is supposed to have said: Judge not lest thee be judged. He never did say how to prevent this. It is interesting to note that this same philosophy is shared around the world. This leads to the conclusion that this piece of philosophy may be Gnostic.

**Dharma**

Dharma has already been used in this chapter. In this chapter I referred to Dharma as the sacred texts of Buddhism. As sacred texts, the Dharma is the teachings of Buddha Gautama. These texts are the "law" or way of Buddhism. As a word, dharma means law. This is misleading though. In the context of religious Buddhism, Dharma is an appropriate name for the sacred texts. In Zen, this is only partially true.

The zennist will read Buddha's sermons, in the form of sutras. Sutras are also the teachings of other Buddha's and masters. The sutras are commented on in works called shastras. The shastras are interpretations, written by masters. Often these shastras are further commented on, or another master simply does away with the original commentary, replacing it with his or her own. The irony of the whole situation is that the Dharma is not sacred in Zen. The sutras and shastras are not sacred either. The reason for this is in the quote stated earlier, where Gautama said that the true Dharma could not be put into words. This removes the Dharma from the sacred in the eyes of Zen.

This discarding of the Dharma is not done blindly though. Another criticism on Zen is that Zen disregards being canonical. Zen refuses to be stooped to the level of words, and thus disregards words without a second thought. This is not the true way of Zen. I-tuan said, "Speech is blasphemy, silence a lie" (Hyers, p. 62). This also holds true with this. Words are a blasphemy, ignoring words is a lie. We have a continuum again, in which we have words on one side, and wordlessness on the other. How should we take this continuum? The correct posture would be to discard the learned, but not to discard the unlearned. Thus you cannot discard the Dharma until you have learned it. Thus the Dharma has a placeless place in Zen. The Dharma is there until you are worthy and capable of discarding it.

What do I mean by worthy? To read something is one thing. To understand is yet another thing. You can memorize all the teachings, and still not be capable of standing up to a true master. Why? Because you have not attained the spirit of the Dharma. The spirit is wordless. You do not need to read the Dharma to attain the spirit of the Dharma. Many masters were illiterate. This did not disqualify them as masters. If anything, being illiterate was a blessing. This was a blessing because they could enjoy the spirit of the Dharma without being misled by reading it. This is not to say that these individuals were unlettered though. Being able to read and write is not a sign of intelligence, wisdom, or ability. Many sages never wrote a single word of their teachings. This is also not to say that these sages were illiterate. This is meant to indicate that the written word is not always the true teaching, and especially not the factual teaching. I will discuss the principles involved in discarding knowledge in Chapter VII, "Meditation." To discard does not necessarily mean to destroy completely. Read Chapter VII closely to be certain you understand my meaning before you attempt to discard knowledge. You should also read the poem called "Purity" in Appendix B to help you to understand the concept of discarding knowledge.

**Paths of Zen**

I will not pretend that this book will help you to become enlightened. I do recommend that there is a way this book can be used to help you on your journey. First, study each chapter and ask yourself, "What does this mean to me? How can I apply this to my life?" Second, abandon what you have learned. As with any Zen text, this text is wrong. Technically the definitions and history provided here are true and accepted, and I have attempted to maintain as much fact as possible. The definitions and history are wrong in terms of Zen, because Zen transcends words. These words are only the briefest glimpse at Zen. The only true understanding of Zen is to live Zen. That is something no book can provide. The third way is to also read the supplement in Appendix B titled Conquering the Inner Tiger.

Zen poetry also offers a path. They are called fayu in Chinese, or hogo in Japanese, meaning "Dharma words." It is not called Dharma words because it carries pieces from the Dharma, but because it contains personal hints for the student in search of spiritual maturity or enlightenment. Some may even be viewed as koans (a Zen case study used for meditation).

When you have achieved enlightenment then the normal Zen thing to do is discard the book. You may choose to do a number of things, including burning it, tearing it up, selling it, giving it away, or keeping it for your personal library to be used by your own students. None of these are uncommon for Zen masters, as you shall see later in this text.

You will find the word koan scattered throughout this book. A koan is a story used to bring realization or to clarify enlightenment. These stories are often taken from the experiences of a master, or from the interaction between a Zen student and a master (the oral interaction is called mondo). A koan is like a question or puzzle. The solutions to these puzzles can only be found within the individual. The solutions are beyond words; they are experiences. You cannot cheat on this kind of test. Even if you could, cheating would harm no one but you. An example of a koan is, "How many angels can dance on the head of a pin?" This question tied up the Christian intelligentsia for many years. I have two responses to this question. First, what do you believe is the answer? Second, anywhere from zero to infinite, depending on your belief. The Church determined finally that it was 137. How they arrived at this arbitrary number I do not know. Perhaps they asked around, and then averaged the responses. This certainly could not be answered logically, which is what they tried to do.

Something else I will discuss throughout this book will be where you can seek further Zen training. Zen training is very traditional, and there are many avenues that can be followed. Most people are unaware of the various means of studying Zen. Sometimes the students themselves do not realize they are students of Zen. Many discover they are studying Zen after ten years or more. For that matter there are probably students who never know. By being told about these paths and generally how Zen is applied to them, you will be able to make better use of them. This will make your transition into a life of Zen much easier.

## Buddha-mind and nature

What is Buddha-mind? What is Buddha-nature? Forget your questions, and let's have tea instead. Buddha-mind and Buddha-nature are very similar. Buddha-nature is the nature of things, the way of nature. Buddha-nature is the potential for Buddhahood, for complete enlightenment. We all have Buddha-nature in us. Buddha-nature is in all things. Buddha-mind is the attitude, the harmony of the mind with Buddha-nature. Like Buddha-nature, Buddha-mind already exists in all things. Through purity and harmony with ourselves we can attain Buddhahood, by realizing our Buddha-nature and our Buddha-mind. When we awaken, become enlightened, we see that we have these two qualities. We cannot find them if we look for them, or try to attain them. We cannot attain something we already have. We can apprehend something we already have. We cannot find something we did not lose in the first place.

To describe Buddha-nature and Buddha-mind is like trying to describe the way of nature. We can even equate Buddha-nature to the way of nature, and declare Buddha-mind as the awareness of the way of nature. We can also break these words down by defining Buddha. Buddha means "the awakened" or forever enlightened. This helps us to shed some light, in many ways, on Buddha-nature and Buddha-mind. Buddha-nature, according to this interpretation, would be the awakened nature, real nature as it appears in the awakened state. Thus it is the revelation of the way of nature through the intuition. Buddha-mind would then be the awakened mind, the mind that is awake and aware of itself and its Buddha-nature.

By defining these words like this we are intellectualizing them. These definitions are provided to create a framework to build on though. You must remember, and I will constantly remind you, to forget these words and their definitions. These words and definitions are meaningless. Buddha-nature and Buddha-mind must be experienced in order to be understood. Both Zen and Buddhism seek a middle path in everything they do. We can neither escape nor dwell on words or dualism. For this reason, Zen would choose silence, but not complete silence. Like with everything else in Zen we recognize the existence of such a situation, and at the same time we discard it.

## Scholasticism

Although Zen is not a philosophy, the most likely college it will be taught in would be philosophy. It may also appear in the college of religious studies. Studying Zen as a philosophy diminishes the personal quality of Zen. Zen is a way of life, but can be studied as a philosophy. The biggest problem with philosophy classes taught today is that they teach dates and facts. Helmut Brinker in Zen in the Art of Painting noted this problem, stating that the purpose should be to teach students how to philosophize. Philosophy is critical thinking, not memorization. This book is written with the intent to teach critical thinking as a philosophy text should be, not to provide trivia. This is not to limit this book strictly to a school setting. Though I suggest having a background in world religions and philosophies, a layman can also comprehend the contents of this book. What is important about other religions and philosophies I try to report here. I do however suggest not limiting yourself to this book, or to texts on Zen. On the contrary you should pursue the study of other ideologies, because they contribute more than I can ever report here.

There are a number of books that I recommend that discuss the paths of Zen. The books listed in the references section of this book are a good starting point. Nancy Wilson Ross does a particularly good job in her two collections. Of these books, I strongly recommend the following two books, because they make no effort to teach facts. They are:

<u>Zen in the Art of Archery</u>, by Eugen Herrigel. Random House, 1981. This is a classic, first published in 1953, which is only 81 pages long. This book provides a brief chronology of the experiences of the author and his wife, in the Japanese arts of archery and calligraphy, and how they provided a path to Zen.

<u>Zen in the Martial Arts</u>, by Joe Hyams. Bantam, 1982. This is another book that provides a personal account of Zen experiences. Joe Hyams discusses how he learned some of the most important principles of Zen, and how he applied Zen to his life. He does not spend as much time creating a chronology of events, but discusses some of the more important lessons he was taught, and shows how his Zen training helped him in his daily activities, and even saved his life.

There are also books I suggest avoiding. The first on my list is <u>Zen and the Art of Motorcycle Maintenance</u>. This may be a good book for something, such as pleasure reading, but it is not what I would recommend for a student (the author of the book does not also). I would also try to avoid textbooks in general, as well as encyclopedias and dictionaries of religion. The exception to this would be Huston Smith's The World's Religions, and dictionaries with entries written by authorities, like S.G.F. Brandon's <u>Dictionary of Comparative Religion</u>. Even these books have mistakes. It is hard to be always accurate, especially when you are dealing with so much information. When shopping for books on Zen, be careful that authorities write them. Be skeptical of books not written by Orientals. Also be skeptical of books that imply an easy way to enlightenment. <u>The Lazy Man's Guide to Enlightenment</u> can be mistaken for a book on Buddhism or Zen. It is neither. I do not believe that it even comes close to the enlightenment we see in Buddhism. That particular book is perfect for someone who wants to catch the spirit of the late sixties and early seventies: drugs, free love, freedom and anarchy. There is no easy way to enlightenment. Zen requires work, like any other credible philosophy.

Although I am not an advocate of television programming and movies, there is one movie I recommend. The movie Circle of Iron captures the spirit of Zen. It is the only movie I have found that is really about Zen. It was contributed to by Bruce Lee, and was produced after his death in commemoration of him. I have heard criticism that Bruce Lee was not a Zen teacher. The martial arts masters teach Zen through martial arts. There is no doubt in my mind as to the authority of Bruce Lee's Zen teachings. The movie itself is a fantasy, intentionally to show that Zen transcends all the boundaries we believe exist. In this book I will discuss some parts of the movie Circle of Iron. I strongly suggest that you see this movie, in order to get more out of what I say later. It is not essential to see the movie, but it will be helpful.

**Religion or Philosophy**

You are probably wondering why Zen does not fit into either religion or philosophy. To understand this, let us examine the definitions of these two words. A religion is something that brings people together. Religion does not have to have a deity. An example would be science. Science is a religion that brings our technological world together. In today's world we are almost all bound by the religion of science, something we often forget. If we take religion very loosely, yes Zen is a religion. Zen is a religion in the sense that many people practice Zen, and thus have something in common.

Zen is not a religion (Buddhism is), if we take the perspective that we are all human and work to survive, and thus we all have something in common. Zen is not meant to bring people together socially. Zen is very personal, just like living and being human, even though we are all collectively human and alive until we are dead. The fact that people get together as zennists is not because Zen encourages it, but because the people feel they have something in common. What zennists have in common is their differences. Beyond being different, zennists have nothing in common. To create a paradox, this is the commonality felt by zennists that may loosely be interpreted as religious. Zennists also come together to learn Zen. In this they are being religious, because they are brought together by curiosity and will.

Philosophy is the search for wisdom. In Zen there is no search, there only is. A love for wisdom is also associated with philosophy. Love is a dualistic condition, and as such is discouraged by Zen. Loosely speaking, wisdom can be defined as reality. However we see traditional philosophy attempting to categorize and answer questions. The reality of this is that the answers are beliefs. What the philosopher believes is true is the philosophy. Truth is not fact, and fact is reality. This element of truth is shared by religion and science. Zen stands virtually alone in the conviction of fact. Fact is the root of Zen, not conjecture. Philosophy is conjecture, theorizing. In this sense, Zen is not philosophy.

Zen does not provide rites of passage, or a social structure. These are basic elements in all the religions I have ever encountered. Zen does not provide anecdotes of wisdom, or debates. The usual result of a debate or an anecdote is a conclusion. In the conclusion a theory about conduct or existence is postulated. Zen gives no theories about conduct or existence. Zen does provide basic theories on the self. These theories are not meant to be guiding, as philosophy generally is. In philosophy we see "The wise man is . . . " or "The just man is. . . . " We do not see any of this in Zen. The wisdom in Zen is inner wisdom, wisdom of the self. In fact Zen does not necessarily recognize wisdom, but instead encourages intuition. We are often inclined to equate intuition with wisdom. If there is "wisdom" in Zen, it is the wisdom of intuition. If there is "knowledge" in Zen, it is the knowledge of intuition. Zen is a way of living through wisdom and knowledge (perception) of the self.

I am sure Western thinkers will waste a lot of time debating over whether Zen is a religion or a philosophy. Zen does not claim either. Zen is. When Western thinkers can accept this, then and only then will they begin to understand Zen. Any category we put Zen in will only diminish the value of true Zen. In categories Zen will take other forms. To understand Zen takes a non-dualistic, non-categorical, and holistic thinking. Even then Zen is incomplete, unless it is lived. When Zen is lived, then it goes beyond thinking to the Ethical—a universal philosophical conception of evolving to being more human than human. Zen practices what this philosophical conception thinks and debates about.

# CHAPTER II—
# Buddhism

## Origins of Buddhism
Since this is not a book on the history of Buddhism, this will be extremely brief. Let us first start with a quick discussion on the historical framework from which Buddhism evolved. To start this we must go back several thousand years, to the Aryan civilization. If we trace the roots of Eurasian religion we find much of its origins on the steps of Asia, in North Western China. Here there lived a people who would migrate to the Caucasus and then into India and Anatolia (Turkey). We are concerned mostly with their influences in China and India, so we will displace the effects of this people on European and Middle Eastern religions for discussion in a more appropriate place. Suffice it to say, their influence would eventually lead to the development of much of the ideologies that dominate that area of the world, including Christianity, Judaism, and Islam.

When this people arrived in India they were polytheistic nature worshipers. They are now called the Aryans. Their religion is called the Vedic Religion, named after collections of hymns called Vedas. The two most important elements of Vedism for our discussion are the cycle and nature worship. In India the cycle became cosmic. The cycle begins with the creation of the universe and ends with its destruction. The cycle was also applied to life, in the form of reincarnation. The cycle of reincarnation (samsara) created a paradoxical problem: how to escape the cycle. The prime directive of Indian religion, including Hinduism and Buddhism, was and still is to escape the cycle. The second feature of the Aryan religion was nature worship, which often appeared in the form of animal and spirit worship. In some parts of the world this led to such religions as classical mythology, where the deities were humanized, although not always very humane. In other areas this worship was reduced to spirit worship. Turning to India we can still see the effects of nature worship and polytheism in Hinduism. In Buddhism we must look much closer to see an association. The most obvious relationship between Hinduism and Buddhism is ultimate goal of escaping the cycle of reincarnation (samsara) through purification (nirvana).

Gautama Siddhartha (also spelled Gotama) was a prince who lived most of his life in elaborate palaces. Most of the legends associated with his birth and upbringing are not relevant. There is one that is important. This legend states that there had been a prophecy on the soon-to-be-born Gautama. He was either to become a great leader of Siddhartha, or he would become a pauper and a great religious leader. The prophecy warned that if Gautama were exposed to illness, old age, death, and a holy man he would follow the religious path. These are called the four sights or

# An Introduction to Zen Thought

four signs. Fearful of his son being a religious leader, Gautama's father tried to prevent the fulfillment of the prophecy.

To prevent Gautama from being exposed to the four sights he kept young Gautama in the palaces. When Gautama wished to go out, his father would send messengers ahead to clear the path. Eventually Gautama was exposed to all four, and was enlightened to the existence of suffering. This compelled him to learn more about suffering. At the age of 29, Gautama bid his sleeping wife (Yasodhara) and son (Rahula) goodbye, and left his palace life forever. Over seven years later he would return, and his wife and son would join him.

Meanwhile the young Gautama left the palace with an attendant. After they had gone a distance they stopped. Gautama shaved his head and put on the clothes of a pauper. Turning his white horse over to the attendant, Gautama began his quest. The attendant returned to the palace, and is never mentioned again. Gautama wandered, seeking out religious leaders and teachers. Everywhere he turned he was not satisfied with the response to his quest for understanding suffering. Then he went to the yogis in the mountains. According to yogic tradition the only way to find answers is through the personal practice of Yoga (which will be discussed later in this text). So Gautama joined them and practiced their ascetic ways. For the next several years he practiced Yoga. He meditated, mutilated himself, and starved himself. Eventually he realized that he was not getting anywhere. When he left, the other yogis denounced him for his blatant denouncement of their methods.

Gautama wandered along the Nairanjana River. He met a wealthy woman, and found a bo tree to meditate under. Every day the woman would come out, feed him, and massage him. Day and night Gautama sat there. He vowed that he would either be enlightened or die trying. There are stories about temptation and a demon harassing Gautama. These are of particular importance for an experience in Zen that can be called conquering the inner tiger. This is a battle with yourself, your inner demons, dragons, tigers, or whatever. The demon who tried to tempt Buddha, according to legend, was a Hindu god named Mara. From my experiences, this inner battle is the hardest you can ever fight. Our inner demons do not like the idea of losing, and they vanish at the prospect. This is what happened to Gautama. Mara realized he was not going to win, and then he disappeared. He later admitted that if there was anything as compelling and tempting as sex, that he would have lost his fight with Mara.

When Gautama arose from his victory, he was the Buddha, the forever awoken. As Buddha he wandered toward civilization. On his way he encountered the yogis he had abandoned previously. To them he presented his first sermon, the Sermon at Deer Park. In this sermon he laid out the framework that was to become Buddhism. This framework was the Four Noble Truths, and subsequently the Eightfold Path.

Before we discuss this framework, we should first discuss Buddha. Buddha means forever enlightened, or the awakened one. In the movie Circle of Iron we meet a character named Cord. Cord is seeking the book of enlightenment. During his exploits he finds a blind man who is a great martial artist. At one point Cord asks the blind man, "How long have you been blind?" The blind man responds, "How long have you been blind?" The enlightened one is the awakened one. Everyone in the world has their eyes closed, is asleep, except for the Buddha. The Buddha is the one who has his eyes open, is awake to perceive reality. This was the lesson of the blind man. Watching the blind man we clearly see that he is not at all blind. He may not be able to see with his eyes, but he sees even more clearly with his intuition. He is not blinded by what his eyes tell him. Thus it is Cord that is blind, not the blind man.

At the beginning of this chapter I emphasized a relationship between Hinduism and Buddhism. As you read through the Four Noble Truths and the Eightfold Path in the next two sections, you will see some of the relationships that tie Buddhism to Hinduism. As an example, the second noble truth provides a gateway connecting Buddhism and Hinduism through the cycle. As for harmony, the Eightfold Path is harmony. In the Eightfold Path we see that the fourth and fifth elements relate particularly to nature. Finally, in the eighth element of the Eightfold Path we can see a religious function that can be applied to Hinduism. Specifically it provides salvation, an escape from samsara (the cycle of reincarnation). These relationships were not originally intended to be used for religion. They would prove to be very attractive to the Hindus, and a contributor to the assimilation of Buddhism by Hinduism.

**The Four Noble Truths**

The Four Noble Truths, when apprehended through experience, constitute the ultimate reality to Buddhists. Of the Four Noble Truths, the first and last are the most important. The first truth tells us about life, and the last tells us how to escape from it. The first truth is that pain (suffering) is universal. No matter what we do, we create pain. If we are not in pain ourselves, then we are causing the pain of another.

The second truth is that pain (suffering) is caused by greed. Greed gives rise to samsara. Samsara is transmigration, being reincarnated over and over again. In Hinduism this is the cycle of existence, of reincarnation. In both Buddhism and Hinduism samsara is represented by a wheel (or circle) or as a stream. Our greed is based on our physical desires, which are conditioned by our senses. What we perceive through our senses as truth comes forth as wants. In economics we see a distinction made between want and demand. Want is limitless, where demand is what we can and are willing to afford. Demand is the real, what is actually purchased, where want is created in the imagination. What Buddha is telling us is that we let our wants overshadow actual demand, and more importantly our needs.  By doing this we are clouding reality, and allowing our fantasies to dominate.  Particularly, we are allowing our fantasies for wealth and power dominate.  Thus Buddha immediately discourages materialism. Materialism is a popular theme in the West.

Materialism, as I have already illustrated, is a product of our imagination.  Our wants and desires are illusions, fantasies.  The third noble truth is that illusion is the source of greed, and in order to overcome greed we must overcome illusion.  The term used for illusion in both Hinduism and Buddhism is maya.  It is a term used by Hinduism as a key concept in describing reality.  Buddhism has also adopted the analogy between maya and reality.  We find in religious studies a distinction drawn between truth and fact.  The reality that I have so far been talking about is truth.  Truth is what we believe.  This is what blinded Cord in the movie.  He believed he saw things, but he failed to acknowledge the facts.  Like religious studies Buddhism draws a line in the sand, saying that what we perceive and what we believe are real are only truths, only illusion, only maya.  Enlightenment comes only when maya is overcome, when we open our inner or cosmic eye.  We are blinded by the illusion of the microcosmic, which includes our physical desires.

The fourth noble truth is the guiding light.  The first noble truth told us what the problem is (what).  The second noble truth told us what the cause of the problem is (who).  The third noble truth told us where the problem is (where).  The fourth noble truth tells us how to overcome the problem (how).  In each sentence I added what, who, where, and how.  The fifth famous question is when.  The Four Noble Truths do not tell us when, because time is not part of the problem.  How do we overcome suffering?  The way to overcome suffering is by following the Eightfold Path.  Though Buddha says that this is the way, he makes no promises.  This is where there is a fault with using Buddhism for salvation.  The general rule with salvation is that the prophet who preaches a path to salvation will believe completely in their prescription.  The only thing Buddha does promise is that we each have our own path to salvation.  The Eightfold Path is not fixed; it adjusts to the individual.  Thus Buddha's path is pragmatic.

There are many things Buddha told us about the Eightfold Path, and Buddhist practice.  Buddha tells us that indulgence in sensual pleasure is only the surrendering to greed and illusion (fantasy).  Self-mortification is only the surrendering to universal pain.  These are extremes that Buddha avoided and discouraged.  Instead he found that the middle path was better, the path of fact not truth.  To surrender to sensual pleasure is to believe in sensual pleasure, making it a truth.  To surrender to self-mortification is to believe in self-mortification, making it a truth.  Neither is a fact.  The fact is that these are extremes along a continuum.  This continuum does not differentiate between the extremes, but dualistic thinking does.  Rather than look at the extremes separately, Buddha tells us to look at the whole continuum, whole picture, to embody it, to become one with the continuum. This is the middle path. Later when we discuss Zen, you should remember that an alternative name for Zen is the Middle Path.

**The Eightfold Path**
The middle path is the Eightfold Path. Brandon divides the Eightfold Path into three groups. These groups are: faith, morality, and meditation. Faith is not part of the picture, except maybe faith in oneself. The two elements Brandon classifies as faith would be better classified as knowledge. However, in the religious sense, faith would be a logical distinction. Faith is not a distinction in Zen, but it is in the Mahayana and Theravada traditions. Later in this chapter I will discuss the Mahayana and Theravada (Hinayana) Buddhism. I will also discuss faith from the perspective of Zen, which is quite different from traditional religious faith. I am also more inclined to consider what Brandon classifies as morality, as conduct. Buddhism does not regulate morality.

In brief, Brandon divides the Eightfold Path as:
Faith (Knowledge):
   1. Right Understanding.
   2. Right Thought.
Morality (Conduct):
   3. Right Speech.
   4. Right Action.
   5. Right Livelihood.
Meditation:
   6. Right Effort. *
   7. Right Mindfulness.
   8. Right Concentration

That which is in parentheses is how I would classify each of these groups, if I were to classify. It is better not to classify these, but to take them as a whole unit. This is why it is the Eightfold Path, and not the eight paths. I placed an asterisk (*) next to right effort because it also applies under the other two categories (Faith/Knowledge and Morality/Conduct).

The first member of the path is right understanding. Right understanding can be interpreted also as right comprehension. Though we see we do not comprehend. Though we hear we do not listen. Our senses often betray us, and so does our thinking. We can study a subject and not capture the true meaning of the subject. Why? Because we come with preconceived ideas, and we let these ideas dominate. The blind man said that every day he started the day with a blank mind for the world to write upon. To comprehend we must open our minds to everything, without letting other ideas prejudice the new information. This is the way we can have right understanding. Right understanding requires facts. Prejudice clouds the facts. Prejudice is formed from previous information, by what we believe. Thus prejudice is truth, but not fact. Embodying fact is right understanding. For religious Buddhism, right understanding is also the understanding of the sutras, and especially of the Four Noble Truths and the Eightfold Path.

The second element is right thought. In right understanding we get information, we get facts. What do we do with these facts? What we do with facts is think, we interpret the facts. Interpretation is thought. Is there a correct way to think? Buddha said there was, but did not take it the next fatal step. How do we think? Anyone that thinks they know how someone else should think lives in fantasy. This is a fatal step that Buddha avoided. Each of us processes information in our own way. The only requirement in Buddhism is that thought is not based on the ego. What does it mean to base thinking on the ego? This is interpreting things in such a way as to benefit our selves. According to Buddha our ego obstructs the facts. The ego will add to the facts, and will take away what does not suit it. In order to have right thought we must take the facts as a whole, without discrimination. We must allow each fact to carry its own weight. If we add to that weight, or lift the scale to put it off balance, then we are not accepting the facts as they are. Facts must be accepted as they are, so that each fact has "its day in court."

I classified these two as knowledge, where Brandon classified them as faith. By classifying them as faith we limit them to religion. This was not the intent of Buddha. These are to be applied throughout life, and especially to intuitive knowledge. In India knowledge is not raw data, as it is often viewed in the West. Knowledge is intuition, self-knowledge, and insight. The reason knowledge is insight, is that Indian tradition holds that reality is an illusion (maya). If we were to weigh worldly knowledge with insight, in Indian tradition insight would have the greater weight. Buddhism follows this same perception of knowledge. It is important though that this knowledge is both worldly and insightful. To neglect one would be to neglect both. Thus as a category, classifying right understanding and right thought as knowledge is broad enough to capture most of the essence of these elements.

Right speech is the third element of the Eightfold Path. This is the first of the three elements classified as conduct. It is also the next logical element. We have gone from collecting information to interpreting it. Now we must express that interpretation. When we talk we have a tendency to slant our words toward our own prejudices. What Buddhism tells us to do is to report all the facts as we know them. Buddhism tells us to report facts, not truth, not what we believe. In other words, we must report facts so that others have the same opportunity to understand and think right. It is here that we find that Buddhism is not supposed to be inflicted or forced on someone. Unlike Christianity, this is a specific attack on trying to convert people (proselytizing). In converting another to your way of thinking, you will naturally slant the facts in your favor, and even pepper your speech with truth, what you believe.

Actions are our physical expressions of our interpretations. This is a simple form of interaction with our surroundings. What kind of action does Buddha refer to? All action. Essentially right action blends closely with livelihood. Obviously Buddha is intending this to mean action that does not result in gain, especially physical gain. Right action must be done without any personal gain. What we are discussing here is altruism. If you see a stranger with a flat tire on the side of the road, you stop to help for the sake of helping. Most people stop and help for the sake of feeling better about themselves. This is a personal gain motive. Buddha prescribes acting for the sake of acting because it is the right thing to do, not for the sake of feeding the ego.

Right livelihood is not much different. We must each support our families and ourselves. We must be able to subsist. There is nothing wrong in profit, or becoming wealthy. Wealth, when obtained without materialistic intent, is not necessarily bad. What you do with the wealth may be. How you handle wealth falls under right action. Under right livelihood we are discussing what you do to fulfill your needs. Buddhism does not tell you what profession you should go into, or which professions you should not go into. Your choice of profession is entirely your own. What Buddhism does state is that you should not profit from the suffering of others. Since pain is universal, why should we contribute to the suffering? Contributing to the suffering of others is bad. Thus we should profit, but not unfairly. We are not only thinking of our own needs, but the needs of others.

Right effort is important to everything you do. If you do not put in the effort necessary to perform an act right, then the act will fail. If the act fails, then there was no point in performing the act. We see politicians making token efforts all the time. If politicians cared enough they would contribute the effort necessary for success. We can see that they are capable of making a right effort, when they get something done that is beneficial to them. We especially see right effort during election years. Though these politicians are putting in the right effort, their intentions are self directed, which is not right action. It is noble to be a politician that acts with right effort for the good of others. Those politicians that fall outside of this category should be incarcerated for their crimes against society.

Right mindfulness (other authors also use mindedness or resolutions) would fit better under knowledge or conduct, than meditation. Having right-mindedness means to be free from lust, ill will, and cruelty, to be aware. In other words, this requires being mindful (aware) of the needs and sufferings of others. This somewhat fits into right thought. As with each of the members of the Eightfold Path, right mindfulness is closely integrated with the others. Each member is like a strand in a rope. Each strand is equally important. To weaken any strand would be to weaken the entire rope. To try and support yourself off of a weakened rope will only result in failure. To try and support yourself on only one strand of the rope will result in an even quicker failure.  Being considerate of others is essential in everything we do.  That is why right speech consists of facts, not lies.  That is why right livelihood is attained without inflicting more suffering on others.

Right concentration is the last member of the Eightfold Path.  Right concentration certainly implies meditation, and focus.  As focus, right concentration shows us the best solution for right effort.  When we focus our energies, all of our energies, on a goal, we can do anything.  You don't believe this?  Then try to explain how in less then ten years Adolf Hitler went from being in a German prison to becoming the most powerful leader Germany had ever seen.  When Hitler came out of prison he vowed that he would use all his energies for the rest of his life to make Germany the most powerful nation.  He succeeded in less than fifteen years.  The combined efforts of the United States and most of the rest of Europe had difficulty overpowering Hitler Germany.  He focused.  He concentrated his efforts.  Hitler was a remarkable man.  What scares us, is that he abused (to understate the facts) the rights of people.  In Buddhism our focus is on being mindful of the suffering of others.  Our concentration in meditation is a focus on our inner selves.

In meditation we begin simply, by concentrating on our breathing.  Later we improve this, concentrating on a problem or issue.  Then we begin to concentrate on concentrating, and finally we concentrate on not concentrating, and we just be.  Concentration leads to discipline.  When we begin meditating we are learning discipline through concentration.  When we have become disciplined, everything we do is in concentration.  When we meditate we then go beyond concentration, because concentration has become our nature.  This state is difficult to explain.  This state of being is called satori.  Satori is not nirvana or enlightenment, but it is a state of self realization.  This is where we find most bodhisattvas and teachers.

Samadhi is the Buddhist term for concentration.  Buddhist schools have developed three degrees of intensity.  These are: preparation, beginning, and attainment of concentration.  Yoga has two forms of samadhi, which are closer to the Zen interpretation of samadhi.  The first, and lesser form, is concentration on an object or idea.  This is called samadhi with support.  The second, and higher form, is concentration without an object or idea.  The second form is called samadhi without support.  These forms are what I am referring to in the previous paragraph.  The first form develops discipline, and the second form develops satori and sunyata (emptiness).

### Satori, Nirvana, Enlightenment

Satori is a Japanese term often associated with enlightenment and nirvana.  It is the state of consciousness to Buddha-mind, to Buddha-nature.  This is not true enlightenment or nirvana, which it is often mistaken for.  This is a mild enlightenment.  Earlier in this chapter I defined Buddha as being the awakened one.  Necessary to this definition is that not only is

Buddha awake, but his eyes are open. To define satori we can use this model. Satori is a state in which we have self-enlightenment. To compare, one who has attained satori is either asleep and knows he or she is asleep, or is awake with his or her eyes closed. Satori is a semiconscious state, where Buddhahood is a completely conscious and aware state. Buddhahood is not the ultimate attainment in Buddhism though. Many books use the word satori as bate. It is a slab of meat luring you into the teachings. It is a false goal. It is presented to Western audiences as a goal, because Westerners need a feeling of direction. Satori is used for this, until the need is no longer necessary, then it disappears. Brandon does catch a significant aspect to this word, which is "essential wisdom (prajna)." In a sense satori is the pre-knowledge of wisdom. It is not the wisdom itself. This is where the mistake is often made in regard to satori. Thus satori is not complete enlightenment, Buddhahood, or nirvana. Western texts over rate all of these words. Brandon even makes this mistake.

Enlightenment is only one step beyond basic satori. An enlightened person has become conscious, but has not yet opened his or her eyes. Enlightenment goes beyond satori, because the one that is enlightened has realized that there is something beyond the self. This is a quality that one who has attained satori does not have. Thus the enlightened one is only slightly more conscious.

Both Buddhahood and nirvana are often mistaken for the highest level that can be achieved in Buddhism. What is nirvana? Nirvana is not really definable, because it is an experience. To define nirvana is like trying to define the taste of an apple. For the sake of this discussion though, it is necessary to give nirvana a framework. Nirvana consists of both escaping from and joining with existence, without dying. Essentially nirvana is the ultimate form of harmony. It is the escape from samsara (the cycle of reincarnation). The word nirvana comes from the Pali word nibbana. Nibbana is associated with a verb that means to blow on in order to cool. This is often applied as the cooling of a fever of greed, hatred, and delusion (maya--illusion). By reducing the fever we are purifying. Thus nibbana and nirvana can be seen as purification.

When a person attains nirvana, that person has opened their eyes, and has become aware not only of him or her self, but also of everything else. To attain nirvana is to attain Buddhahood. Nirvana is as pure as we can get in our life. Nirvana is not the highest state a Buddhist can attain. Nirvana does provide an escape from samsara (reincarnation) though. This is compelling for those who believe in reincarnation, but is not the goal of Buddhism. In fact, satori seems to be sufficient to many, sometimes even less, depending on the individual's religious beliefs. In Buddhism the goal is harmony with reality.

When Gautama developed Buddhism he evaded any reference to the metaphysical. He declared that he was not made by a god, sent by a god, nor was a god himself, but he did not attack religion. This is why the goal of Buddhism is reality, and not a religious goal, like salvation. Salvation is in religious Buddhism, notably in the Theravada and Mahayana traditions. In Buddhist traditions, harmony with reality is not complete with only nirvana. Another point of importance is that the different stages mentioned (satori, enlightenment, and nirvana) are not inclusive. You can attain enlightenment, skipping satori, and you can attain nirvana without ever attaining satori or enlightenment. When you attain nirvana you are aware of the other levels of consciousness.

The highest level of harmony that can be attained in Buddhism is para-nirvana (pari-nibbana). Para (pari) means death. Thus para-nirvana means purity in death. Since all of us will die, we know that we will reach para-nirvana. If we believe in samsara, then we will have had to pass through the other stages in order to have salvation. Para-nirvana is ultimate purity, ultimate harmony. For those that understand this principle, they can understand why Buddhist monks seem to place such little value on their lives. Suicide is not uncommon among the semi-conscious Buddhists. For the enlightened, death becomes something that is looked forward to, but not sought. For a Buddha, death is accepted with a smile. To enter para-nirvana is to have your body become one with reality. For one whose mind is already one with reality, to have the body become one with reality becomes yet another achievement.

**After Gautama**

When Gautama Siddhartha, the Buddha, died his teachings began to be interpreted. He would not have been happy with the interpretations. His successors tried to understand his teachings through his early actions. The first school to form was a school of ascetics called the Theravada. The Theravada did three things that were against the teachings of Buddha. First, they were ascetics, and used Sanskrit (a dead language) in their practice, both of which Buddha discouraged. Buddha wanted his teachings to be given to the people, not restricted to a few ascetics. Thus the practice of Buddhism was supposed to be in the vernacular, the language spoken by the people. He also denounced self-mortification, and other techniques employed by ascetics. Second, they idolized and virtually deified Buddha. Buddha was very specific that he was not a god and not sent by a god. He was also very specific that he did not want to be idolized, that he wanted the people to study the spirit of his teachings more than they studied him and his activities. The third thing the Theravada did, was they followed the actions of Buddha up to his enlightenment, creating a specific path. Buddha had said that his path was the wrong path. The Theravada had turned Buddhism into a religion for a select few. Buddha did not consider his teachings as a religion, and he wanted his teachings to go to the masses.

# An Introduction to Zen Thought

In the third century B.C.E. (before the common era) the Emperor Asoka (Ashoka) came to power in the Mauryan Empire in Northern India. Asoka expanded his empire throughout most of the Indian Subcontinent. One day he witnessed a particularly bloody battle, and was moved by the pain and suffering. This touched him so deeply that he adopted Buddhism and its doctrines for peace. Asoka was to become a major player in the history of Buddhism. It was Asoka that made Buddhism a world religion. Asoka began to erect pillars around the Mauryan Empire, to mark the boundaries. On these pillars he had his edicts and Buddhist teachings inscribed, so that the neighboring people would be exposed to Buddhism. He also invested a great deal of manpower and resources into spreading Buddhism throughout Southern Asia. He sent missionaries to the southern tip of India, Ceylon (Sri Lanka), and east to Burma and Thailand. Though Asoka declared the religion of his empire to be Buddhism, he was tolerant of the numerous religions in India. Certainly his belief in Buddhism helped it to spread quickly in India, but his missionaries had the greatest impact. Today Buddhism is virtually extinct in India. All the countries that Asoka sent missionaries to still practice Buddhism. From Burma and Thailand, Buddhism continued to spread east slowly. Buddhism would not reach the east coast of Asia until the Chinese influenced the Vietnamese. There is speculation that Buddhism was assimilated into the Hindu mainstream in India. Considering their similarities, this is the most likely reason for the apparent absence of Buddhism in India. Looking at Hinduism we find that Hinduism is a very compelling religion in India. Hinduism has repeatedly absorbed other religions, notably Jainism and Yoga. Though both Jainism and Yoga still exist, they are in the shadow of Hinduism, as is Buddhism in India. Jainism is slowly disappearing into the mainstream of Hinduism. Even Huston Smith discusses Yoga in terms of Hinduism.

Asoka's efforts helped to give rise to a second school of Buddhism. Like Buddha, Asoka wanted Buddhism to be spread to the people. The new school that developed called itself the Mahayana. Maha means greater, and yana means raft. Some translators refer to the Mahayana as the Greater Vehicle. The Mahayana labeled the Theravada as the Hinyana, or the Lesser Raft (Vehicle). Why the distinction in size? The Mahayana are the greater raft because they are ferrying the masses, the general population, to salvation. The Hinyana are the lesser raft because they only have to ferry themselves, the ascetics, to salvation. The word salvation has religious connotation. and this is intentional. Both the Theravada (Hinyana) and the Mahayana are religions.

What else distinguishes the Mahayana? We can differentiate between the Mahayana and Theravada by looking at the life of Buddha. The Theravada follow Buddha up to the time of his enlightenment. The Mahayana follow the teachings of Buddha after his enlightenment. What we find is that the Mahayana are also at fault with Buddha's teachings. Toward the end of Buddha's career he said that his teachings were not the

**23**

true path either.  He encouraged his disciples to follow the spirit of his teachings, not the words of his teachings.  Buddha had recognized a problem with being a great teacher.  In the West we are used to religions of the book.  These are religions that have their teachings written down.  Many people have studied these teachings and attacked inconsistencies.  People have begun to study religions not for their spirit, but for concrete information, the facts.  Buddha did not want this.  Being only a human, and restricted to the language of humans, Buddha could not keep his teachings pure, but was able to convey the spirit of his teachings.  He did not want his words twisted and interpreted.  Another problem was that Buddha knew that each person had to follow their own path, which they would have to find.  He knew that if people looked for their path in his words, they would not find it.  This is why Buddha said that his teachings were wrong.

Like the Theravada, the Mahayana had a specific path, which was wrong.  Several sects of both schools also deified Buddha.  What the Mahayana did that was right, was they took Buddhism to the people.  In the Mahayana school the monks become bodhisattvas.  A bodhisattva is one that forgoes nirvana to spread the word of Buddhism.  They are Buddhas to be.  Originally Buddha used this term (in Pali it is bodhisatta) to refer to himself before he became the Buddha.  This is the way bodhisattva is used in the Theravada school.  In the Mahayana school the bodhisattva does not place emphasis on the self, and the self-fulfillment of enlightenment.  Instead the bodhisattva is altruistic, seeking the enlightenment of even "the last blade of grass" before his or her own fulfillment of nirvana.

Another thing the Mahayana do, as a result of this, is actively seek to convert people (proselytizing).  Buddha did not seek to convert people.  People came to him because they wanted to convert or hear him speak.  Buddha did not go to people in order to convert them.  He was a very charismatic person, and a great speaker.  Though he did not seek to convert people, his very presence and speech was enough to convert them.  If there is something that is originally Buddhism, it is the conversion of people not by force, but by the charisma of the teachings themselves.  Asoka's efforts were obviously copied by the Mahayana.

Another area of difference emerged between the Mahayana and the Theravada.  Although it seems small, it is illustrative of the goals of both schools.  The Theravada used the Sanskrit language to inscribe their sacred texts.  Sanskrit was and is a dead language.  As a result very few people could read or understand the Buddhist texts in the Theravada school.  The Mahayana used the vernacular language, the language of the people.  The Mahayana texts are also filled with Sanskrit terms, the traditional language of Vedism and subsequently Hinduism.  The common terminology and language made the teachings of Buddhism easier to spread to the people, and provided a means for the people to relate Buddhism to their old religion.  As a tool, the vernacular language was an

# An Introduction to Zen Thought

excellent choice of the Mahayana for attracting the masses from Hinduism to Buddhism. The Sanskrit terminology provided an avenue for Hinduism to assimilate Buddhism though.

The Theravada and Mahayana schools are distinctly Buddhism as a religion. The word religion comes from the Latin word religio, which means to bring together. The Theravada brought ascetics together under the aegeus of Buddhism. The Mahayana brought the masses together, with the promise of salvation through Buddhism. Salvation was the central theme of both schools. Salvation from what though? Salvation from samsara—the cycle of reincarnation. Thus the cycle of reincarnation was another force that brought people together. Faith is an integral part of religion. If you do not believe in something, then you do not have faith in it. If you believe in something, and get together with others who believe the same thing, then you are forming a religion. In this case the belief was in samsara, and the belief that Buddhism is the way to salvation from samsara. Thus these schools are distinctly religious.

## The School of Zen

In the late fifth century, early sixth century of the Christian era Bodhidharma brought Zen to China. In China, Zen is called Ch'an. Bodhidharma felt that the building of Buddhist temples and the reciting of sutras was futile. He brought with him the essentials of Buddha Gautama's teachings, the spirit of Buddhism. Buddhism had already arrived in the form of the written and spoken word, but its spirit had not yet arrived. By this time, Buddhism was almost one thousand years old. Buddhism had virtually lost its spirit in the religious teachings of the Theravada and Mahayana schools. Dwight Goddard and Huston Smith both agree that Zen captures the spirit and essentials of the original teachings of Buddhism.

How is Zen so different from the Mahayana and Theravada schools? Zen relies on very few of the teachings of Buddha. The teachings that Zen relies on are: the Four Noble Truths, the Eightfold Path, and Buddha's commitments to being available to the masses and attracting the masses through charisma alone, not by actively seeking converts. Zen also pays particular attention to what Buddha said with regard to his teachings and his own path; that he had denounced his own path and teachings as wrong. Finally, Zen embraces with all its force one of Buddha's most important sermons. The sermon Zen embraces is the one in which Buddha transmitted enlightenment to one of his disciples. One day Buddha was given some flowers and asked to give a sermon summarizing his teachings. Buddha agreed, and set himself before his disciples for the sermon. He then held up one of the flowers, and that was his entire sermon. When he held up the flower his disciples did not understand. The exception was a disciple name Kasyapa. When Buddha held up the flower, Kasyapa smiled in understanding. Buddha then gave Kasyapa the flower.  This was what is called the first transmission of the lamp.  From then on Kasyapa was called Mahakasyapa, or Great Kasyapa.  He was great because he had great insight.  Mahakasyapa was the immediate successor to Buddha, as the principle teacher of the Dharma (law).  He was the first Dharma-heir.  This wordless transmission is the centerpiece of Zen.

Where the Theravada and Mahayana rely on the sutras (sermons/teachings) and shastras (commentaries on the sutras), Zen burns its books.  Zennists study Buddha up to the point where he states that his teachings are wrong.  Then the Zennists burn their books.  Zennists study the path that Buddha took to enlightenment, and when Buddha says that his path was wrong, they abandon his path and seek their own, which is what Buddha implied.  Though Zen emphasizes the Four Noble Truths and the Eightfold Path, they are lost in word, and maintained in spirit.

Where many schools of Zen can be found at fault, is that many focus on asceticism.  Though their doors are open to all, to become a Zen monk is to become an ascetic.  The true spirit of Zen is not found in the monastery.  The true spirit of Zen is found in the culture and the people.  The monasteries do serve their purpose though.  The monasteries provide a formality, something that creates an illusion of the existence of Zen.  Without the monasteries, Zen would be a cultural entity only, and would be lost in name as a specific discipline.  This is fortunate, because it has provided a focal point for promoting its own existence.

The biggest problem with the monastery is that it is not the real world.  A monk or nun can live his or her entire life within the confines of the monastery.  Monasteries are self sufficient, and require little from the outside.  What monasteries need from the outside, they are given willingly by the people.  The monasteries lack the qualities available to living in the general populous.  These qualities include sex, alcohol, social interaction within the culture and with other cultures, and interactions within the work force.  Thus monasteries have become an escape, a fantasy.  Many monks have had difficulty interacting outside the monastery because they have learned to live in the fantasy of the monastery.  This is not true Zen.  Many other monks have refused to be confined to monasteries, and have spent their lives wandering or leading regular lives.  This is true Zen.  True Zen is a way of life for the people, not to be limited to a small number of people.  Looking through the history of Zen we can see what has made the true masters of Zen.  The masters all left the monastery and experienced regular life.  Zen monks have begun to realize the fault in being confined to monasteries, and are beginning to leave their monasteries to live normal lives.  The monks have begun to even marry and have children.  Without the experiences of normal life we cannot fully understand the Four Noble Truths.  This is what has begun to be realized in Zen monasteries.

# An Introduction to Zen Thought

Though Zen has its faults, Zen is receptive to new thought. Unlike its contemporaries, true Zen does not profess a goal. The existence of monasteries suggests a general goal, and a religious connotation. Gradually these monasteries have been transformed into learning centers. A zendo is a learning center for Zen, translated as the way of Zen. It is a place where the way of Zen is taught. Monks have been transforming into teachers, with regular lives outside the zendo. Certainly there are still monasteries and ascetic Zen monks. What is important here though is the existence of the zendo. The zendo is the avenue for sharing Zen and Buddhism with the masses. The zendo is also the charismatic embodiment of Zen, in a formal location. Merely by its own existence, a zendo attracts fresh minds. These fresh minds come curious to see what is taught there. The people are not formally converted. Some leave confused and not interested. Most stay by their own choice. This is the way Buddha would have preferred it.

Another thing that Zen practices is extreme tolerance of other religions and philosophies. Zen is literally affirmative in its approach to religions and philosophies. Buddha taught that his disciples should make an effort to study other teachings, including religions and philosophies. Zen also encourages this. Zen also encourages individuals to maintain their original religious beliefs. The reason for this is that Zen asserts that it is neither a religion nor a philosophy. Previously I defined religion as bringing people together. Does not Zen bring people together? The answer to this is both yes and no. When people go to the zendo to study Zen they are coming together for a common purpose, to study. In the zendo each person is a complete individual, thus the people that have come together are only physically together, not mentally. When the people leave the zendo they return to their normal lives. They do not continue to congregate, to come together. They do not get together to worship, or to practice. If they wish to continue their formal education, they can go back to the zendo, but again what is bringing them together is the will to learn. Thus Zen is and is not a religion, depending on your personal interpretation and how broadly you define religion. For these reasons, Zen can maintain its posture of indifference and tolerance of religions.

The encouragement of studying and practicing religions is unique. The Chinese religions/philosophies do not do this. They do have a characteristic of complimenting each other though. Each of the Chinese religions/philosophies applies to different aspects of life, allowing each individual to have equal commitment to each. This is a sharp contrast from Western thought. Western religions like to isolate themselves from each other. This has been the source of conflict throughout Western history. This isolationist attitude makes acceptance of other schools of thought difficult for Westerners, and has resulted in conflicts between the West and the Orient. These conflicts have risen from a Western desire to inflict their beliefs on the Orient. The Orient cannot help but be disenfranchised by the self-centered attitude of Western thought. The Orient otherwise accepts Western teachings as subjects for study but not for adherence. Zen and Buddhism support this study of Western thought. Zennists are very interested in studying the West, because the West is their new frontier. Zen does not aim to supplant Western thought. Zen aims to become a part of Western thought, just as it has become a part of Eastern thought. In this, Zen is a way of life, not a philosophy or a religion. We find that Zen is non-competitive. We do see competition between schools of Zen though. But is this entirely true?

There are numerous schools of Zen. On the surface we see that these schools have differences. As Westerners we fail too look for their similarities. Although different schools of Zen exist, true Zen schools do not compete. Students may feel animosity toward the teachings of other schools, but the masters do not. Thus the competition among schools of Zen is merely a surface issue. Deep inside the real masters agree that Zen is Zen, no matter what school you go to. Some radicals that believe they are masters, or capable of teaching, break away and form their own conflicts. As they try to compete with the true schools of Zen, the true schools ignore their antics. The true school of Zen emphasizes harmony, and discourages any conflict. For this reason you would not see masters competing, but you would see the students competing.

**Harmony and Nature**

Harmony is central to Zen and Buddhism. To the true school of Zen, there is no distinction between Zen and Buddhism. This attitude itself is illustrative of the principle of harmony. In Buddhism we are supposed to attain harmony with ourselves, our surroundings, and with reality. To tie this all together we can call this collectively harmony with nature.

In Buddhism we see the existence of Buddha-nature. Buddha-nature is in everything. What is Buddha-nature? Buddha-nature defines itself, as the awakened state that is everything. Nature is everything, including our environment and ourselves. This is a complicated situation that will be discussed with Tao and Taoism later. Buddha-nature implies interconnectedness in everything. If all things have Buddha-nature, then all things are in some way connected. This holistic view encourages the Buddhist to look within themselves. Why? Because we each understand ourselves better than we understand anything or anyone else. If this were true, why would we ever seek the answers in something we understand less than ourselves? This is the biggest mistake people make, seeking the path outside themselves.

When we attain harmony with ourselves, then we will have harmony with nature. We attain harmony with ourselves by awakening to our own existence, through meditation. From this Zen derives its name. Zen literally means meditation. In Zen we meditate to establish harmony throughout ourselves, and our environment. Our environment includes our religious and cultural background.  In this sense Zen compliments the individual's own beliefs, by providing harmony.

**Faith**
Faith is a belief.  In Mahayana and Theravada Buddhism adherents believe in samsara and salvation in nirvana.  In Zen adherents believe in themselves, and in the wholeness of reality.  In Zen there is not a religious faith, but there is an almost philosophical faith.  Faith assumes an altogether different role for zennists, than we would expect in a religious faith.

I have given non-denominational sermons before groups of people of a variety of religions.  My emphasis has always been on faith, because faith is the central element of religion.  Many people wonder what religion they should follow.  Never seek your religion in books or temples.  This is the way of Zen.  First we must all have faith in ourselves.  Then if we still have some faith left, we should devote that faith to reality.  Then if there is still faith left, then devote that faith to a religion that fits your beliefs.  If you do not agree with the religion you are practicing, then it is the wrong religion for you.  If you are not happy with a religion you will not have faith in it.

Faith is like love.  We cannot have faith in anything unless we first have faith in ourselves.  This is one thing that Zen provides.  Zen is a way of developing faith in the individual.  If the result is a stronger faith in something else, that is okay.  Most spiritual and religious problems are rooted in faith.  This is where Zen compliments personal beliefs and religion in general.  Zen is without goals.  The way of Zen is through what Taoism calls wei wu wei.  Wei wu wei means action non-action.  Without having any goals or a prescribed way, Zen does not provide any space for disappointment.  We cannot live Zen wrong.  Thus Zen gives us assurance, confidence, and subsequently faith.

# CHAPTER III—
## The Evolution of Zen

To understand Zen we must understand the evolution of Zen. We have already discussed the Buddhist origins of Zen. Now we need to examine how Zen developed historically with the arrival of Buddhism in China. To create this outline, Dumoulin's books, Zen Buddhism: A History, volumes one and two, are the primary source. I highly recommend these books to the researcher of Zen history.

Buddhism began to arrive in China around the year 62 C.E. At first Buddhism was accepted, particularly because of its similarities with Taoism. By the fourth century Buddhism had flowered. Buddhism arrived by way of India through the steps of Asia, into Northwest China, and then into Central China. The form of Buddhism that came to China was Mahayana. In the ninth century Buddhism was persecuted for a short period, dating from 841 to about 846. By the end of this short period all that was left was the Pure Land Buddhists, and the school of Zen. The reasons Buddhism was persecuted are many. Among these are: a conflict generated by the doctrine of celibacy, which conflicted with the Chinese family system and social structure; immunity from taxation and social service; failure to contribute to the Chinese economy; and the biggest blow was they were becoming too involved in the government. It should be noted that one of the reasons Zen had survived was that Zen monks were productive, contributing to the Chinese economy agriculturally.

Pure Land Buddhism was founded by Hui-yuan (ca. 337-417 C.E.). This sect was a religious school of Buddhism. It focused on something the Chinese already believed in, which was Heaven. Heaven was the Pure Land, the place where adherents would go after death, a western paradise. This school emphasized salvation through devotion to Amitabha Buddha. You should remember that the Chinese only believed in a Heaven and Earth, and did not believe in Hell, Purgatory, nor reincarnation. This did provide a narrow avenue for the acceptance of the Pure Land sect. What this school emphasized was meditation in order to see the Pure Land and Amitabha Buddha. In a sense Amitabha was deified, but really he was revered as being the spirit that had guided in the creation of the Pure Land sect, and the spirit that would take the dead to the Pure Land. He was also the spirit that would take the adherents to the Pure Land. It would be natural for them, especially since traditional Chinese religion is the worship of the spirits of ancestors, to worship one spirit out of respect.

Dumoulin begins his first volume with a review of Buddhism and Yoga, then moves through the early history of Buddhism of China. The last section of the chapter on early Chinese Buddhism, is devoted to a person named Tao-sheng (ca. 360-434 C.E.). Tao-sheng is very important, because he has been called the founder of Ch'an (Ch'an is the Chinese name for Zen).  Calling him the founder of Ch'an seems warranted. Dumoulin states that Zen, as Ch'an, originated in China as a meditation school of Mahayana Buddhism.  Tao-sheng was a Mahayana Buddhist, with beliefs that diverged significantly from Mahayana to Zen.  First, Tao-sheng believed in sudden enlightenment, a sharp contrast to the Mahayana and Theravada traditions.  Tao-sheng was raised in a Buddhist monastery.  He embraced Buddhism completely, but was also deeply interested in and influenced by Taoism.  Some of this influence can be found in Tao-sheng's distrust in words and images.  Seng-chao (ca. 384-414 C.E.), a prominent and respected monk, also felt that true wisdom transcended words and concepts.  Seng-chao had also studied Taoism, and seems to be representative of Buddhist thought at the turn of the fifth century.  For this discussion you should realize that in comparison, Buddha-nature and the Tao are synonymous when we examine Taoism and Buddhism one on one.  Tao-sheng adopted the belief that enlightenment is the realization of Buddha-nature.

In the previous chapter I defined enlightenment as a realization that there is something beyond the self, that enlightenment is only one step beyond satori.  According to my definition, "An enlightened person has become conscious, but has not yet opened his or her eyes."  This fits with what Tao-sheng believed.  Enlightenment is a state of awareness where one is aware of one's Buddha-nature.  Buddha-nature is beyond the self, and it is within the self.  Buddha-nature is in everything, just as the Tao is in everything.  The distinctions between satori, enlightenment, and nirvana emerged with what Tao-sheng taught.  These distinctions are very important in understanding Zen.  Particularly of importance is Tao-sheng's concept of sudden enlightenment.  This concept suggests that the distinctions do not lay out steps, but rather a continuum.  By creating categories we violate the quality of our perception of the continuum.

## Bodhidharma

In the early sixth century another person appeared.  He is called Bodhidharma.  Where Tao-sheng contributed to the evolution of a formal school of Ch'an, Bodhidharma gave that school life, spirit.  Bodhidharma is commonly credited with being the founder of Ch'an.  Let us examine his story briefly, according to tradition, assuming he was the person who popularized Ch'an.  When Bodhidharma brought the spirit of Buddhism he popularized a new school of Buddhism called Ch'an.  We do not know whether Bodhidharma wanted to do this.  For that matter, we are not certain that Bodhidharma was actually a man.  For our discussion, we will take Bodhidharma's existence for granted, and assume that there is a central figure to the development of Ch'an.

In the previous chapter I mentioned that Bodhidharma felt that the building of Buddhist temples and the reciting of sutras was futile, that they have no merit and are not productive for individual progress.  The central element of Ch'an is its quality of decentralization. True Ch'an is the epitome of informality. Thus it would be logical that the person that popularized Ch'an would feel that building temples would be futile. True Ch'an also emphasizes wordless teaching. Again it would be logical that Bodhidharma would find reciting of the sutras futile. What is the point that I am making? Simply that we see in all schools of Zen (Ch'an) these two elements: the wordless transmission and individualization. If we see the same elements between schools we can assume a point of origin, either embodied in one person, or a group working together. For this reason we will examine Bodhidharma as the originator of this school, regardless of his existence as an individual or as a group.

The teaching of Bodhidharma brought together an old but new concept of Buddhism. Since we do not see Zen in Indian Buddhism, we can easily criticize where Bodhidharma came from. According to legend Bodhidharma came from Southern India. Historically we have no evidence of this. The absence of Zen (Ch'an) in India suggests that Ch'an originated in China, not India. Something else that supports this, is that Bodhidharma wandered all over China teaching Ch'an. He left a distinct trail, which we can trace back to India only through the martial arts he brought with him (Karate). He may have claimed he was from India to give authority to his teachings. Another inconsistency is that Bodhidharma claimed to be 150 years old. I am inclined to consider Bodhidharma as the first eccentric Zen master. This eccentricity would be the spirit of Zen, which has lasted up to now. Being an eccentric he would attract a lot of attention. Hitler once said that effective propaganda required big lies and going straight to the masses. Hitler's rise to power still mystifies historians. Through lies, Bodhidharma was able to attract a lot of attention. He got the attention of the masses. Where Tao-sheng affected a few scholars, Bodhidharma was able to take the teachings to the people. For this, we must give Bodhidharma credit.

The evolution of Buddhism toward Ch'an in China seems inevitable. Bodhidharma was successful also because Ch'an was more acceptable to the Chinese people. The Buddhism that originally came to China was religious in nature. The Chinese had no use for escaping samsara. With this concept, the Chinese could not relate. In fact, the Chinese could not relate with the concept of salvation. There was no idea for the need of salvation. As exhibited by Taoism, the Chinese could relate with self-realization and harmony. Thus it would be logical for the Chinese intelligentsia to cut out the religious connotations that had been attached to Theravada and Mahayana Buddhism. When they did this they removed that which had been added to Buddhism after Gautama's death. The Chinese captured the spirit and essence of the original Buddhism. The result was the formation of Ch'an.

If there was a Bodhidharma, he was not attempting to form a new school of Buddhism. Like many religious leaders, Bodhidharma only aimed to reform Buddhism, and to get the teachings to the people. We see this exhibited in Western religion, especially in Christianity and Islam. Westerners are fond of viewing Christ as a savior, a Messiah. What was Jesus? Historically Jesus was a man, who was a rabbi. He was the third of six children of Mary, and was married himself. He was aggravated by the conduct of the Jewish community, his own community. He retaliated, forming a group of followers who agreed with his views. His goal was to reform Judaism, not to form a new religion. He wanted the people to see the faults of their practices. It was his disciples that glorified him, making him the founder of a new religion. The irony of this is that Christianity, which formed later, was not a reform of Judaism. Christianity emerged with completely different customs and rituals.

We see this also in Martin Luther. In 1417 Martin Luther became aggravated by the sale of indulgences. The Catholic Church had taken to selling indulgences to raise funds. Indulgences were pieces of paper that guaranteed time off in purgatory. This bothered Luther so much that he wrote his 95 theses. The recent invention of the printing press caused these theses to be circulated rapidly throughout Europe. The end result was not a reform of Catholic Christianity, but the emergence of Lutheranism. Though Lutheranism is Christianity, it divided Europe religiously. One of the important things Luther did was he translated the Bible into German. This allowed for the common people to read the Bible. This along with the printing press contributed to the realization that there were inconsistencies within the Bible.

Islam is not much different from Christianity. Mohammed (6th century C.E.) was disgusted by local polytheism, and by Christianity. Like Christ he felt that Judaism needed reforming. He went a step farther, stating that Christianity had failed in its reforms. He also said that the Talmud and the Bible were not accurate, because men wrote them. His accusation was right, the Talmud and Bible were written by men. He believed that his Koran came directly from God. Of all the prophets and other figures in religious history, who started their own religion, Mohammed was the only one who wrote his own teachings. All the other figures orally taught their disciples. In most cases it would be centuries before the disciples would write the teachings. Even Confucius did not write his analects. Christianity did not begin to be written until eighty years after the events. Some of the writings, like Luke, were written over a century later. How accurate can these be? Mohammed put forth a good argument for his Koran. There was no middleman involved, no oral tradition that could be exaggerated by individuals. Mohammed claimed that God made him memorize parts from a book in Heaven. From this he named the book Koran, which means recitation.

Both Tao-sheng and Bodhidharma also took this perspective. Buddha never wrote his teachings. Buddha's teachings could not have been accurately transmitted by word of mouth, until it was written. The spirit of

Buddha's teachings was within the literature though. Certain key teachings emphasized this. Among these teachings was Buddha's assertion that the spirit of his teachings should be studied, not him or his words. Buddha knew his teachings would be distorted through oral tradition, and the Chinese got the message almost a thousand years later. The result was the wordless Ch'an. The light along the path, the lamp, was transmitted not by the words but by the concept, the spirit of the teachings. We find ourselves looking at the first transmission, to Mahakasyapa and the flower sermon, for support of the wordless spirit of Buddhism.

To the Chinese this was an old concept. This concept had already been accepted for at least a thousand years. In the Tao Te Ching, Lao Tse tells us that the Tao that can be told is not the eternal Tao. He also states that those who know do not speak, and those who speak do not know. Confucius also supported this throughout his teachings. Already ingrained in the Chinese culture was the preference for silence. Even today a man who works quietly in the fields, so I am told, is very attractive to the women. Boisterousness, verbosity, and garrulousness are not socially accepted in China. They are accepted in Western culture though. As a result of the Chinese attitude toward silence, the Chinese would accept Bodhidharma's new view on Buddhism with open arms.

As a religion in India, Buddhism vied for public support, not unlike Western religions throughout the history of Western civilization. When Buddhism arrived in China it found a receptive audience because of its relation with Taoism, but an unreceptive audience to active conversion. The Chinese were used to the integration of different schools in individual thought. An assertive religion was a threat to Chinese society. Buddhism became so assertive that it vied for political power. This would cause Buddhism to become very unpopular in China. Eventually the Chinese government would condemn Buddhism, burning temples and killing monks. Buddhism would become virtually extinct in China. After 846 only Ch'an and Pure Land Buddhism were left. Pure Land was acceptable because it fit in with Taoist mysticism and traditional Chinese religious thought.

Ch'an was acceptable because it was not assertive. Ch'an did not mind sharing its space with other schools of thought. Assertive and religious Buddhism naturally brought conflict. The Chinese already preferred to live in peace. Ch'an did not threaten to disrupt this harmony, and even encouraged the principles of harmony and peace. With these qualities that were already widely accepted by the Chinese people, Ch'an was easily accepted. We could say that Buddhism had been sinocized (assimilated by Chinese culture) when it became Ch'an. If we take the view that stripping Buddhism of its unpopular religious elements is sinocizing, then it is. We may also take the view that the Chinese did not add anything; instead they removed what should not have been there in the first place. In that case Buddhism was not sinocized. The argument created here is not what is important. What is important is that the

Chinese did this. They removed but they did not add. Taoism would act as the catalyst in the transformation of Mahayana Buddhism to Ch'an.

Later in this text Taoism and Confucianism will be discussed. It is easy for you to think that these are Chinese traditions added to Ch'an. Taoism was not added to Ch'an. Taoism only complimented Ch'an. Buddhism and Taoism are very similar, making it only natural that they would support each other. When we examine Ch'an we see a distinct influence from Taoism in the form of wordlessness. Ch'an borrowed much of the terminology of Taoism, as Buddhism was brought out in the vernacular language, the language of the people. Confucianism did not add to Ch'an either. What is important about Confucianism is that we see it employed by all the countries that Zen has flourished in. Confucianism is integrated throughout the entire society of each of these countries. To ignore Confucianism would be to ignore the socialization of all the people involved. Though Confucianism neither adds nor directly compliments Ch'an, it is essential for understanding the original perspective of the people who practice Ch'an. This is an essential element that is frequently overlooked in the study of Zen (Ch'an).

## **Cultural and Historical Influences**

Nothing has helped to perpetuate Zen more than the cultural and historical forces involved in the evolution of the Orient. The Chinese culture dates back over four thousand years. Though China has had its periods of disunity, and changes in government, China has remained as a cultural unit for this entire time period. This makes China the longest-lived advanced society. Certainly there are remote cultures that may be older, but these are not world cultures. The Chinese culture has included as much as one-third of the world's population at one time.

The size and longevity of this culture have had their effects. With early civilization came early technology. The Chinese began to look on themselves as civilized, and the surrounding cultures as "barbarians." This is not uncommon anywhere in the world. Feeling in the middle of all these barbarian cultures, China came to view itself as the "Middle Kingdom." This middle kingdom occasionally annexed more territory, and continued to grow through the millennia. It was not the intention of the Chinese to dominate the known world though. China did not want to bring these barbarians into their civilized country. On the contrary, they preferred that their neighbors pay them a tribute. The tribute was supposed to be for China's compassion, recognition, and for the protection from invasion by other cultures. When we think of tribute we often think of blackmail. This kind of tribute appears frequently in history. The Chinese were probably not innocent of this either. Generally the tribute was not forced. The tributes received by nearby cultures were generally very regular. These tributes may have been forced. The further we go from China though, the

# An Introduction to Zen Thought

less frequent the tributes. This seems to indicate a tribute out of respect more than from fear.

We also see, attributed to these gifts to China, the exchange of cultural and technological information. All the surrounding cultures looked up to China, as they would a divine being. In a sense these cultures worshipped China, and studied it closely, trying to imitate. Japan was close, but not too close. Like the other cultures, the Japanese sent missionaries and tributes. Like the other countries, Japan sought to learn everything about the Chinese culture. When China would suffer disunity, her neighbors watched attentively, and studied what had caused the problem. When China was conquered by the Mongols, China's neighbors watched to see how they could defend themselves. It should be noted that Japan was the only Eastern culture that was able to stop the Mongol invasion of their homeland. This was due to two factors. First, the weather did significant damage to the Mongol ships. Second, the newly formed samurai, practicing Zen, defeated the ground forces. When this happened Zen found its home in Japan, and the Japanese people.

Zen came to Japan through the usual channels. According to Dumoulin, Buddhism made its first official appearance in Japan in 552 C.E. This came from Korea to the Emperor Kinmei's court. This event was followed by missions to China. From the ninth to the twelfth centuries the Japanese increased their efforts, sending numerous missions to learn more about Buddhism as well as other institutions and ideologies. Dumoulin reports also that official reports on Zen are present in Japan as early as the seventh century. This would be logical, since Japan was one of the leading and most attentive of China's pupils. The first Zen master did not arrive in Japan though until the eighth century.

Buddhism was not quickly accepted in Japan. After centuries of conflict, Buddhism would take root in Japan, and became a leading participant in the Japanese culture. By the twelfth century the exchange of information had become regular, and Buddhism had established a strong foothold. Toward the end of the twelfth century the power of the aristocracy had diminished, and the gap was filled by the first shogunate, the Kamakura (1185-1333). Japan would go through three shogunal governments, lasting up to the middle of the nineteenth century. This form of government was called the Bakufu, meaning literally tent government.

What is important about the Bakufu government is the element of Zen. As previously mentioned, Zen played a key role in defeating the Mongol invaders. The Japanese warriors, called samurai, adopted Zen for many reasons. First, Zen develops discipline. Discipline is essential to an effective military force. Second, Buddhism in general removes anxieties about death. The paramount issue on the minds of most soldiers is their life. There is a constant fear of being killed on the battlefield. Unfortunately this fear is distracting, and is thus self perpetuating. By overcoming their fear of death, through Zen, the samurai were able to devote themselves entirely to fighting. The combination of discipline and no fear made the samurai extremely fierce warriors.

Another thing that came with Zen was the martial arts. Monks would be bored in their monasteries, and would wrestle and mock fight with each other for leisure and exercise. Through the years they began to formulate styles of fighting that were very effective because of the constant need for harmony. Thus the martial arts developed as harmonious fighting that required little strength, but a great deal of skill and discipline. This sport made for an ideal training instrument for the samurai. With the adoption of Zen and the martial arts, the samurai were able to be some of the best warriors the world has ever seen, maybe even better than the Spartans.

**Popular Zen**

When the United States dropped atomic bombs on Nagasaki and Hiroshima, and Japan surrendered, the atomic age had begun. Nuclear energy became very popular, but this popularity was short lived. The rise of the samurai was Japan's atomic bomb against the Mongols. The success of the samurai made them very popular. The samurai in turn blessed Zen for its invaluable contribution. Today we live in a world filled with nuclear power plants and arsenals. For the most part we are happy with the power plants, but not happy with the arsenals. The same held true with the samurai and Zen. People became unhappy with the samurai, but increasingly happy with Zen.

Zen became the religion of the samurai, and subsequently the official religion of the Bakufu. Shintoism was not thrown away, but was rather put on a different burner. The people also recognized Zen, and were willing to adopt it. Unlike the samurai, the people did not adopt Zen as exclusive, but rather as something additive. Zen became integrated in every part of Japanese life. You may say Zen was japanized, but what really seemed to happen was that Japan was zenicized.

In the earliest contacts with China, Japan had adopted much of Chinese art and culture. Included in this is language, calligraphy, painting, sculpture, and Confucianism. All of these acquired a special Japanese flavor, as the Japanese adjusted them to their own will and needs to fit their culture. When Zen came it was no exception. Certainly Zen adjusted to the Japanese needs, but Zen also changed the Japanese significantly. The arts became zenized, including calligraphy, painting, sculpture, and fighting. The Japanese culture and Zen molded into one solid unit, making Zen, in many instances, impossible to distinguish from the culture. Though the people were not comfortable with a military government, as we are not comfortable with nuclear weapons, they embraced Zen as an integral part of their culture.

At this point Zen seems to have moved from China to Japan. In reality, it virtually did. Zen had become very popular in China, but had become too popular. In India, Buddhism eventually disappeared into the larger

# An Introduction to Zen Thought

conglomeration of Hinduism. This seems to have also taken place in China, but not to the point that Zen completely disappeared. Zen had become so ingrained in the culture, that it was hard to formally see. There are still Zen monasteries in China, but they have lost their prominence as they have been assimilated into the culture. Somehow, in Japan, Zen managed to survive this, at least to some extent. As Zen became an element of the culture, it managed to maintain its identity. Zen became what might be termed a civic religion. That is, Zen became what brought the Japanese community together as a society, apart from Shintoism. Monasteries became formal representatives of the society, to the society. In the monastery one learned how to be a better member of society. Unlike the Mahayana though, Zen did not get involved in politics. Zen could not get involved in politics because it represented the society, not the individual, or groups of individuals. Thus Zen maintained its decentralized and neutral stance. This helped Zen to survive Buddhist suppression in both China and Japan.

One historical factor that pushed Buddhism onto Japanese soil was the oppression of Buddhists in China during the ninth century. The Chinese became alarmed about the influence of Buddhism on politics, and retaliated. They burned temples, killed monks, and forced Buddhists to go elsewhere. The result was a large migration of Buddhists from China into Japan. By the time these Buddhists arrived, the Japanese were beginning to be more receptive to Buddhism. Their arrival brought the fertilizer that would help Zen to grow, though Zen was not included in the Chinese oppression. Eventually the Buddhists would become to politically active in Japan as well, but the Japanese did not act so violently. This helped to set the standard for the acceptance of Zen in both China and Japan. By staying out of politics, Zen had escaped suppression in both China and Japan. This certainly had some affect on zennists who had any political aspirations, and further encouraged Zen neutrality. By being neutral, Zen was attractive to all the people, especially of Japan. For the Japanese it acted as a binding agent. Where the Chinese had a central culture for thousands of years, the Japanese culture was still relatively decentralized. Zen would act as the agent in giving the Japanese an identity. Eventually, as Shintoism became accepted through out Japan, Shintoism would also be an identifying agent in Japanese culture.

From all this we can say that Zen became a cultural entity. Zen literally became the culture, and the culture became Zen. Shintoism filled in where Zen did not provide for religious needs, such as worship and divinity. Where Shintoism did not provide for philosophical and spiritual needs, Zen filled in. Even today the Japanese faithfully practice all the rituals of Shintoism and Buddhism. Zen dissociated itself with religious Buddhism, but remained Buddhist. As a result, the Japanese had to be a combination of Zennist, Buddhist, and Shintoist. Buddhist religious rituals remained, right along side with Zen. The irony here is that Zen is very iconoclastic.

Iconoclasm in Zen has contributed to the reduced adherence to Buddhism as a religion. Though it was not the intention of Zen to bring about the demise of its partner, this happened anyway. If there is a point where many Christians will have a problem with Zen, this may be it. Catholicism in particular enjoys the use of numerous icons. Zennists will faithfully remind Catholics of the Ten Commandments (EXO 20:2-5), in which is said:

"I am the Lord thy God, who brought thee out of the land of Egypt, out of the house of slavery; thou shall have no other gods before me. Thou shall not make for thyself an idol, whether in the form of anything that is in heaven above, or that is on the Earth beneath, or that is in the water under the Earth. Thou shall not bow down to worship them; for I the Lord thy God am a jealous God. . . . "

The difference will be, that Zen has no personal relationship with Christianity. Since Zen came from Buddhism, it is only natural that Zen would attack the idols associated with Buddhism. Historically, to my knowledge, zennists have not gone out to destroy idols that were not Buddhist. This should be reassuring to Christians who are paranoid about losing their religion. Zen has traditionally not felt in competition with other religions, including other schools of Buddhism and Zen.

## **The Schools of Zen**

Every ideology has its schools. Buddhism has four major schools. These schools are the Theravada (Hinayana), Mahayana, Vajrayana, and Zen. Each of these major schools has numerous lesser schools associated with them. Zen is no exception. For our purposes here, we will only identify two major schools of Zen, though they are far from representative of all. These two very important schools are the Soto and the Rinzai schools of Zen. Of these two, perhaps Soto Zen has had the greatest impact on the West. To separate these two schools though would diminish them as individuals, as they are somewhat dependant on each other. To help understand the development of these two schools, we must also look at two other schools that are Pseudo-Zennist. These two schools are the Tendai and Shingon.

The Tendai (T'ien-t'ai in China) School was introduced to Japan by Dengyo Daishi when he returned from China in 805 C.E. What Dengyo emphasized was the universality of salvation. This became the leading force of religious faith and philosophy, along side Shingon, in Japan. According to this school, Buddha was a savior, and an embodiment of Buddha-nature. It is also believed that Buddha will return (Maitreya) as a new incarnation to finish his work of saving everything from samsara. The easiest way to describe this school is by relating it as a Taoist manifestation of religious Buddhism. The primary teaching of this school holds that Buddha-nature flows through everything (similar to the Tao of Taoism). The ideal goal is then to attain full realization of one's Buddha-nature. It is similar to Pure Land Buddhism, in that this school emphasizes faith in Buddha Gautama. This includes adoration and worship of Buddha, dependent on the teachings of Buddha, and harmony and identification with the universal self of Buddha-nature.

This is distinctly a Mahayana school more than a school of Zen. However, this school does emphasize contemplation, or meditation. Though this school is too indoctrinated with scripture and religious faith to be technically Zen, this school is important to Zen as an ideology. It is through schools like this that the teachings of Buddha are maintained. It is essential to formal Zen training to study the teachings of Buddhism, in order to qualify an individual to disregard the teachings. In this way the Tendai School is important for the preservation and providence of the Dharma and Buddhist ritual. Many great masters have attended the Tendai School, and studied the Dharma intensively, before they abandoned the Tendai School for a "higher learning." Dogen, for example, was bothered by philosophical questions that could not be answered through the scriptures and the study of the Dharma. For this reason he left the Tendai School. Other masters have likewise been dissatisfied with blind faith in scripture, and have left to seek the spirit of the Dharma, outside the words.

Kobo Daishi founded the Shingon School in Japan in 806 C.E. This school emphasizes mysticism and harmony with nature. In this respect the Shingon School is more like the mystical schools of Taoism, than Zen or Mahayana Buddhism. This is a cosmic Buddhism, in which Dainichi Buddha comprises the whole cosmos. This school recognizes other religions, declaring the deities and demons in other religions are manifestations of Dainichi. The universe is dynamic, changing, and potentially holistic. This may sound odd as a contributor to Zen, but it is really very important. What is important about this school is its emphasis on holisticism.

When we examine schools of Zen there is one dominant feature that stands out along side meditation/contemplation. All schools of Zen believe in a holistic reality. In the Shingon sect this has been raised to a religious form, almost cultist, but certainly magical and mystical. In the true forms of Zen there is no mysticism, but there is recognition of the holistic, and a desire for universal harmony. Holisticism may seem like a complicated idea, but it is not. A holistic view would see everything as being interconnected. If you have good, you must have evil, and you must also have varying degrees of good and bad. Good and bad exist on a continuum, similar to the colors in a rainbow existing on the continuum of the color spectrum. The existence of one necessitates the existence, or potential existence, of all the other members of the continuum. If the cosmos and everything in it is a continuum, then everything must be interconnected. If we have trees, then we have soil, water, and a solar energy source. If we have soil this soil must be attached to something, like a planet.  The existence of one thing necessitates the existence or potential existence of all.  Thus each thing is representative of the whole, and the whole is representative of each thing. The two are inseparable.

This is an essential element of Buddhism and Taoism.  The Tendai sect emphasized the existence of Buddha-nature in all things.  This is also holistic.  The Tao exists in all things, thus Taoism is also holistic.  What we find is that Eastern philosophy holds a holistic view of existence.  Even Confucianism emphasizes the society over the individual.  We are not individuals, but representatives of the whole society, and the whole society is representative of us.  There is no I, me, or my only us and we collectively.  This collectiveness is essential for the view of a collective consciousness, described as a constituent of Buddha-nature.  It is logical to assume if everything physical is connected, then everything mental and spiritual should be as well.  Then this is taken a step further, by declaring that the physical, mental, and spiritual are also holistically connected.

This view sets an important framework for Zen, perhaps more important than studying any particular school.  From this we can see the emergence of ideas of beauty.  Beauty is a characteristic of Zen that helped, perhaps more than anything else, to popularize Zen among the Japanese people. Along with beauty, we see the existence of the concept of holisticism.  This holisticism provides an identity.  We all want to know who we are, why we are here, and where we are going.  These questions are answered through holisticism.  We are part of a cosmological whole, and can identify ourselves as constituents of that whole, and as participants.  This further propagates national identity, which was also nourished by Confucianism. In this way the Japanese were able to identify themselves as Japanese, and as their society as an element of the Earthly whole.  Further the Earth becomes an element of the cosmological whole.

The beauty derived from this holisticism is expressed in Zen art.  Rather than bore you with details of Zen art, for which there are a lot of books published, let us summarize Zen beauty and art.  Zen art originates in China.  This art became more representative and beautiful in the hands of the Japanese.  This was not because the Japanese artists were any better, because the Chinese artists were truly brilliant in their simplicity.  The Japanese maintained the simplicity, and added spirit to the art.  What brought this was a much deeper rooting of Zen in the Japanese culture.  Where the Chinese Zen art is mostly paintings, calligraphy, and sculpture, the Japanese turned everything into art.  In this way regular work became a form of art, and art subsequently had to assume a higher form in order to stand out.  We see this beginning to form with Dogen, the founder of the Soto school of Zen in Japan.

The fundamental concept of the Soto School is the one-ness of everything, the wholeness.  It was originally founded in China by Tung-shan and Ts'ao-shan in the ninth century, named after its founders Tsao-tung.  Dogen is credited with bringing the teachings of this school to Japan.

## An Introduction to Zen Thought

What he brought was more than just the teachings of this school though. In order to understand what he brought back with him, we must look at Dogen's life.

Dogen was born in about 1200 C.E., to an aristocratic family. At the age of two, Dogen's father died. His mother died when he was seven. Before she died she told him to become a monk. These two tragedies were hard on him, and he would carry this burden for many years. This tragic experience introduced him to the impermanence of life. His mother may have realized the effect her death would have on him, and knew he would be empty without an understanding. Thus her advice seems to have been intended for her son's psychological welfare. After his mother's death, Dogen lived with an uncle. Just before he was to turn twelve he ran away, to keep from becoming his uncle's heir and successor as a nobleman. From there he went to another uncle, and pleaded to be trained as a monk. This uncle finally gave in, and directed young Dogen to the Tendai School at Senkobo Monastery.

At Senkobo, Dogen was ordained at the age of thirteen. He continued to study the Dharma, but was wild minded and filled with questions. Finally one question would drive him out of Senkobo. At about the age of seventeen Dogen wondered what the difference was between original and acquired enlightenment. His masters failed to answer this question adequately for him, and he was compelled to leave by his own desire to find an answer. He then wandered around Japan seeking a master that could settle his restless mind. Eventually he entered into the instruction of Master Myozen. Myozen also failed to satisfy Dogen. Dogen had given up on Japan, and figured that perhaps the older Chinese schools could better answer his question. He asked Myozen for permission to go, and Myozen insisted that he accompany Dogen on the mission.

So Myozen and Dogen went to China. When they landed Dogen was left on the ship for several months, possibly due to difficulties with Chinese immigration officials. While Dogen waited a cook, who wanted to purchase some Japanese mushrooms from him, visited him. The cook intrigued Dogen, because the cook was a Zen monk. Still young and curious, Dogen ventured to ask the cook how he practiced Zen. The cook told him that cooking was his Zen practice. This was confusing to Dogen, because he had thought the only Zen practice was scripture study and contemplation (zazen). In a later meeting, Dogen would ask the cook about scriptures and practice, still thinking they were one and the same. The cook responded, "Scriptures and words are one, two, three, four, five. Practice is revealing everything in the universe." In other words, scriptures are simple, empty, and lead to endless paths, but practice is the true way to find the spirit of Zen. From this Dogen learned that everything is practice, unleashing his mind from the boundaries established by declaring meditation as practice.

Dogen would wander around China for several years, going to many different schools. Still he could not find his answer. During his wanderings though, Dogen took an active interest in Zen history and genealogy, studying historical records at numerous Chinese monasteries. In 1224 he was getting ready to return home, when he found out that the abbot of Mount T'ien-t'ung, Wu-chi, had died. This abbot had been in charge of the first school that Dogen had gone to in China. What was important about the news, was that Wu-chi was going to be replaced by a highly repudiated master named Ju-ching. Dogen thought that perhaps Ju-ching would be the authentic teacher he sought to answer his question. Ju-ching emphasized meditation beyond all else. He himself meditated from three in the morning until eleven at night, every day. After studying under Ju-ching for a while, Dogen became enlightened. Ju-ching had given a sermon in which he told his disciples they would have to shed off their mind and body in order to attain enlightenment. This statement answered Dogen's question, and he was enlightened. Dogen would stay at the Mount T'ien-t'ung monastery until 1227, and would leave for Japan with only his enlightenment and education.

What Dogen Zenji brought back is what characterizes Soto Zen. The focus of Soto Zen is meditation, with little use of koans and scripture. Scripture remains of as much importance to the Soto School as any Zen school, which is not saying much. The student is the center of education in the Soto School. The student is responsible for deciding how he or she is going to practice, and what koans he or she will study. The student also chooses his or her own methods of meditation and breathing, presenting these decisions to the teacher. In this way the student becomes his or her own guide, following his or her own path, instead of one directed by the teacher. This is important because this is basically the same format emphasized here in this book.

Another important aspect of the Soto School is meditation. In this text I introduce you to the basic forms of meditation. I also introduce you to zazen, which is not really meditation. Meditation implies concentrating on something. The ultimate goal though is to concentrate on no-thing (mu). To concentrate on no-thing means to stop thinking altogether, and just be. This is zazen. Zazen is what is emphasized in Soto, not meditation. Meditation may be used to condition the student for zazen though. This is the method that I propose in this text, so that the student can work gradually into this seemingly complicated state of no-thing. A point where the Soto School diverges from the Rinzai School is that the Soto practitioners face the wall when they practice zazen. This is not the way I recommend for zazen. Instead, I recommend what is comfortable for you. A final element of Soto zazen is that it is practiced without any intended or unintended goal. You practice Zen for the sake of practicing Zen. I support this statement throughout this book.

# An Introduction to Zen Thought

At about the same time as the development of the Soto School in Japan, the Rinzai School also emerged. These two schools are the dominant schools of Zen thought in Japan and China. In some ways these two schools appear to be oppositely polarized. However, it is interesting to find that these two schools often exchange ideas and practice many of the same techniques. Of the two, Rinzai is considered the most unorthodox. As we will see throughout this text though, there really is no orthodox manner of Zen training. In my own teaching I feel it is better for the teacher to adjust to the needs of the student. For this reason I fully employ methods of both the Rinzai and Soto schools. If we can venture a distinction, we would be inclined to view Soto as conservative, and Rinzai as liberal and unrestrained. The liberal and unrestrained quality of Rinzai makes it the school of the spirit of Zen. The conservative formalism of the Soto School makes Soto the body of Zen. These do not exist apart from each other, but are integral to the entire picture of Zen. We find formality and conservatism in Rinzai, and liberalism and freedom in Soto. For this reason, to study one without studying the other is to mislead. To practice one without practicing the other is to but only half practice. Full practice is essential, so practicing both is also essential.

The Rinzai School was founded by Eisai Zenji (1141-1215), who introduced the koan as a form of Zen training in Japan. As with Soto, Rinzai was one of five schools that formed in eighth century China. Of those five schools, only Soto and Rinzai survived. Eisai, like Dogen, went to China and brought back Rinzai. Also, like Dogen, Eisai is reputed to have become a monk as a young boy, being ordained at the Tendai monastery at Mount Hiei. Eisai visited China twice. Like Dogen, he discovered the spirit of Zen in China. If there is something that both Dogen and Eisai can be credited for, it is the bringing of the spirit of Zen to Japan. In this they parallel Pu-tai and Bodhidharma. Where Bodhidharma was the unmoving conservative zennist, so too was Dogen. Where Pu-tai was the eccentric and informal, Eisai was also eccentric and informal. This parallel undoubtedly is what helped to give China the spirit of Zen (Ch'an), just as it did with Japan.

Eisai found enlightenment in the Lin-chi school in China. He then took this and transplanted the teaching to Japan. This was not an easy task for him, because he found opposition in the Tendai School. He was fortunate to get the protection of the Kamakura shogunate, and was thus able to begin a school at his temple in Hakata on the island of Kyushu. Here the Rinzai School began its unorthodox training programs, which were teacher oriented, instead of student oriented. In Rinzai, the teacher provides the student with a koan, which is used as a tool during meditation. In the Soto school, the mondo, or student and teacher exchange, is the source of koans, thus drawing the koans out of the students. In either case, the koan is contemplated until the student has reached an understanding beyond logic, rationality, and creativity.

An important feature of Rinzai is the style of zazen practice. In the Rinzai School zazen is practiced facing the center of the dojo. The teachers wander around the dojo checking the students to make sure they are practicing correctly. To correct the students, the teachers will yell at them or strike them, either with a convenient object, a hand, or a kyusaku. The kyusaku is a "stick of awakening." It is a long thin stick, flattened on one end. The usual place for striking is between the neck and shoulder. This is supposed to both stimulate and relax, inspiring sudden enlightenment, and according to reports, it has worked. This has often been related to humor in Zen, because of the strange methods these masters have employed on their students. One master, for example, yelled at a student so loud that the student was deaf for several days, but was enlightened by the experience. The key word here is experience. For masters in both the Rinzai and Soto schools, experience is essential.

Experience requires a specific condition in order to evoke the desired effect. For this masters are forced to stage the experience at the right time and place. This means that this form of training can be very time consuming. For that matter, there does not seem to be a form that is not time consuming. What consumes the time is preparing the student and the environment for the experience. The next difficult step is providing the right experience to fit into the conditioning the student has been exposed to. Generally this experience contradicts everything the student has been conditioned to expect. In this way, the student is faced with a very special and personalized koan, a perplexity of the conditions and situation. The perplexity is the continuum, upon which we build dualities. Realizing the absurdity of the dualism, the student realizes the continuum, abandoning dualism. At this point the student has become enlightened.

This is not to say that verbal and physical abuses are the entirety of Rinzai teaching. On the contrary, zazen is still essential. Zazen plays an important role in the conditioning process. Sometimes enlightenment is attained during zazen. Sometimes the master is not the one who invokes the enlightening experience. There are stories of enlightenment in which the student was struck by a falling object, such as a rock. Though this was not intentional or staged by the master, enlightenment was still achieved. In these ways, the Soto and Rinzai schools cross paths, and even blend into each other.

## **The Form of Zen**
As a whole, Zen has been shaped in much the same way as its enlightened adherents, through experience. Zen has been formed out of the body of Mahayana Buddhism by social and historical conditions. The arrival of Zen in Japan was timely, enabling it to enter the hearts and minds of all the people. In China, Zen just blended in with all the other traditions. This was not a timely situation, but Zen was still able to build a foundation. It is hard to say just how much Zen affected China. Though it still exists in

# An Introduction to Zen Thought

China, it is minuscule in comparison to the influence of Japanese Zen even today. Several masters, such as Taisen Deshimaru, Shunryu Suzuki, and Nyogen Senzaki have recognized the need for Zen to move again. Japanese Zen has been fortunate enough to maintain its identity after a thousand years. I tend to agree with these masters that Zen is becoming stagnant in Japan. As an element of Japanese culture, Zen is bound to lose its identity, and eventually fade away. The West has shown an insatiable hunger for new ideologies, as Westerners feel unsatisfied with their old traditions. While the spirit of ideologies still live, they must find new soil and fresh minds, so that they can evolve to suit the needs of the future.

When an ideology loses its dynamic quality, it stagnates and dies out. Shunryu Suzuki emphasizes this in his book Zen Mind, Beginner's Mind. It is the mind of a child that is most pure. The mind of a child is empty, and this is what we should get from Zen practice, an empty mind. The beginner's mind is void of preconceived ideas. The person who struggles because they feel their practice is inadequate, will achieve the most. When one believes they have already achieved, then they have imprisoned themselves by their beliefs. The same holds true for a culture. Japan is too zennist, and Zen is being taken for granted. The West is fresh soil, with clean minds for Zen to write upon (erase if you will) and grow.

In order for Zen to truly be transplanted, no school can be ignored. No single school of any ideology can be completely representative of the entire ideology. Though Rinzai and Soto are not the only schools, they are important for an understanding of Zen. These two schools are not only the leading schools of Zen, they represent opposite ends of a continuum. Where Rinzai is the profane, Soto is the sacred. Other schools also fall along this continuum. Not only this, as I have already pointed out, these schools often exchange roles. Thus the purpose of this was not to show you this dualistic situation, but to illustrate the continuum as a whole. Transplanting the continuum is the only way to be effective. From the continuum new schools will develop to fit the needs of the new soil. With the entire continuum at our disposal, individuals are provided the opportunity to find their own paths.

The individual path is the most distinctive characteristic of Zen. Every school must provide elements of the whole continuum. The difference becomes an emphasis on certain features of the continuum, not taking some features and ignoring all others. This is why all schools of Zen are important. This is also why there is little animosity between schools. In fact, masters tend to respect other schools, knowing that no school is exclusive. This is what you must remember as a student: no school is exclusive. Study each school at least as much as you study the school you belong to, with at least the same amount of respect. Not only should you study other schools of Zen this way, you should study other religions and philosophies with equal effort. You cannot discard something until you

An Introduction to Zen Thought

have earned the right. You have not earned the right until you are correctly educated (right thought, right effort, right comprehension).

# CHAPTER IV—
# Yoga Tradition

According to legend, Bodhidharma came to China from India, over land through the West. There is no solid evidence that Bodhidharma came from India. There is no visible trail of his teaching Zen in India. There is the possibility that this legend may be true though. It has already been mentioned that Hinduism absorbed Buddhism. It is also possible that Bodhidharma's teachings would have been absorbed into the mainstream of Yoga and Hindu tradition.

Bodhidharma emphasized sitting meditation above everything else. According to legend, Bodhidharma meditated facing a wall for nine years until his legs withered away. This sounds peculiarly like something a yogi would do. He was notably interested in Buddhist tradition, and frequented Buddhist monasteries. He was approached once and offered one of the Chinese classics (most likely one of the classics of Confucius). Asked to comment on the classic, Bodhidharma held it up to his nose and said, "There is a kind of quarrelsome smell about it!" (Hyers, p. 14). His iconoclasm did not stop there. The emperor of China approached him once and asked what merit he had earned from building temples, translating sutras, and having monks ordained. Bodhidharma simply replied, "No merit at all." These had no merit because they were not done out of right effort, a distinctly Buddhist principle. Bodhidharma's point was that Buddhism was not a religion of worship, and that you cannot buy the Eightfold Path or enlightenment.

In spite of this distinctly Buddhist view, Bodhidharma had definitely adopted the Yoga perspective of Buddhism, the meditation perspective. Gautama, as you should remember, practiced Yoga as an ascetic. This had not satisfied him, though he did maintain the Yoga tradition of meditation. Tao-sheng followed this doctrine, emphasizing sudden enlightenment through meditation. Bodhidharma comes onto the scene as an extremist. He is not alone in Zen history for extreme displays of meditation. His effort was a model for others to go by. Whether he really sat facing that wall for nine years or not is not the issue. It does seem obvious that he spent a remarkable amount of time meditating, enough that stories like this developed.

Whether Bodhidharma came from India or not, is also uncertain. One thing that is certain is that Yoga has had a profound impact on Buddhism. This influence dates back before Gautama became the Buddha. Yoga appears to be the direct ancestor of Buddhism, and Zen is a return to that ancestry through Buddhist eyes. All other influences have remained secondary, in comparison to Yoga. This is apparent through the main element that distinguishes Zen, and is the meaning of the word zen: meditation. Meditation is the root of Zen. This is not just sitting in contemplation, but walking meditation (kinhin), working meditation (samu), and so on. Thus all of Zen and life are meditation. In this way, Zen has taken meditation perhaps a little further than we would expect in Yoga. To understand some of the Zen perspectives on meditation, we must look at Yoga.

**Principles of Yoga**
Buddhism is a direct descendent of Yoga. The influences of Yoga on Buddhism in the creation of Zen are obvious. Yoga itself is of questionable origin. Yoga predates Hinduism. Hinduism may have resulted from the interactions of the Vedic religion and Yoga. After Hinduism developed Yoga seemed to integrate with it. At a certain point it becomes difficult to differentiate between Yoga and Hinduism. Except for the emphasis on meditation in Yoga, the basic beliefs are almost identical now in India. Huston Smith in The World's Religions includes them in the same chapter, as if they are interdependent. This is interesting, but not of importance to us. What is important here is the influence of Yoga on Buddhism and Zen. To recognize this influence we must examine the four paths of Yoga.

The four paths of Yoga are ways of reaching a goal. This goal is self-awareness (purity) and escape from the cycle of life-death-rebirth (samsara) that we find in Hinduism. Self-awareness is the means of escaping from samsara, the cycle of reincarnation. To achieve this, the Hindus believe they must look inward, and turn to Yoga to learn this art. It is interesting that the philosophies of South and East Asia share this same principle, despite being separated by the tallest mountain range on Earth. The general belief is that all the answers to all the questions are inside each of us. Everything is manifested and represented in even the smallest object, animate and inanimate. Simply, the parts comprise the whole, and the whole comprises the parts.

In the West we see religions emphasizing the "out there." We go to Church, the Mosque, Temple, or Synagogue to worship. For Christians, God is usually not believed to be inside us, but is somewhere out there. Christians have a tendency to view God as being a "mighty whitey" in the sky, pulling the strings of all the puppets. The Christians have pointedly made God in their own image, with the help of Michael Angelo and other artists. By doing this they have typecast God into being an old white guy in the sky. I must retract my assertion that this is a Western norm. By saying this I neglect Judaism and especially Islam. To the Moslem, God is within. As we move further east, the concept of "God" becomes more vague, until it is lost in the self. In this, the further East the ideology, the more call is given for looking into oneself. It is interesting to examine the ideologies across the Eurasian continent. In Britain we see Christianity with its outward search. In Japan, on the opposite side of this great continent, we see the inward search of Zen. Perhaps this is an over simplification, but it certainly illustrates a continuum. Finally the cultural conflict reaches its peak in the "Western" hemisphere, in the Americas. In the Americas the West has encountered the East. The West has become the East, and the East has become the West. This paradox has turned the Americas into a cultural grab bag, where the continuum has discovered itself.

The path in Yoga is not a simple one. To determine the path that should be taken, the master must first understand what kind of person the student is. From this assessment, the master determines which form is most suitable for the student. This sounds easy, but it is not. The reason is that no one specifically fits into any of the four categories to be chosen from. Instead the student will represent varying degrees of each. Here is another principle that Oriental philosophies share. The instruction is very personal and individualistic, because the Hindu and Yogi realize that we are all different. There is no one path. The path for each person is different. Thus these four paths are really points along a continuum, and are not independently exclusive.

## Jnana Yoga

Jnana Yoga is the path of knowledge. Knowledge, in this respect, is not raw data. This is not knowledge that can be gotten from a book, but an intuitive or internal knowledge, Gnostic knowledge. Gnostic knowledge is knowledge that is so pure that it cannot be explained or proven wrong, because it is real fact transcending time and space. This is a common definition for knowledge in the Eastern religions and philosophies. Zen also maintains this definition of knowledge.

The approach in Jnana is conceptual. Intellect is not necessarily capable of grasping the concepts, such as the infinite within the finite, or the whole in the parts. This requires perception beyond the senses, a self-perception. Most people do not have this talent, thus few are able to follow this path. This is the shortest path to enlightenment, and the hardest. We can compare this form of Yoga to mountain climbing. One mountain climber, with a lot of upper body strength, decides to go up the face of the mountain by pulling himself up with rope. Another mountain climber, with less upper body strength, chooses to walk around the mountain, and finds a way he can walk up. Assuming that neither climber gets tired before they succeed, the one climbing the rope will get to the top faster. He does it because he is able. He will also expend his energy in a shorter period of time, requiring greater endurance. His path was not easy, but it required ability and hardship. Jnana is not the easy way, and only a small number of people are capable of achieving it. Jnana is the quickest way to enlightenment though.

It is common for Westerners to seek an easier alternative. Neither Zen nor Yoga offer an easy alternative. You must do what you are capable of. As such, you must expect an appropriate amount of time and energy required for the method. As with the mountain climbers, you do what you are capable of. One may be able to walk, another to run, and yet another can scale the face even quicker. There is also the possibility that another can walk up with numerous rests, and great hardship. The end result is completing the climb. It does not matter which alternative was used. The one that tries a form they are not capable of will never reach his or her goal. He or she will expend all of his or her energy prematurely. You may ask how long it takes. This also depends on your capabilities, assuming you are practicing correctly. There is no set time frame for any method. The same holds true for the amount of energy required.

Jnana Yoga is specifically meditation as we are used to thinking of it. It is sitting in focused contemplation. You will see in this chapter, and Chapter VII, that meditation is not just this, but assumes many forms. These forms are countless, because our applications and actions are countless. In Zen we practice all the forms of meditation discussed here, in varying quantities depending on our needs and environment. Jnana is fundamental to bring out the knowledge and emptiness. By using this form we empty our cup, so it can be filled from our other activities. Where the other forms focus on particular aspects of our daily activities, Jnana summarizes them, and empties us from our attachments to them.

The first story in Zen Flesh, Zen Bones is a story about a tea lesson. According to the story, a university professor went to a Zen master named Nan-in to ask about Zen. Nan-in began by serving tea. He filled the professor's cup, and then kept pouring. The professor watched until he could not restrain himself any longer, and said, "It is overfull. No more will go in!" To this Nan-in replied, "Like this cup you are full of your own opinions and speculations. How can I show you Zen unless you first empty your cup?" (Reps & Senzaki, p. 5). In Zen in the Martial Arts, Joe Hyams tells a similar story, with the same moral. The purpose of sitting meditation is to empty your teacup. In Zen correct meditation is actually zazen, which is not meditation. Zazen is emptiness, no-thought. Meditation implies contemplation, which in itself is insufficient. As with the teacup, you must empty in order to fill again. By concentrating you are not completely emptying the teacup, because it is still a teacup. It is still a teacup because you have left a residue. Thus the teacup cannot hold as much as it can hold. Also, because of the residue, the cup has retained the identity of a teacup. If you put something else in the cup, it will be tainted with the taste of tea. Thus in zazen the teacup loses itself and its identity, and it can be filled with something else.

**Bhakti Yoga**

Bhakti Yoga is the form of love. This is not to say that love is the only part of this Yoga. Love is an emotion. With love we find all our other emotions. Even emotions like jealousy, hate, and reverence stem from love. Our emotions are our fantasies. These are sensations we feel internally. We do not get these fantasies from our natural perceptions, but from our emotional and creative mental faculties. For this reason, emotions are harder to describe than even physical sensations. Though you know the smell of a flower you cannot describe it. Likewise, the emotions are beyond our capacity to communicate. We can say we love someone or something. This only tells others that you have a strong positive feeling toward that person or thing. Love has more positive emotion than like. The word love does not state how much, or in what way. The word does not describe the fantasy associated with it, an image that is different within all of us. Since no two are the same, we have no way of communicating our emotions effectively.

In the religious sense, Bhakti Yoga represents a reverence for God. In Pure Land Buddhism we see a reverence for Amitabha Buddha. In the Tendai sect we see a reverence for Buddha Gautama. From the perspective of Zen I am inclined to equate this with faith and love, not reverence or worship. Both love and hate are very strong emotions. If we direct our energies toward love instead of hate, we feel more positive about our surroundings and ourselves. By loving ourselves, we can love others, and feel better about others even in the face of hardship. This is also a matter of survival. Survivors of Nazi prison camps all had a positive outlook and feel little animosity toward the German people, because they have no room in their hearts for hate. This also provides a faith in the self. In loving oneself one also has faith in oneself. Faith in oneself is important to success. If you do not believe in yourself, then you will prevent your own success, creating a self-fulfilling prophecy. Having faith in oneself, one is also going to create a self-fulfilling prophecy, only with positive consequences.

In the non-religious form, Bhakti Yoga does not attempt to define or describe the emotions. The goal is to be in touch with the emotions. It is important to learn to control fantasy. It is our fantasies that blind us (illusion is the source of greed). We may believe something, thus making it a truth, but that is not reality. By controlling our fantasies we can learn to differentiate between them and reality. You might say this is the reality check of Yoga. It certainly is a method for learning harmony with the emotions, fantasy, and the subjective. If we imagine something then it is true. That is not the goal of either Zen or Yoga. The goal is reality. If our emotions dominate us, then we will never know the difference. An irony in Zen is the respect for the blissful. The blissful often live in a world of fantasy. They have an advantage over those who are not blissful. The advantage is that they are not concerned with what concerns the non-blissful. The blissful do not believe that anything can go wrong, their fantasies paint over even the negative parts of reality. Inanimate objects are viewed as being even luckier, because they are not constrained by the troubles of the conscious or the fantasies of the blissful. A sort of emotional limbo is optimum in both Yoga and Zen.

## Karma Yoga

Karma Yoga is the Yoga of work. The definition of work has a physical element to it. When we think of work we think of manipulating that which is outside our physical being. The actual definition of work is very long. You should take the time and look in a dictionary for this word. You will be surprised at its length. We will leave it at the simplistic definition I have posed here, because this fairly well generalizes the dictionary definition. In the religious form, Karma Yoga refers to action in the form of fulfilling one's ethical and religious duties. This means the fulfillment of ritual practices (li in Chinese). In Buddhism this is identified in the Eightfold Path as right action. For the religious Buddhist this entails the fulfillment of ritual. Zen is empty of ritual. Work is essential to Zen though. This work is the work we do to survive, the work we do for the betterment of others. It is work that is not done for the purpose of personal gain.

If we look on work as the manipulation of that which is outside of us, we realize that we are discussing that which is not ourselves. Living requires work. Living requires interaction with our environment. In our interactions we find that all things are interconnected, the wholeness of reality. We can get in touch with ourselves through our interactions with our environment. We are members of that environment, so we are a part of the whole. Since each part contains in it the whole, our interaction with the environment becomes an interaction with ourselves. This is the point of Karma Yoga.

The work ethic of Ch'an helped to preserve Ch'an during the Buddhist suppression of the mid-ninth century in China. Ch'an monasteries were productive. They produced their own food and other commodities. The excess commodities were released into the general economy. One of the major complaints against other schools was that they did not contribute to the economy. Instead, the other monasteries acted as parasites to the community, begging and tithing. In the Ch'an monasteries, work was a form of meditation. Ch'an is not an idle school of thought. This has also helped Zen to be integrated with all levels of society, and to become more of a culture than a religion. The Japanese, a very productive people out of the necessity brought on by their environment and limited resources, were easily able to adopt the Zen culture because of the Zen work ethic.

We should also examine the word karma. Karma, in Hindu tradition, is our record, the record that stays with us throughout our incarnations. This is the record of our past actions, for which the consequences are based on our intentions, not the result of our acts. In the Hindu faith, the karma determines the form we will be reincarnated in. Being a record, karma implies something physical. The record itself is of our interactions, both with ourselves and everything else. In this instance the emphasis is on our intentions with everything else. By achieving a pure interaction with our environment we attain an understanding of ourselves. We also cleanse our karma. Thus the goal is to erase the karma, so that it has no reason to be reincarnated. We can do this through our work, our interaction with everything outside of ourselves.

In Michael Talbot's book The Holographic Universe, Talbot discusses near death experiences. People who have had near death experiences often have reported that they had lived several other lives. These people report that they were reincarnated to resolve a problem, to get them closer to enlightenment, or to balance their karmas. These problems are unresolved situations, where in one life the individual indulged too much in one thing or another. To balance out the indulgences the karma plans out a new life, and is reincarnated. Though near death experiences are more of a metaphysical issue, they pose as an example of applying Karma Yoga. Those who have near death experiences report that their interactions outside of themselves are what is significant in reincarnation. Thus it is the goal of Karma Yoga to cleanse the karma through work, through interactions in this life.

Karma is not an issue with Zen. Karma is metaphysical. The issue in Zen is to create a balance, and to come in touch with yourself and reality. Since Buddha-nature is in all things, we can learn from our interactions with things outside ourselves. We learn through work. Specifically, we attain a better understanding of ourselves through meditative work. Our work becomes meditation, as we harmonize with the unfolded reality, the reality of our senses. In the unfolded we find the enfolded. This opens up the student's mind to perceiving the enfolded in everything, including themselves. This perception clears fantasies, and eventually dualities cease to exist as the enfolded and unfolded melt into each other.

Samu is the name given to working zazen. Zazen is beyond meditation, in that it emphasizes no-thought. We put ourselves into our work and become the work. The identity of the individual is lost, as the individual permits the way of nature to take its course. By working in this way equilibrium is achieved within the individual. This equilibrium is the state of no-being. This is the abstract conception of sunyata, which is emptiness existing in the unempty. Sunyata is not a state where there is nothing, but it is a state of no-thing. It exists without existing. Thus the cup has been emptied, and then the cup has been erased. When the cup has been erased, the cup cannot be filled. The cup exists in a state of ultimate emptiness, no matter how much tea is added. Thus the presence of tea does not determine emptiness; rather the presence of the cup measures the degree of emptiness. In the terminology of Bohm, the cup is unfolded when we perceive it, and enfolded when we do not perceive it. When the cup is enfolded, it is dissolved into the Holographic Universe, and is no longer an obstruction.

### Raja Yoga

Raja Yoga is what Huston Smith calls the "Royal road." It consists of psychophysical exercises. From the word psychophysical we can see that

## An Introduction to Zen Thought

Raja Yoga is dealing specifically with the mind and the physical body. In the West we usually see Raja Yoga in the form of yogis distorting their bodies by twisting their limbs into shapes similar to a pretzel. This physical exercise is intended to create harmony within the body. Raja practice entails learning to control your physical being. It also entails learning to control your conscious being. This seems like a very strange technique. In performing the physical exercises the yogi has to focus his or her attention completely on the exercise. This is why the exercises appear to be so difficult. If the exercises were simple, then the conscious mind would find something else to do. Huston Smith reports psychologists as saying it only takes three seconds for the mind to get bored and change direction. Smith also mentions a passage in the Bhagavad-Gita where it is asserted that the wind is no milder than the mind.

The idea behind Raja Yoga also applies to Karma Yoga. By keeping the mind busy, focused on one thing, the mind can be cleansed. We see in Jnana Yoga a focus of the mind on something within. In Bhakti Yoga the mind is focused on an emotion. In each case the mind is being focused on something. The ultimate goal is to train the mind to focus well enough to focus on no-thing. No-thing is not nothing, or even something. Focusing on nothing is also focusing on something. When our body is conditioned so as to not interfere with our mind, then we must condition our mind not to interfere with our mind. The first part is the immediate goal of Raja Yoga. The second part comes partly as a result of the first. From our physical well-being we can build our meditations. By focusing on our physical well-being, we have already begun to develop our meditation.

There is an argument in Western philosophy about the mind and the brain. The fundamental question is, are the mind and brain separate or the same? According to Zen tradition, this question is paradoxical, in which both possible answers are simultaneously right and wrong. On the one side we can say that the mind is not physical, where the brain is physical, and thus they are separate. On the other side we can point out that the mind does not function without the brain. In Hindu tradition the atman is the self, the mind, the soul. The atman floats in a vast ocean of souls called the Brahman. The Brahman is the great power and soul of the entire universe. When we die our atman is supposed to dissolve into the Brahman, as salt dissolves in water. Though our atman cannot be perceived, it still exists. From the Hindu perspective, the mind and brain are separate. Scientists have also noticed that there appears to be a separation between the brain and mind. The mind, in science, has become our identity, where our brains are merely like computer processors. In this way, the brain taps into the Brahman to reach our atman, creating a link between the physical and metaphysical. The problem, when brought to Zen, provides a new question. How can you define the difference between the mind and brain? The point here is to try and find a boundary, to categorize. This is impossible to do. For this reason Zen tells us that this is another continuum. This is the continuum of the physical and the metaphysical. The difference between mind and brain lay next to each other on this continuum. The fact is that the continuum exists. The truth is what you believe the answer to these questions to be.

We exist on this continuum of physical and metaphysical. We have qualities and characteristics that are featured throughout the continuum. As was previously mentioned, by controlling the physical we can also learn to control the metaphysical. Mind and matter appear as two separate things, but are really connected in the cosmic whole. Since they are connected we must control both in order to control one. This is the ultimate goal of Raja Yoga, to control the continuum of the physical and metaphysical, to control reality. In this way, Raja Yoga is directly related to Zen. Zennists do not, generally, put themselves through the forms of physical exercises prescribed in Raja Yoga. Instead the emphasis is placed on physical exercise that has utility. For zennists it is important to be productive. On the other hand, there are also times for non-productivity. These periods gave rise to the development of the martial arts as a form of physical exercise. Where Raja Yoga does aerobic exercises, Zen does martial arts. Do not be misled though; a lot of martial arts are aerobic exercises, such as the practice of kata. The complexity of kata helps to make up for the reduced strain that is a quality to Raja Yoga. A well-practiced martial artist usually has little problem with Raja Yoga exercises. I do not know about the other way around though.

**Yoga and Zen**

In reviewing these forms of Yoga we can see the relationship with Zen. Since Zen is beyond words, Zen does not bother with dividing the forms of meditation. Instead Zen takes all four of these and applies them together, without creating distinctions. Creating the distinctions to a zennist is a waste of time. Applying these forms appropriately is not a waste of time. On the contrary, it would represent right action, right practice, right Zen. Right Zen requires accepting continuums as wholes, not by accepting their parts separately. Though studying the four personalities of Yoga is important, it is also important to recognize their interconnectedness. How these four came to be named I do not know. On inspection, it appears that these were labeled for academic purposes, not for purposes of practice. For purposes of practice these four are combined, and issued according to individual need. To determine issuance, it is necessary for the teacher to recognize elements in a personality that needs to be balanced out. These elements require personal attention, making for a pragmatic technique. Later in this text I will discuss Zen gatherings called sesshins. When you attend a sesshin you will exercise each of the forms of Yoga, in one degree or another. If you live Zen, then you will apply each form every day of your life. Every day our lives include knowledge, love, work, and psychophysical exercise. If we recognize these as ways of meditation, then everything we do is done in meditation. There is a story about a Zen teacher who went to give a lecture before a group of nobles. He sweated and was nervous throughout the presentation. When he returned to the monastery, he surrendered his position, because he realized he did not have every moment Zen. We never take off our Zen—it is always with us. When we have Zen every moment, then we live Zen.

If we examine the four paths of Yoga we can see a pattern. We find that the forms of Yoga are divided between the perceived and the intuitive. Karma represents the physical, and our interactions with the physical. Raja represents our mind and body, and our interactions with our mind and body. Bhakti represents the emotions and our interactions with our emotions. Jnana represents intuition, the metaphysical, super-physical, and our interactions with the intuition. We can perceive the physical, emotional, and somatic (soma means body). The mind and the metaphysical are intuitive. Metaphysics is not an ingredient in Zen, although a good argument could be made that it is present. Where David Bohm divides the universe into the enfolded and unfolded, Zen sees the whole universe. In David Bohm's theory the enfolded would be relative to the metaphysical, where the unfolded would be relative to the physical. What we perceive is the unfolded universe. Enlightenment is the unfolding of all that is enfolded, and the enfolding of all that is unfolded. In this holistic thought neither the metaphysical nor the physical can be differentiated; they become a whole, they become reality. This is why metaphysics is not an ingredient of Zen, and why all forms of Yoga are applied in Zen. The illusionary distinctions cease to exist.

Where Huston Smith seems to fail in his book is the ultimate goal of religious Yoga. This is the same goal as Buddhism, to escape the cycle of reincarnation (samsara). True and original Yoga was most likely exactly like Zen. Being assimilated into Hinduism, Yoga took on a new job, a religious function. Not only does Yoga offer an escape from the cycle, it now offers a path to God. Whether this is the way contemporary Yogis see themselves or not, I cannot say. Certainly a lot of people that practice Yoga are intent on its religious function. In the West, Yoga has assumed the form of psychophysical exercises (Raja). To some degree people pursue Raja Yoga in the West for spiritual and religious reasons. Many treat it as a form of exercise. Certainly Yoga has been metamorphosed by the West, and probably underwent a similar metamorphosis in India with the rise of Vedism and subsequently Hinduism. If this is true, then Zen has embraced the spirit of Yoga, and is perhaps the best representation of the ancient tradition. We cannot prove this with much certainty because early Yoga predates written history. The similarities are numerous though. Considering that Buddha practiced Yoga before he was enlightened, he may have captured the essence of Yoga and applied that in his own meditations. Naturally this would have been reflected in his teachings, and subsequently in all the schools of Buddhism that followed, including Zen.

The biggest difference between Zen and religious Yoga can be found in Huston Smith's headings on the four paths of Yoga. Each heading has "The Path to God" in it. The difference between religious Yoga and Zen is the same as the difference between theology and religious studies. In theology and religious Yoga you try to improve your religion, try to get closer to God. In Zen and religious studies, it is not their original intention for you improve your religion studying them. Both Zen and religious studies emphasize reality over truth. Truth is tainted by beliefs, where reality is not. Philosophical Yoga does exist. This is Yoga that is not interested in paths to "God." In the West we usually see this as more blind than philosophical. As blind, Yoga assumes no philosophical or religious role, it just exists. You may even say that Yoga is a fad, because much of its substance is ignored in the West. Many Westerners turn away from blind Yoga, because of its lack of substance, to Zen.

Zen and religious Yoga do follow a similar principle though. It is said that you cannot pursue God, the divine, the sacred, but you can apprehend God. This same sense of apprehending is found in both Zen and Yoga. We do not pursue enlightenment, satori, or nirvana. We apprehend enlightenment. It appears to us not because we want it to, but rather when it is. This is what Rudolf Otto called sui generis (of its own kind). It is because it is, no other reason. See Chapter VII, on the use of koans, and the apprehending of nirvana as opposed to seeking it.

### Eight Elements of Yoga

Yoga is a meditation school. There are eight essential elements to Yoga meditation. Where Buddhism had to deal with religious issues that had arisen from Hinduism, Yoga did not have to. Later, however, these elements would be applied to the Hindu faith, but their essence is still present. In Buddhism we have the Four Noble Truths, and the Eightfold path, which are a response to the notions of karma and samsara, as well as atman, Brahman, and the caste system. To understand the relationships, let us first look at the similarities and differences between Buddhism and Hinduism in terms of samsara and karma.

We find that both Hinduism and Buddhism are interested in escaping the cycle of reincarnation, samsara. The Hindu tradition holds that only members of the Brahmin caste, the priestly caste, can experience moksha, the Hindu escapes from samsara. These persons must maintain a clean karma, a clean record. Their record must be balanced for all their past lives, including their present life, in order to attain moksha. Persons belonging to the other castes also must strive to keep a balanced karma, so that when they are reincarnated as a Brahmin they will be able to attain moksha. Buddhism does not follow the caste system. Escape from samsara is nirvana. Nirvana can be attained in this lifetime, despite the caste you have been born into. What is shared here is the notion that the karma must have balance in order to attain moksha or nirvana.

An Introduction to Zen Thought

The karma is a permanent record that is transferred from one life to the next. This record is not the soul, the atman. Each incarnation has its own soul. Thus several souls through time-share one karma. The karma is a record of past actions, throughout all one's lives. The consequences for these actions are determined by the intention behind those actions, not in terms of human judgments of good or evil. When a person dies their karma is passed on to another incarnation, unless they attain moksha. The atman (soul) does not die, but rather is dissolved into the cosmic ocean called the Brahman. The Brahman is the cosmic soul. In this way we find the concept of cosmic interconnectedness in Hinduism.

The atman represents the individual in Hinduism. That is, the atman is personal, one and only, the specific life force occupying a particular form. For Hinduism this is representative of the self. In Buddhism, the self must be surrendered to sunyata. Sunyata is the cosmic wholeness, in which there are no distinguishing marks, no dualisms, being of non-substance without birth or death, nor having a self-nature. Sunyata is the non-empty emptiness, in some ways equivalent to the Brahman. In essence, Buddhism emphasizes the return of the atman to the Brahman before death. In this way the karma is brought to the surface.

The karma is then balanced by following the Eightfold Path, so that the escape from samsara is made possible in one lifetime. By shedding the atman, there are no longer class or caste distinctions. The individual becomes comparable with all castes and none simultaneously. The ego, the self, ceases to exist. In its place is the emptiness. The teacup has been erased so that the cosmic ocean, the Brahman, the Tao, Buddha-nature can flow without hindrance. How is this done? Through meditation, and subsequently zazen in Zen. It becomes essential to practice correct meditation, or as stated in the Eightfold Path, right concentration. For the source of meditation we must turn back to Yoga, and the eight elements that comprise Yoga practice.

The first element of Yoga practice is yama. Yama is restraint. The word Yoga is equivalent to yoke, which means to restrain, to control. The restraint here is both physical restraint, and the restraint of the mind. Though karma is a record of actions, the consequences are based on intentions. Thus it is necessary not only to control your actions, so as not to create bad karma, but also to have the right intentions, the right state of mind. Living requires action. If you pray with the wrong intentions, then even if the action is right, the state of mind was wrong. It is then better not to do a good thing if your intentions were self motivated, selfish. Performing actions for the sake of personal gain is not good karma. However you might be forced to do something that is not good, but with good intentions. Though this would generate good karma, the karma could be improved. The way it could be improved is by performing a good act with good intentions. This requires discipline, restraint. You must restrain

## Yool—Introduction to Zen Thought

yourself from doing wrong, and from doing good with wrong intentions. This is what must be done to fulfill the element of yama in Yoga.

Niyama is the second element in the path of classical Yoga, which means disciplines. In some ways this is a further affirmation of yama, it is a greater state of yama. Discipline however also means a school of thought. In religious studies it is said that "to know one is to know none." It is important to be versed in the procedures and rituals of your discipline. It is also important to understand those practiced by persons of other disciplines. Not only will this improve your own practice, it will also enable you to be mindful of their needs and situations. If you are not mindful of the needs of others, then you may perform an act with the right intentions, and on the surface it may be good, but it will not be good for others. Again this is a situation of improving the karma. We must balance our karma. Even slightly bad karma weighs on the negative side. The purpose is to equal the karma out, not to create more work for the balancing process. The more balanced your karma is, in Hinduism, the closer you are to being incarnated in a higher caste, and closer to moksha. You do not want your karma to be trapped in one caste. In Buddhism this is even more important, because you only have one life in which to balance your karma.

The third element of classical Yoga is Asana, which means postures. With postures we are entering into the field of meditation. Posture is essential to meditation. An uncomfortable posture does not permit for a productive meditation. On the contrary, poor posture breaks down meditation. Poor meditation does not offer the opportunity for self contact. It is in meditation that we learn restraint of both our minds and our bodies. We learn to be tolerant of others, and mindful of their needs. We empty ourselves, putting aside prejudice so that we can think clearly when we are not meditating. Even when we are not meditating we must maintain a good posture, so that the mind can function at its best. So long as the mind is functioning at its best, it can make the right decisions, and be able to weigh the ethical problems associated with an action. When a decision is made to act, then that decision can be made with the right intentions. In this way posture becomes essential in the process of balancing karma. Our physical posture is representative of the posture of our mind and our karma. A balanced posture helps to balance the mind and the karma.

Breathing control is the fourth element in the path of classical Yoga. This is called paranayama. You may recognize that this is the composite of three words. Para means death, an means breath, and yama means restraint. Breathing is essential to life. In the words atman and Brahman, the an helps to create the element of soul in their definitions. Thus breathing control is restraint of the soul, and restraint of death. By controlling your breathing you are restraining death. Remember the concept of sunyata. Sunyata is emptiness, with an absence of both birth and death. Without birth there is no death. Without death there is no birth. These cannot exist without each other. It appears that classical Yoga agrees with Buddhism in terms of sunyata.  We must restrain these concepts, if we ever hope to transcend them.  By controlling our breathing we discipline ourselves, our minds and our bodies.  We are also disciplining our souls, our atman.  This is a balancing technique that is both important to meditation, and to the concept of escaping samsara.

In classical Yoga the fifth element of practice is pratyahara. Pratyahara is the elimination of the outer perceptions.  This is the elimination of the five senses of sight, smell, taste, sound, and touch. Meditation can be correlated with the numinous.  It is Gnostic, in the sense that the experience is so true and well understood by the individual that it cannot be explained. Many call this experience "other worldly." Meditation is not meant to be other worldly, it is meant to bring forth the inner perceptions, the intuition.  Through the intuition reality is revealed, so that there are no misconceptions.  The senses are deceitful and our perceptions are clouded by the prejudice of our learning.  To prevent the interference of memories with the interpretations of the information received from our senses, we must not use our senses.  Our minds interpret our senses, and what we perceive is what we believe.  What we believe is truth.  Truth is not fact.  By eliminating the senses we are forcing ourselves to accept fact without the delusion of truth.  Illusion is a central element to Yoga, Zen, Hinduism, and Buddhism.  The name for illusion is maya.  Maya is the source of greed, in Buddhism, which is the cause of suffering.

Dharana means concentration, which is the sixth element in the path of classical Yoga.  This is not the same concentration that is referred to in the Eightfold Path.  Dharana is only part of the eighth element in the Eightfold Path.  Here concentration is not meditation, it is focus.  Under the eighth element of the Eightfold Path I suggested that focus was one part of that element, and the other was meditation.  In the Eightfold Path, meditation is the predominant theme associated with right concentration.  Here concentration is focus; focus on duties, rituals, mindfulness, livelihood, and so on.  When we do something, no matter what it is, we must contribute the right amount of concentration.  We must devote ourselves to doing that something.  In the Eightfold Path this was distinguished more by right effort than by right concentration.  Again we look at this in terms of karma, and we can see how this is important.  We must have good intentions to go with our good acts.  If we have good intent, then we will devote the right energy and effort to getting the action done.

The seventh element is meditation.  From the Yoga term dhyana, Zen and Ch'an were transliterated and adapted to Japanese and Chinese. Meditation is the most obvious of the eight elements, and is the way most people visualize Yoga practice.  This oversight leaves a lot of misunderstanding, both for Yoga and Zen.  Meditation is necessary for self contact, in the effort to maintain a balanced karma.  These eight elements can also be viewed as steps or stages of practice.  As you complete each step, you bring that forward to the next step. By the seventh element you will be practicing all seven simultaneously. Meditation is the ultimate form of cleansing and balancing. It is followed naturally by a higher state of being.

The higher state of being is samadhi. Samadhi is a state of concentration, in which a higher trance is attained. In a sense this is like enlightenment. If we were energetic we could say that there are actually nine elements in the practice of Yoga. However the ninth element would be applied only to the religious functions of Yoga, since the emergence of Hinduism. This ninth element would be moksha, the escape from samsara. Only the brahmin would make it beyond the stage of samadhi though. To attain samadhi would be to attain a taste of moksha. Certainly, in the Hindu tradition, samadhi would be indicative of being able to progress to the next caste in the next life. However one experience of samadhi would not be enough, because the karma would still have to be maintained and balanced. Samadhi is a state where one is absorbed and attains harmony. In Yoga there are two forms of samadhi. The first is with support and the second is without support. Samadhi without support is the greater form. To attain samadhi with support requires concentration on something, either real or imagined. To attain samadhi without support requires concentration on no-thing. This is pure consciousness without object.

In Buddhism, samadhi is literally concentration. As with Yoga this concentration can be either fixed on some object, or on no-thing. This is done to discourage the mind from wandering. For Buddhism there are three stages of samadhi, which are: preparation, beginning, and attainment of concentration. These three stages of samadhi can also be applied to Yoga. In either case, sufficient practice leads to the ability to attain samadhi at will. It is the state of one-ness, in which there is enlightenment, and subsequently nirvana. For Yoga it represents the liberation, bringing a new and existential understanding of both ultimate reality and the self. The release would be moksha in Hindu tradition. Moksha would thus be viewed as either a phantom ninth element, or as integral to the eighth element of samadhi.

# CHAPTER V—
# Taoism and the Arts

### Introduction
Taoism is one of the most difficult topics to write about. Taoism may even be more difficult to write about then Zen. The reason is that Taoism is not based on another written ideology, as Zen is based on Buddhism and the thousands of volumes that comprise the Dharma. Taoism is based on 81 poems, consisting of about 5,250 words. This does not leave much to go on. There are other Taoist works, such as the Chuang-tse, that can be used. The problem with these secondary documents is that they represent an interpretation of the original work. When reporting on a topic neutrally, primary sources are essential. Interpretations only mislead. It is better to have access to the original information, and for each person to interpret that information in his or her own way.

Taoism is paradoxical. The poems of the Tao Te Ching can be confusing to the unprepared. Being able to understand the poems is not a scholastic achievement, which means it cannot be taught. The necessary understanding is intuitive. This is typical of poetry. Recognizing this problem I have made an attempt to translate the concepts of the poetry into prose. To explain the poetry is impossible. To discuss the concepts of the poetry is possible through examples. This is not to say that all the concepts in Taoism, specifically the Tao Te Ching, are covered here. Instead, a small number of important concepts are discussed. These concepts are even deeper then they are portrayed here. No amount of words can do any concept justice. Many volumes could easily be written on these concepts, and the many other concepts of Taoism. Since this is not a book on Taoism, it is essential to limit our review of this topic. Though the concepts discussed here are important to Zen, these are only the primary concepts. All the Taoist concepts have some significant role in Zen. The relationship between Taoism and Zen is extremely intimate.

A famous theme in Zen art is the picture of three sages. The three sages are Lao Tse, Buddha, and Confucius. They are portrayed laughing as they prepare a stew or soup in a large pot. That stew is Zen. This theme is symbolic of the intimacy of these three ideologies with Zen. We cannot say that Zen is only Buddhism, or only Taoism, or only Confucianism. Zen is a composite of all three of these ideologies. Upon the formation of Zen from these ideologies, Zen attains its own identity and becomes completely severed from its parents. Zen loses its heritage. To understand Zen thought it is thus essential to understand the perspectives of Zen's heritage. The next step in understanding Zen thought is to erase the heritage from the picture. Admittedly this is a paradox that is difficult to comprehend. Do not attempt to comprehend it, just allow it to exist. When you allow it to exist, then you will catch the spirit that is at the root of all these concepts.

## Evolving Eastern Thought

The two most influential philosophies on Zen are Taoism and Buddhism. Certainly Yoga had a significant impact as well, but it should be noted that this impact comes through the Buddhist roots more than from a direct contact. Taoism is related to Buddhism through the Aryan civilization and their tradition of Vedism. The nature worship of Vedism is reflected in Taoism's distinct slant toward nature, especially in the meaning of Tao. Tao will be further defined later in this chapter. For our purposes here, we will define Tao as the way of nature. Though the Aryan influence is most obvious in India, it stands to reason that this same group left some influence in China. Unfortunately we have no record of this influence. Records on Vedism do not begin to appear until Hinduism began to emerge. At that time the Vedas, collections of religious hymns, were written down. The Vedas are the only reference we have to go by for our understanding of Vedic tradition. They were recorded about one to two thousand years after the Aryans left Western China. From what little we know of Vedism, we can see certain relationships. (In Appendix A is a chronological table that illustrates the relationships being discussed here.)

There are definite similarities between the later recorded Vedism, and the Chinese ideologies. This is most apparent in the ancestor worship that was the closest thing to a traditional "religion" in China. To help with this picture we must look at what these barbarians brought with them to India. The Vedic religion of the Aryans had certain elements we see throughout Europe and Asia, from about the twelfth century B.C.E. until the early Christian Era. Among these is a worship of spirits, who in most cases became humanized and deified. It is interesting to note that this polytheism was adopted throughout India and Southern Europe, where the invading barbarians were the most prominent. The polytheism resulted in division, where adherents to one god would try to dominate others. Eventually, urbanization would help to do away with polytheism, and monotheism would arise. In China the spirits remained as spirits, never assuming a deified role. As a result, neither polytheism nor monotheism developed.

One element of Vedism that was carried through Europe, China, and India was the concept of Heaven and Earth. This is a basic concept in which there is more than one plane or level of existence, where the spirits and the living are separated. In Chinese ideologies much emphasis has been placed on Heaven (T'ien). This rises from the traditional ancestor worship, something none of the Chinese ideologies argue with. If anything, they argue over rituals for practicing ancestor worship. The belief is that ancestors supervise human destinies, reward and punish, and demand the obedience of their descendants. The dead become spirits, and can only be contacted through divination and sacrifices. Heaven is not necessarily a place above or below. It is not a place in the clouds, but more of an alternative dimension existing within our reality. Something we see in Western religions is the existence of numerous planes of existence. An example of this would be the various planes of Hell. Western religion also contains the element of judgment. When you die you are either selected to go to Heaven or Hell. This is not a written belief, it is an oral tradition. The concept of Hell may come from Classical Mythology, in which Hades was the god of the dead, and ruler of the underworld, Hell. When all people died they either went to Hell, or they wandered the Earth as spirits. The belief, at that time, was that wandering the Earth as a spirit was a curse.

The Greeks also had judges of the dead. These judges would determine what Hell was going to be like for the deceased. Some were punished severely. The myths do not, however, mention anything other than punishment. This made it easy to adopt by Christians, who could use Hell as a tool of fear. Heaven became the place of "God" and Hell became the place where bad people were sent. There is no judgment of the dead in Chinese Ancestor Worship. There is no Hell to send bad people to. Instead, if you are bad, then you are punished during your life. When you die, you are released from worldly desires and pleasures, making you supremely wise. This concept is very important to understanding Taoism and Zen, because in Taoism and Zen you are supposed to remove your desires and pleasures to become wise and achieve harmony.

Both China and India also have a cycle. In Europe this cycle is a giant cycle involving the relationships of the gods, and an eventual revolution of the gods (Ragnarok in Scandinavia). But in Europe this cycle was not as important as the cycles that would be adopted in China and India. The cycle in China is relatively simple. This cycle is based on the reign of a dynasty. The way the Chinese viewed this reign was that a dynasty would begin with the support of Heaven. As this cycle progressed the support of Heaven would weaken, mostly because the rulers would not treat their people right, and thus would not have support of their ancestors and Heaven. Eventually this support would diminish until another dynasty would take over, that had support. In India we see two distinct cycles. The first cycle is the cosmic cycle-the cycle of existence. The second cycle is the one of life, and reincarnation, samsara. Neither of these cycles is explicitly provided for in Chinese ideologies. The exception to this may be found in Taoism, where the Tao is somewhat equivalent to the cosmic cycle in India. Even with this, there is not a complete equality. What is important are the similarities that these cycles have. Similarities make the acceptance of seemingly new ideas easier. Although it is unwise to prejudge, people do it anyway. If people cannot relate to an idea with their own preconceived ideas, they tend to ignore the new idea.

Vedism had one last important characteristic, which helps to tie all of Eurasian religions together, and this is nature worship. It does not take careful scrutiny to see the nature worship in such religions as Classical Mythology. Certainly Classical Mythology personifies characteristics of nature. The Greeks, and especially the Romans, were fond of creating a deity for virtually everything. They had river gods, fountain gods, a goddess of menstruation (Mena), muses, fates, and many more. For that matter, it appears that Vedism was excessive as well. In Hinduism each person practices in his or her own way, and worships his or her own god or goddess. For Classical Mythology I have cataloged over 265 gods and goddesses, Egyptian Mythology is credited with having thousands of deities, and India has been accused of having 330 million deities, and more. The influence of polytheistic nature worship is obvious in India. To see the impact of nature worship on China we have to turn to Taoism. Original Taoism is a philosophy, not a religion. Its focus is harmony with nature. The way to achieve this harmony is by following the Tao, the way of nature. Harmony with the self and nature is where Buddhism and Taoism most importantly coincide.

Buddhism formed during the decline of Aryan unification of India. It was a reaction to the ascetic ways of Hinduism, providing a way to escape samsara for everyone. To over simplify this, Buddhism provided a way to achieve harmony with oneself and nature. Centuries later there would be a major debate between Buddhists and Taoists in China, because of this similarity. The two schools took turns declaring their founders had lived earlier in history, and had been responsible for the founding of both schools. Upon examining the canonical works of both schools we can easily see their similarities. At the same time the differences are also obvious. If we were to compare Lao Tse (Taoism) with Buddha Gautama, we would find that Buddha was full of things to say, and wasted no effort holding these things in. The teachings of Buddha became the thousands of volumes that comprise the Dharma. On the other hand Lao Tse's teachings are quite different. Upon the request of a border guard, wondering how the Tao should be learned and followed in Lao's absence, Lao wrote the Tao Te Ching. The Tao Te Ching consists of 81 poems, and it is only about 5,250 words long. There are more volumes in the Dharma then there are words in the Tao Te Ching.

Although the schools of philosophy debated with each other, and vied for power and popular support, they complimented each other. In Europe and the Middle East, and even in the Western Civilizations of today, members of one religion or philosophy usually reject other schools. Where Western people tend to focus themselves on one school, the Chinese do not see a conflict between the schools, practicing and applying the teachings of each school throughout their daily activities. What does this do? Each person takes the best of each philosophy, and applies that philosophy where it will do the most good. This is an ironic picture of the Chinese mind. Westerners have a tendency to view Chinese as closed minded. On these grounds, it seems more like the Westerners are the ones who are really closed minded. There is one aspect of Chinese thought that does create closed mindedness. Upon contacting Westerners the Chinese treated their visitors like they treated all foreigners, as barbarians. In being too open minded they had actually closed their minds, in a paradox not unlike the paradox between good and evil in Taoism. This image is important though, to help understand the evolution of Zen.

The connection between Taoism and Vedism seems very strong. The problem becomes an argument over time, in which millennia had passed before Taoism formally emerged from the Aryan background. There is a strong supporting argument from sociological historians that religions and beliefs do not just spring up. With this I tend to agree. A religious belief does not just materialize out of nowhere. Two religions that come to mind are Christianity and Islam. Christianity developed directly from Judaism, and was greatly influenced by the Romans, who borrowed from the Greeks. Islam developed from Christianity, Judaism, and Arab polytheism. Though both Christianity and Islam, on the surface, seem to have appeared by the will of one person, neither did. Jesus was a Jew and a Rabbi. Displeased with the ethics of his countrymen he aimed to reform Judaism. Whether Jesus intended to form a religion is not certain. His disciples certainly worked hard to make it a religion though. It was not Jesus that made Christianity a major religion, it was the Roman Empire. Likewise, Mohammed did not start with nothing. These men did not invent a religion, if anything they canonized a religion. They put together what was already there.

The same can be said for Taoism. To believe that a mysterious old man named Lao Tse single handedly started Taoism is absurd. Whether this man lived or not is not the point. If he did, he canonized something that already existed. This holds true for Confucianism and Buddhism as well. No one can deny the importance or genius of these men. We must be skeptical though to think that they started from nothing. For these reasons it seems logical that Taoism existed long before Lao Tse.

Why is there a gap? The gap exists for the same reason the Vedas (the canonical writings of the Aryan religion) were not recorded until much later. Early religion was often restricted to a small number of religious people, because of the need for specialization. Earlier religions were not restricted like this, all members of the community memorized the religious teachings. The teachings were transmitted by word of mouth, which eventually led to a sort of evolution. Many of the great sages never wrote any of their teachings. Even Confucius did not write down his own teachings, though he wrote six classics. If Lao Tse did exist, he may have been an ascetic. When he wrote the Tao Te Ching he most likely did not write specific teachings, but restricted himself to the conceptual framework. Considering the context of Taoism, his choice was wise.

## The Tao Te Ching

The Tao Te Ching (pronounced Dow Deh Jing) is a collection of poems that represent the hub of Taoist ideology. There are only 81 poems in this collection, with a total of about five-thousand Chinese characters (words). It is claimed that this little book was written by a man named Lao Tse, around the sixth century B.C.E. Research also suggests that the Tao Te Ching could have been written as late as the third century B.C.E. The actual date is uncertain, but it is most likely that the Tao Te Ching was compiled by the fifth century. This would place the Tao Te Ching after Confucius. Lao Tse is often claimed to be an older contemporary of Confucius.. His life and existence are uncertain. There are no facts to support his existence. It would seem that someone had to have done this work though, so we will refer to that someone as Lao Tse. Lao Tse means literally "Old Master." With so little known about Lao Tse, it is hard to document facts, or to recognize the significance of the person. The most important thing about this person is the Tao Te Ching, since we have nothing else to go on. Where in Buddhism and Confucianism we have historical facts, and can understand their perspectives better, we do not have this option with Lao Tse. Thus what is more important than the author, is the content of the Tao Te Ching.

Tao Te Ching means the Classic (Ching) of the Way (Tao) and Power (Te). There are three ways that the way and power can be interpreted from this. First would be the cosmic way and power. This would mean the way and power of ultimate reality, all of reality. We cannot limit this to the word reality though, because the unreal also exists in the real, making the unreal real. Ultimate reality would have to be everything, real and unreal, imagined and invisible. From the Tao everything is born from, and returns to upon death. The Tao, the ultimate reality has all the power, without beginning or ending. It controls everything, not because it wants to, but rather because it exists. The second way the Tao Te Ching can be interpreted is as the power or driving force of the universe, of nature. In this sense we are talking about the living universe, where the Tao is the principle that gives order to life, and is life itself. The third way the Tao can be interpreted is as the way of human life. In this sense the Tao assumes an ethical and moral role.

The Tao Te Ching does not show any concern for rituals, religion, or deities. It is more of a testament on nature, a revelation of the way of nature. There is no heaven or hell, but every action has a reaction. In Western ideologies we find jealous deities. In Taoism there are no deities and the Tao, nature, is nonplussed. In other words, the Tao does not care whether you believe in it or not. It will do its thing no matter what you believe or do. The Tao Te Ching does not attempt to state all that the Tao can do, because that is limitless. Instead it testifies to this limitlessness, and to the undefinability of nature, the Tao. The Tao Te Ching suggests to attain harmony with nature, rather than try to oppose an insurmountable force.  The logic of the Tao Te Ching is obvious.  In some ways it is syllogistic.  If you do one thing, something else will happen.  If you go against the way of nature, nature will win over.  If you have harmony with nature, and go along with the way of nature, then you will be able to use the power of nature.  You cannot manipulate the power of nature willfully.  Thus you must have the same goals as nature.  You must be free from desire, and you must be emotionally neutral, as is nature.

We have two concepts that we can use to relate Taoism and Buddhism.  The first concept is the cycle.  The second concept is harmony.  Previously I mentioned a simple cycle which was adopted by the Chinese.  In Taoism the cycles become unified in a cosmic cycle.  I have also mentioned that Buddhism is directed toward a state of harmony referred to as Nirvana.  Harmony with nature is also central to Taoism.  Let us examine each of these individually.  In order to understand the cosmic cycle of Taoism thoroughly you should read the Tao Te Ching.  A summary does Tao no justice.  In Taoism the cycle is called the Tao, the way of nature.  According to the Tao Te Ching, the Tao has no beginning nor ending.  If we take this literally, especially from a mathematical perspective, a circle has neither beginning nor ending.  This is further implied throughout the Tao Te Ching, and is illustrated in the Chinese arts.  The Tao flows like water.  Circles also flow.  When we think of a cycle, we think of a circle.  When we think of flowing we think of water.  Circles and water are both very important to Taoism and Buddhism.  For both Taoism and Buddhism, the circle represents oneness and a cycle.  The fluidity, flowing, of this cycle is described using water as an analogy.

Harmony is pivotal in Buddhism, Zen, and Taoism.  What these schools have in common is manifold.  First, harmony with oneself is necessary.  Second, harmony with one's surroundings must be established.  Third, harmony with nature, with the cycle, creates ultimate harmony and "salvation."  It is no wonder that Buddhists and Taoists fought over their founders.  They both felt that they had the same founder, and then argued over who received his teachings first.  The similarities are unsettling if they are not examined deep enough to discover their origins.  Beware of using the term salvation.  Salvation is an abused term, as are many Western terms when used in reference to Oriental ideologies.  In this context salvation does not mean being transmitted to heaven for redeeming oneself.  Salvation is not something that is sought after in either Taoism or Buddhism.  Salvation is something that is apprehended through right conduct, following the right path.  To seek salvation, to try and capture it, is like trying to grasp water.  For Taoism salvation is harmony with nature.  Is this really salvation?  It is not salvation for Westerners.  Westerners expect to gain something from salvation.  For the Taoist the only gain is harmony.

An Introduction to Zen Thought

## **The Tao**

Tao is pronounced "D ow" and is often spelled Dao, depending on the transliterator's Romanization preferences. I will spell it Tao for the fact that this is the way it usually appears before Western audiences. The reader who is familiar with Chinese and Japanese will notice a slight difference in connotation between the words Tao and Do, that the reader of this book should also recognize. These words also provide an avenue for us to examine some of the effects of Taoism on Zen.

Tao is not a simple word, and nor is it taken lightly. The Tao Te Ching makes a strong case for the significance of Tao, saying:

> In the beginning was the Tao.
> All things issue from it;
> all things return to it. (52:1-3)

This passage illustrates a cycle. This passage also sounds much like Christianity. Christianity is much simpler than the Tao though. In the Bible we see God creating the universe and man. In this sense God is personified, especially where God created man in His own image. To attack this with logic, this statement is circular. It can be taken as God created man in God's image, or God created man in man's image. It is much better to say that man created God in man's image. God creating man in His image is a belief, not a fact. Though Jesus was a Jew, he is often portrayed as a white man with blonde hair. Jews do not have blonde hair or white skin, at least not the ethnically Semitic Jews. Looking at the work of Michael Angelo we see Moses, another Semitic Jew, given characteristics of a white man. Again man created God in his own image. From a logical perspective, the Bible can be very complicated.

In Taoism the Tao is not a god. The Tao assumes no personified or deified role. The Tao exists, but does not exist. The Tao does not have a beginning nor an ending. So the Tao is never born nor does it die. But in the Tao all things are born and die. This is exemplified in 34:2-3 and 14-15:

> All things are born from it (the Tao),
> yet it does not create them.
> ....................
> (The Tao) is not aware of its greatness;
> thus it is truly great.

Also in 1:1-4:

> The tao that can be told
> is not the eternal Tao.
> The name that can be named
> is not the eternal Name.

The last two lines are interesting if they are compared to Judaism. The name for God in Judaism is not pronounceable, though Christians have transliterated the name as Jehovah. In essence it is a nameless name. Despite this God is still personified throughout the Torah, Talmud, Koran,

72

and the Bible.  Essentially what the Tao Te Ching is saying, is that Tao is not a name for something, it is an action.  Tao is literally the way.  The way needs not be a physical or imagined path.  It is a non-distinctive and non-directive improper noun.  Because of these qualities it probably should not be capitalized in translations of the Tao Te Ching.  This problem assumes another form, in that tao is both a proper and improper noun.  This creates a problem for the translator.

A sentence that really creates a problem would be "the way of the Tao."  In Chinese it would simply appear as tao tao.  Which should be capitalized?  Which goes first?  This also translates as the Tao of the way.  We find that the connotations here must be intuitively understood, not intellectually.  This is not the only paradox that appears in Taoism, as has already been illustrated.  Taoism thrives on oppositions which neutralize themselves and flow into each other.  An example of this is the famous yin and yang symbol.

In the yin and yang symbol, both good and evil exist independently and together, represented by the colors black and white.  This is a symbol of the principle of polarity in Chinese cosmology, in which the opposite poles eventually blend and become one another in a cosmic connectedness.  The conflict of black and white, and their cultural meanings help to reassert this meaning of the yin and yang.  It is also interesting to note that black and white are technically not colors.  White is the presence of light, where black is the absence of light.  These are conditions, not colors.  We label them as colors even though they really are not.  This contradiction is also supportive, as the connotations blur at this point, becoming one.

Taoism is also profound.  The Tao is something special that cannot be understood with logic.  Like much of Zen and Buddhism, intellectual analysis is impossible.  The Tao transcends categories and words.  In 56:1-2:
> Those who know do not talk.
> Those who talk do not know.

Again in 70:1-4:
> My teachings are easy to understand
> and easy to put into practice.
> Yet your intellect will never grasp them,
> and if you try to practice them, you will fail.

The Tao is something that is special, and only a few will find harmony in it and follow it.

In 41:1-8:
> When a superior man hears of the Tao,
> he immediately begins to embody it.
> When an average man hears of the Tao,
> he half believes it, half doubts it.
> When a foolish man hears of the Tao,
> he laughs out loud.

> If he did not laugh,
> it would not be the Tao.

The qualities of Tao do not completely define it. Tao escapes true definition because it exists without existing. Earlier in this text I stated that Tao was the way of nature. Can we define the way of nature? No. We can attempt to describe it, but our description will be limited to abstract and meaningless words. That is why the Tao Te Ching tells us that "Those who know do not talk," and that the Tao cannot be told. Like Zen, Taoism is beyond words.

The way of nature is not a name, it is an abstract phrase that embodies everything and nothing all at once. Nothing can stop or control Tao, not even Tao. It is without independent thought, but it continues its course without effort. It is a series of events that are cosmic. For this reason not even the cosmos can control the Tao. In trying to control the Tao we are only following the Tao. The Tao itself does not try to control, and that is why it is so powerful. It is truly great because it does not know its greatness. The Tao is. This is a famous approach in Zen: just be. The other side of this is being in the now.

Time is not of significance to the Tao. Like Zen, all dualities are exterminated. Thus there is no future or past. One Zen master said that the present leads to the past. The future also leads to the present. We are often concerned with direction, especially East and West. Since the Earth is round, how far east is West? When we go west are we not also going east? If you were to fly over the North or South pole, to a point on the opposite side of the globe, will you have gone east or west? These questions of relativity are just what Taoism and Zen transcend. The Tao does not concern itself with direction, either geographical or in time. The Tao exists, but cannot be touched or sensed in any other way. The Tao also does not exist, because claiming its existence is to try and give it form, which it does not have.

## **Do in Zen**

One of the principles of Taoism is wei wu wei. This means literally action without action (action inaction). This is important to our perception of existence and of Tao. The true way is to let nature act. This does not mean to become lifeless and do nothing. It means to establish harmony with the Tao, so that your actions are not actions. In martial arts the ultimate form is the art of peace. By encouraging your enemy, by fighting, you are not acting in harmony. Through the act of inaction you can create harmony. Instead of viewing the contest as a win or lose system, which is dualistic, you let conflict be. In doing this no one loses or wins. Everyone does benefit. Thus Tao (the way of nature) is wei wu wei. This is the same state which is optimum in Zen. We find that wei wu wei is the strongest link between Tao, Do, Zen, and the arts. Before Zen, Taoism was the driving force of the Chinese arts. With the evolution of Zen, we find that Tao assumed a new role and companion, in Do.

Do also means the way, suggesting a path. But Do is not as limiting as Tao. Tao specifically addresses the way of nature, where Do does not claim any direction whatsoever. The way of Zen has been compared to riding a train, in which the tracks are the way. This train leads nowhere, and yet it leads everywhere. The track has no beginning nor ending. The train appears to move, but is stationary. The track is infinitely long, and at the same time it is infinitely short. Do becomes simply the way. It needs no direction or purpose. It has no limitations. Tao is almost limited. Nature is everything and nothing, but nature is still nature. Nature has a name attached to it, which gives it a form, albeit this form is formless. Do does not have this limitation, although it may not appear to be a limitation. Do is often attached to other words though, that appear to limit it. By limiting Do we diminish its infinite quality.

We often see Do attached to the name of arts. We are especially familiar with the martial arts, which all end in Do. Each of these arts uses Do in two ways. The first way is to signify the way of the art itself. The second way is to signify the way of Zen. These combine into one harmonious unit. To study one of these arts is to study Zen. But the art itself is not necessarily the direct path, and there should be no misconception that the art is the path. On the contrary, Zen is necessary to truly master each art.

As Westerners we cannot help but wonder if Michael Angelo or any of the other great artists of early Western history, were also Zen masters. To be a good artist does not mean to be a master of oneself. In the Orient less attention is paid to the form or to the product of art. Often the art appears to have been done by a child and is very simplistic. But one quality the art has is harmony. Erasing is not necessary, because the artist has developed harmony with the art. This harmony is developed from harmony with the self. Art and artist have become one.

**Power in Taoism and Zen**

Ki and te are essential elements of Zen. Ki is the power of the spirit, the inner being. Te is power, both physical and spiritual. Both of these are centered just under the naval. By focusing these on this point they are easy to control and to distribute where they are needed. In the West we are accustomed to the belief that our thinking and energy are centered in our head. In the West we think with our head. In the Orient we think with our mid-section. The expression "gut feeling" seems to be very fitting to Oriental thought. We equate a "gut feeling" with something that we cannot intellectualize or explain rationally, an intuitive sense. This is exactly the perspective of Oriental thought, permitting the intuitive. It would also seem logical for the mid-section to be the source of energy. This is the same area of the body we "feel" unusual sensations, and where our food is digested and absorbed. Our mid-section is definitely a source of energy. It is where the external is placed and transformed into energy. The idea of the mid-section being the source of thought and energy is intuitively right.

Science has recently begun to realize that the brain is not where the mind really is. The brain is physiological. The brain is an interface point, a memory bank and a processor. Computers also have memory banks and processors, but they do not have a mind, they are not alive. Research is showing that the mind is throughout the entire body, and is not trapped within the boundaries of our skin. Mystical Taoism led to the development of much of Chinese medical knowledge. Among this knowledge is a concept of ch'i, the energy of the spirit. This energy flows throughout the body.

Ki is a Japanese word somewhat equivalent to ch'i in Chinese. Ch'i, however, is more like a life force. The Chinese used acupuncture and acupressure to affect the ch'i flow, and subsequently regulate body functions. Much of martial arts relies on pressure points, whose origins are found in ch'i and Taoism. Some of these points are even deadly. In my dokusan sessions with Chinese zennists (Zen is Ch'an in China) I often substitute Ch'i for Ki. This is an awkward and perhaps not completely accurate substitution. It creates a minor language problem, which is solved with the de-emphasis placed on language and words in Zen. For our purposes we will focus on ki and te.

Te is also adopted from Taoism. Huston Smith notes three forms of te: physical, philosophical, and religious. The physical form of te is optimized power, specifically relative to ch'i. Through this form practitioners seek to increasing their power by tapping into the powers of nature, by experimentation. It is interesting that these people still emphasize selflessness. Efficient power is the philosophical form, embodied in wei wu wei. The idea of efficient power is to manage your natural power. Finally, the religious form of Taoism is vicarious power, attempting to get power through ritual. We find elements of all three of these forms of te in Zen. In general, te refers to the power of nature, power in general. Both Zen and Taoism emphasize harmony, both with oneself and with nature. By learning to control your own te you will learn to control the cosmic te. This creates harmony. Harmony with te enables even the weakest individual to manipulate great things with ease. This is because you allow the te of what you are manipulating to power itself. Perhaps where this is most obvious is in Aikido, where even the smallest person can fell an opponent by using the opponents own power.

Ki follows this same pattern. In Taoism and Zen ki is the power of the spirit. To translate Aikido literally, it means the way of spirit harmony. Looking at a martial artist in a tournament, especially a skillful one, we would be more inclined to think they have harmony with te, physical power. This is not the purpose of any martial art. The founder of Aikido, Morihei Ueshiba, wrote a book called The Art of Peace. The art of peace is an alternative name for Aikido. From this we can see that the true purpose of Aikido is ki, not te.

It is easy to have harmony with te. It may even be a stepping stone to spirit harmony. One can achieve spirit harmony, and in doing so would automatically achieve harmony with te. The martial arts are designed to work in stages. The student is unaware, generally, that they are studying Zen. For this reason the student works very hard to master moves, and to manipulate power. Around the stage of black belt the student has learned to manipulate power, and how to keep it under control. Usually they are still limited in their ability to manipulate power. Even a black belt has not achieved spirit harmony. Spirit harmony is what separates the masters from the other martial artists.

When the student has achieved a high enough rank to be a teacher, the student is not yet a master. At this stage the student feels they are a master, but may recognize that there is something else beyond. Without spirit harmony martial arts training is not even half complete. The teacher is still a novice. When spirit harmony has been attained, the teacher becomes a master. The master is a student. This last sentence may seem confusing. The problem with having become a teacher is that many feel they have no more to learn. The master realizes that existence is static, ever changing. To maintain spirit harmony the master must never stop learning. For this reason the master becomes the student, where the teacher does not. This should not be mistaken though, because there are varying degrees and individual differences at each stage. The master has both ki and te harmony, and has become the student. As a student the master has the advantage of pre-knowledge. The master as student has to maintain harmony.

## The Ego

Why is the teacher so limited? At the third dan a student may be authorized to teach. To be a teacher is to achieve a status. By achieving a new status, especially one that deserves respect, the student feeds his or her ego. Each of us develops an ego, but through Zen training, this ego is discarded. It is still there, but it no longer dominates. What happens is the ego resurfaces and creates a block. At this point in Zen training it is not uncommon that the student is given a special lesson in humility. C.W. Nicol describes such an occasion in his book Moving Zen. He tells about a student who was being advanced to the status of teacher. The masters brought him in for a special lesson, in which he sparred with the masters. For an hour they fought with him, traded places, and berated him without rest. Anyone who has ever been in a fight knows how exhausting fighting can be. Professional boxers get numerous rests, and their fight is only a matter of minutes. Imagine this student's exhaustion. By the end of the session the student could barely kick or perform maneuvers. The student was told how horrible he was, that he did not know how to stand or fight.

As this hour of humiliation was drawing to a close one of the masters told Nicol that the student had done very well, despite the verbal abuse.

The only problem with something like this is that it too can add to the ego. The student was proud when he left the dojo. Not because he had achieved a higher status, but because he had earned the special attention of the masters. This made him special. He was honored to be beaten and berated by the masters. This is not unlike a child being disciplined by its parents. When the child is disciplined it is receiving attention. Psychologists have illustrated that this can be counterproductive because children are hungry for any attention, either good or bad. Social death, or not acknowledging undesired behavior, has often been proven to be more effective than physical punishment. Unfortunately the environment must be right for social death to work.

Nicol also described an occasion that a master was suspended from the Karate association. The master violated the principle of being peaceful, when he got into a bar fight and put several people in the hospital. His suspension was ineffective though, as his students still came to him and so did his friends. The only change in his life was that he was not allowed in the dojos. If these people had not sympathized with him, on the basis that he was defending himself, he would have been shunned. This would have been an effective punishment. However, their acceptance illustrated a social philosophy that justified violent self defense. The students and friends made the environment wrong for effective social death.

You may say, What is wrong with self defense? A conflict in which blows are struck leads only to everyone's loss. A conflict which is settled verbally is won by all. When I was younger there was always opportunity to fight. Like most young men I was tempted. This philosophy held me up though. I would go as far as to lie, saying that I did not know how to fight, when a belligerent individual would not back down. I am not proud of the fights I had when I was younger. By beating my opponent I had disgraced myself. I turned to the art of peace. For years I turned the other cheek. In most cases I was antagonistic in doing this, laughing at my opponent or tantalizing them with slighting words. On the surface I lost those fights. Those that I inspired through my poor choice of words, I lost against myself. I did win them psychologically with my opponents though. If you hit someone in the face as hard as you can and they laugh at you, not even blocking or fighting back, how would you feel? After several blows most opponents will feel disgraced, even more so if they hurt themselves and you are still laughing at them. I would not suggest doing this unless you know how to take blows.

Another dimension to this is the bystanders. They watch the whole event, and imagine themselves in both places. When your opponent leaves disgraced with himself, the bystanders will respect you. I guarantee that they will think twice before trying to pick a fight with you. The person that takes the blows as if they were flies landing on him scares people more than the person that fights back. Why is this? The bystanders will be thinking, "If he could take those blows like that, imagine what would happen if he decided to hit back!" They do not understand. In the West they are also inclined to think in terms of violence. Some will actually respect you. They know that you will not stoop yourself to a petty level of violence. We try to teach our children that violence is immature, animalistic, subhuman. At the same time we do not practice what we preach, and it is our practices that our children learn from.

There are also occasions in which you are attacked. This is very uncommon, especially if your body language is right. Attackers want an easy victim. If you do not look easy, then they will leave you alone. Size is not an issue, the issue is attitude. There is also the rare attacker who feels threatened, and this feeling inspires them to attack. Never make your attacker feel threatened. I once made this mistake, by inadvertently using a word that hurt my opponent's ego. I did not hurt my opponent. Instead I diverted the blow and restrained him. The crowd and him were both disappointed, because there was no fight. This was very humiliating for him. Years later, when we met again, we became friends. This is the advantage of the art of peace. My word choice was bad, but my actions were righteous.

How does all this relate to te and ki? With the power of the spirit (ki) you are holding yourself back. With te you are absorbing the blows. If you have harmony with te you can hurt your opponent without ever being aggressive. When you are struck you are supposed to breath out. If you have control of your te you can focus your energy on the point of impact just after the impact is absorbed. This sudden change will be a shock to your opponent physically. Your opponent will no longer be prepared for the blow that was struck, because his focus is no longer in the blow. What happens? If you are good at this your opponent will break his own bones. But this is not necessary. By practicing peace you do not want to intentionally hurt your opponent. You build your own ki by absorbing the blow. If the opponent hurts themselves, it is not your fault. You have won without winning.

When you make your enemies your friends you must be doing something right. You do not gain respect through violence. Violence breeds more violence. By avoiding violence you gain the respect of your opponent. When you have done this you have created harmony. Since harmony is what you wanted in the first place, you have won. This builds the spirit. It also makes people devote themselves to you. When people devote themselves to you, they will help you. You have thus created harmony with their te. If you treat them with respect, not abusing their devotion, then you also feed spirit harmony with them, and they will follow you to the ends of the Earth without being asked.

# CHAPTER VI—
# Confucianism

The relationship between Taoism and Buddhism seems obvious, but Confucianism appears to fall outside. Hinduism and Yoga also have this fate throughout most of the available literature. In this chapter we must address the concepts of Confucianism, because they are also integral to Zen. Confucianism is most important because it acts as a cultural outline for China and all the countries China has had an influence on. Confucianism sets up a social structure, and a method of governance that has been important to the history of Asia. This ideology sharply contrasts, in many respects, Taoism. Where Taoism emphasizes nature, anarchy, and emotionlessness, Confucianism emphasizes structure, society, and emotional recognition. Confucianism may in some ways be compared to Jean Jacques Rousseau's theory of the social contract. This contract requires the existence of a society, with a structure created by the people, with a government based on the needs and wants of the people. The Chinese people have lived with a theory similar to the social contract theory for thousands of years. Confucius did not do anything special in creating this atmosphere. Instead, he gave it formality.

A central concept in the teachings of Confucius is the Tao (Way) of Heaven (T'ien). To Confucius this Tao was the essential path of all men. His teachings are thus ethical, in the sense that they are focused on the interactions of people within a society. He wrote five classics. These five are: I-ching (Classic of Changes), Li-ching (Classic of Rituals), Shih-ching (Classic of Songs), and the famous text the Spring and Autumn Annals (Ch'un-ch'iu). Confucianism would firmly take root during the Han period (202 B.C.E. to 9 C.E. and 25 C.E. to 220 C.E.). During this period tests were formed, based on the classics and the Analects of Confucius, and used for appointing people to public offices. By 150 B.C.E. Confucianism was definitely adopted as the official orthodoxy of the Chinese government.

The tests were open to everyone. All the people were very excited about getting involved, or knowing someone that was. This provided an opportunity for anyone to become a statesman. Certainly the wealthy were more likely, because they could afford formal education. Many did, however, rise up from the farms, self taught, to become statesmen. This testing system would remain in effect until the revolution of 1912. Today Confucianism is still taught in the public schools in China. It is still important and integral to the Chinese culture. Confucianism is even reflected in Mao Tse Tung's works, but is more of an underlying theme, rather than the dominant role it had played for over two millennia. Mao Tse-tung's works have a definite Marxist slant.

## Confucius the Man

Confucius was relatively unsuccessful in his lifetime, as far as status and wealth are concerned. He was not a religious leader, but his school attracted a large following. His real name is K'ung Fu Tse, the Master (Tse) K'ung. He was born at Tsou in the state of Lu, ca. 551 B.C.E. He was orphaned at a young age, and though he grew up in poverty he managed to get a good education, devoting himself to study at the age of 15. He was married at the age of nineteen, and had a son and a daughter.

He never held an important nor influential position in government himself. He was appointed to one office that was all title and no responsibility. Recognizing that he was being "put out to pasture," K'ung abandoned the office. He was very ambitious about politics, believing that he had a mission. This mission was to bring "peace and good government" to the Chinese people (Brandon, p. 204). It is interesting to note that Confucius did not begin to be politically active until he was fairly old. He wandered around from state to state, observing, teaching, and gathering a following. Among the subjects he taught were history, music, poetry and tradition. He demanded of his followers that they "practice the virtues of sincerity, justice, benevolence, courtesy, respect for older people, and ancestor reverence" (Runes, p. 273). He never found a ruler that would give his teachings a chance. Finally he returned to Lu, as him and his followers were often given a hostile reception (Waley, p. 15). Upon his return, Confucius opened a school.

Great men arise during times of great need. The ideas of Confucius fit into the needs of his time. He lived in what is called the Spring and Autumn period (722 to 481 B.C.E.). This period was characterized by the struggle of the Chinese states for power, which would continue into the Warring States Period (403-221 B.C.E.). The regional states vied for power, each wanting to be the one to control China. The center of this conflict was to become unification of China, a theme that was already ingrained in Chinese tradition. In 221 B.C.E. the Ch'in succeeded in unifying China, but quickly lost power when the first Ch'in emperor died. The Han then succeeded the Ch'in, and implemented Confucianism as the state orthodoxy.

As we can see, Confucius never saw peace in his own time. He also never got to see a unified China. The closest thing to unification he saw was the Chou government. The Chou Dynasty was unsuccessful as a central government, losing its power to the regional governments. With power comes greed. These states would make China physically divided, although it still had the facade of a central government. The position Confucius had been appointed to was intended to get him out of the political picture. He was opposed to war, as most philosophers are. Naturally he was a thorn in the side of the regional governments. The regional governments understood him all too well, and knew that given a chance his teachings would dominate the scene. How right they were. By pushing him out of the official government picture, Confucianism would have to wait three centuries before it could really take root.

The life of Confucius was somewhat tragic. He lived for about seventy-seven years, long enough to outlive his own son. Having lost his parents when he was young, K'ung had an early start with tragedy in his life. With a long life, K'ung was also bound to have experienced the tragedies of losing many friends and relatives. Within his family, K'ung was head of the family, despite the fact that he had an older brother. The reason that is given for this is that K'ung's older brother was handicapped, and was unable to take on the responsibility. When K'ung died, ca. 479 B.C.E., he was only an obscure and impoverished teacher. He never sought to make a fortune off of his school. He wanted his teachings to take root, and not be just limited to the select wealthy elite who would want to pay for tuition. He is acclaimed for accepting anything for his teaching services, even a piece of meat. A man who offers his services like this does not acquire material wealth. The wealth he attained was greater, as he was able to teach people from all walks of life. All they needed was the will to learn.

**The Classics and Teachings**

Though Confucius made numerous references to Heaven, he did not teach a religion, nor did he express a belief in a supreme deity. In his teachings Confucius set the framework for a social system that resembled a grid. He did not believe that we should love universally, but rather classified love under categories of duty. For example, the father-son relationship would have the appropriate virtue of filial piety, the ruler-subject relationship would have loyalty, brother-brother would have brotherliness, husband-wife would have love and obedience, and friend-friend would have faithfulness. These appropriate virtues were not "one-way streets," but were rather shared virtues. To some extent these are taken as one-way, for example the father-son and the husband-wife relationships. However, when we examine the other three key relationships we see that the appropriate virtue must be shared by both parties. Confucius does not speak much on husband-wife relationships, but he does emphasize filial piety. Confucius also emphasizes the need for loyalty of rulers to subjects and subjects to rulers. Later interpretations have added to the brother-brother relationship, a greater respect for the elder brother. This seems to be consistent with the teachings of Confucius, since he does emphasize respect for elders.

Hucker recognizes seven themes that Confucianists, despite their disagreements, have in common. First, everything is governed by an impersonal Heaven. In comparison to Taoism, this first idea seems traditional to general Chinese thought. Second, the will of Heaven is that men are happy and live in harmony with the cosmos (Tao). Third, to live ethically and virtuously is to live in harmony. Fourth, virtue (as te) is developed through ritual (li), where the emphasis is on what a person does, not what a person professes to do. Fifth, knowing the Will of Heaven is not easy in times of crisis. Sixth, proper conduct requires the study of history and prior sages, as well as the correct effort to mold oneself according to what is learned. Seventh, both man and society are perfectible.

Looking at these precepts we get a sense of affirmation and optimism. Without the optimism, especially illustrated in the seventh precept, there is no point in trying to change. In essence, there is no destiny or divine force that predetermines the results of actions. In order to get desired results we must have a good knowledge of history so that we understand causes and effects. In essence, this makes Confucianism a means-end system of analysis, but not a means-end morality. The morality and ethical basis of Confucianism is based in duties and ritual. This is a sharp contrast to Taoism and Buddhism.

The classics help to support the Confucian system of ethics, ritual, and duty. It almost seems ironic that one of these classics deals specifically with merriment in the form of singing. Something that Confucius would be criticized for, by Mo Tse, was this call for merriment, as well as his call for elaborate rituals. Confucius did not recommend these things for economic reasons. These were not done for the sake of being a means to an end. Rather these were done for the sake of morale. This is what Mo Tse did not recognize. To Mo Tse an activity had to be profitable in order to be good. Mo Tse's materialism overlooked psychological needs, with the impression that those needs were economically costly and unproductive. Mental health is very important, and I am inclined to argue that this is perhaps the main reason for the death of Moism.

The Book of Changes (I-ching) was originally a diviner's handbook. Essentially this book illustrates the relationships of things, especially with relation to the yin and yang. The yin and yang are cosmic opposites, polarities. At some point these polarities cancel each other out, and exist in harmony despite their opposition. This book is a cosmological analysis of relationships and changes. The changes occur along a continuum between extremes, where at various points specific changes can easily be noted. This is a gradual change though. As with any continuum there is an infinite number of possible combinations. The actual use of this book has been used for fortune telling and "mystical insights into the nature and workings of the cosmos" (Hucker, p. 72). The I-ching is particularly interesting, because the subject matter has been used for metaphysical purposes. It does however illustrate the need for change, the fact that all things change, and the power of change.

The Classic of Writings (Shu-ching) is particularly important to Confucianism. Something that Confucius was fond of doing, was citing the activities of "sage kings." He liked looking back into history, especially into the Shang and early Chou dynasties. This book is a collection of documentaries, which are attributed to legendary rulers from the Shang and early Chou dynasties. It is believed that the documents on the Chou Dynasty are authentic, though those pre-dating the Chou are not thought to be. Confucius was a scholar, and was enamored by history. It is very likely that the Shu-ching is the product of his studies and research. Whether they are accurate and truly representative of the historical personages is uncertain. They are most likely true to the resources Confucius had available to him. What is important about the Shu-ching is that Confucius is telling us about his background. This background is important for understanding his teachings. Also, this background is on prior sages, which is an important topic for study in Confucianism (the sixth precept requiring education for right conduct).

The Spring and Autumn Annals (Ch'un Ch'iu) is also important in terms of the sixth precept. Not only does this book provide information on Confucius' knowledge, but gives us a picture of the environment he lived in. This book covers historical events from 722 to 481 B.C.E. Since Confucius died in 479 B.C.E., we can see that he wrote this in the last years of his life. From this we can see that a large portion of this book was very personal to him, especially since he had lived through it. He even wrote this book from the perspective of Lu, his home state. It is a year-by-year, month-by-month, day-by-day chronology of events and historical personages. As Hucker notes, this compilation gives us an understanding of Confucius' value judgments. Certainly, his choice of entries would provide us with an insight of what he felt was important. This book becomes a treatise, a listing of causes and effects that could be used by future Confucian scholars. This is most likely what Confucius intended this book to be.

The Classic of Songs (Shih-ching) is actually a collection of 305 ritual hymns and folk songs. Confucius selected these from a collection that had more than 3,000 songs, a collection that was also from Lu. It is asserted that Confucius did not collect or edit these poems, but he did know of the Shih, and liked it. In the Analects, Confucius says, "The Poems, all three hundred of them, may be summed up in one of their phrases: 'Let our thoughts be correct'" (II, 2). The majority of the Shih are folk songs, and the rest are ceremonial hymns used in the feudal courts. Hucker reports that the Shih is the "greatest single literary monument left from China's formative age, and no work is cited more regularly in later Chinese literature of all sorts" (p. 107). Why is this book important to Confucianism? Confucianism is a school on culture, and part of a culture is its folk songs and stories, the ceremonies and rituals. These are important, as was previously stated, for the mental health of people within a culture. It is the ceremonies and rituals that bring the people together to form a culture, and to have a cultural identity. In approving this work, Confucius was essentially saying "This is China. This is the way the Chinese people feel. This is the way the Chinese people must feel in a Confucian culture."

An Introduction to Zen Thought

The Li-ching (Classic of Rituals) is also very important to the Confucian cultural system. Confucius was emphatic about rituals and duties. To him rituals were as much duties as parents taking care of their children are duties. Rituals, to Confucius, are a necessity. The necessity of rituals is made most apparent by the fact that the Li-ching is actually three books. The first book is the Chou-li (Chou Rituals), describing the early Chou government organization, as ideal but not necessarily true to fact. The second book is the I-li (Propriety and Ritual), which continues with the idealized (even idolized) early Chou government, describing "the Chou code of gentlemanly conduct. . . . " (Hucker, p. 99). In this, Confucius describes the organization of archery tournaments, and the correct conduct of diplomats at various stages of diplomatic missions. The Li-chi (Ritual Records) is the third book, which prescribes numerous rituals, including "funerals, mourning, sacrifices, weddings, (and) banquets" (Hucker, p. 99). As with many ancient documents, these books are also not considered completely authentic. However, they are to some extent authentic, at least for Confucianism. As with the other books on history, we are taken back to the "ideal" society of the early Chou Dynasty. It is doubtful that the early Chou Dynasty was in fact ideal. The ideal society that Confucius refers to is excellent though for providing insight into Confucian ethics and teachings. Regardless of their authenticity, these classics have made a mark on history and Asian civilizations.

**Confucianism and Buddhism**
We have already noted the similarities between Buddhism and Taoism. Confucianism also has numerous similarities with Buddhism. To see these we must look at the Sermon at Deer Park, where Buddha Gautama first introduced Buddhism. In this sermon Buddha started with the Four Noble Truths. The fourth truth was that pain could be escaped by following the Eightfold Path. The Eightfold Path consists of right: thinking, action, livelihood, understanding, speech, effort, mindfulness, and concentration. Right concentration consists of meditation and having focus throughout all your activities. When you are reading, you are reading. When you are eating, you are eating. Though this seems to not be related to Confucianism, it is, and so are the seven other members of this Eightfold Path.

It is not uncommon to see the Analects of Confucius divided according to their applications. Confucius addressed broad areas like government, learning, and home life. In each of these he focused his attention on elements of the Eightfold Path. In order to see this, let us examine how he portrayed each element individually. We will see that Confucius took the Eightfold Path a step further, declaring how each element is applied to daily life.

Right thinking: To Confucius right thinking was essential. As I illustrated in the poem Purity, the eight elements of the Eightfold Path are interconnected.  To have right thinking you must have right learning, which requires right understanding (comprehension).  What was right thinking to Confucius?  Confucius took things as they were.  From this we see a distinct relationship between Buddhism, Zen, and Confucianism.  We must remember though that Confucianism and Buddhism developed independently at about the same time, and they did not directly influence each other.  When Zen appeared a thousand years later, we can see how it was easily adopted by the Confucian Chinese culture.

"As (youth) feels an affection for all let it be particularly fond of Manhood-at-its-best.  Any surplus energy may be used for book learning" (I, 6).

We do not have to look far to find examples in the analects.  Here Confucius is discussing filial piety and duties.  Filial piety is respect for one's parents and elders.  By having respect, the individual does their duties without ill feeling.  We can look at this from the perspective of thought, and realize that right thought requires respect.  This respect is necessary not just to elders, but to everyone.  It was not Confucius who introduced the idea that the rulers should respect their people, but he certainly affirmed it.

According to Confucius we must respect one another, both younger and older, and higher or lower in social status.  We should think ethically.  From an ethical perspective we could consider this utilitarian, in that we should always do the greatest good for the greatest number of people.  Confucius would have simply said: do the greatest good, which would be one's duties.  In right thinking we think of how our actions will affect others, and benefit them.  If it is right for others, then it is right thinking.

This brings up an interesting characteristic of Oriental philosophy.  There is a tendency to emphasize the society first, then the individual.  A Chinese friend of mine, named Wu Yuan-cheng said that "I" should not be capitalized in English.  This is a very accurate observation.  Westerners have a tendency to overemphasize the individual.  In Chinese history we see a conflict that arose over just this issue.  Mo Tse was very utilitarian, from an individualistic point of view.  He felt that good required benefit, especially for the individual.  Second he felt that for society to be good, the society had to be profitable.  This went against the Confucian ethics of placing society before the individual, and doing good for the sake of good alone.  It should be noted though that Confucian ethics did not hold the patent on these ideas.

Confucian ethics co-existed with other philosophies, such as Legalism.  Legalism removed the individual from the picture, creating a bureaucracy.  This is not unlike Western society today, where each person is identified by the government, with numbers.  We have a birth certificate number, a drivers license number, a tax number (social security in the U.S.), and many other numbers.  According to Confucius right thinking is thinking in terms of the society, not the individual, the ego. This is a trait we see carried over and common to other societies throughout the Orient.

Right Speech: As with Taoism and Zen, words are not looked upon favorably. In Chinese society, according to Wu Yuan-cheng, the man who works quietly in the fields is very attractive to the women. In Western society women expect men to be very conversational, and are often disappointed. "Silence is golden." Though this is a cliche, we often neglect its philosophical foundation. We find that Confucius upholds this strongly:

"The Excellent man will always have something to say, but those who do speak are not necessarily Excellent men" (XIV, 4).

"To engage in gossip is to cast aside Excellence" (XVII, 12).

"Clever talk and a domineering manner have little to do with man-at-his-best" (I, 3).

You may have noticed "Manhood-at-its-best" and "man-at-his-best" in the two quotes here. I am taking these from James R. Ware's The Sayings of Confucius. Ware had a translation problem with this, because he was trying to maintain the spirit of what was being said. Arthur Waley uses the word "Good" in these places, but in doing so creates a duality. Ware also creates a duality, but is attempting to de-emphasize it and spread it out. By spreading it out he is making the reader think more about the implications. You may substitute a much longer definition here, of one who is following the right path or ethic; one who is acting ethically. To be ethical, or act ethical, is not right or wrong. It is only a way of life, and according to Confucius it is our duty. You may say one who lives this way of life.

All dualities and translation problems aside, this definitely illustrates the wordless ethic. Those who know do not speak, and those who speak do not know. In Confucian ethics this again suppresses individualism, suppressing it on the individual level. This ethic also encourages right action, by treating others with compassion (humaneness/ren).

Right action: Right action requires right intention. For Confucius, right action is doing one's duties, which include ritual. In the analects Confucius said:

"It is flattery to make offerings to the dead who do not belong to your own family. It is cowardice to fail to do what is right" (II, 24).

If we were to expand on what Confucius is saying here, and catch his implied meaning, we can see how right action is possible. In this Confucius feels that paying respects, through gifts or other actions, when it is not a duty is "flattery." In a sense he is saying this is a way of trying to impress, persuade, or coerce. If the intent is not to persuade, impress, or coerce then the gesture is being made without any desire for gain. To seek gain from an action is not right action. This is also the view of Zen and Buddhism.

In Buddhism when we meditate we are not meditating for any reason. We do not expect to gain anything. We just sit. This is Zen. Right action, even to Confucius, is action without the desire for gain. To expect something in return is unethical. Confucius takes this a step further by declaring that a person is a coward for not doing what is right. Confucius outright attacks unethical behavior. Buddhism does not generally do this, though we do see Buddha defining the actions of the fool in the Dhammapada. We can see how Confucian ethics could dig its roots so deep in Asian civilizations. He prescribes a specific set of ethical responsibilities. These are right actions. Failure to act right is repulsed by society's right reaction, lack of social recognition. This creates a framework for social death, a system of punishment far more effective than prisons, beatings, and executions. In this Confucianism differs from Buddhism. Buddhism is tolerant, where Confucianism basically lays down the law of behavior for the government and the individuals. With the fool, Buddhism takes pity, but does not attack or punish. By "laying the law" Confucius created a degree of intolerance, designed for a social structure. Confucius also recommended a social structure. Buddhism is not interested in social structure, and even transcends social structure, as has already been noted. Where Confucianism states what we should do in affairs with others, Buddhism directs us to understanding ourselves. This does not create a conflict. Instead we find that they work well together, and compliment each other because they provide for different needs.

Right livelihood: Religions of the world have a habit of telling us what we should do for our livelihoods. Philosophies are more personal and less dominant. The general perspective of philosophy is to do that which is satisfying to your individual needs and goals. Confucianism is a slight exception to this. The entire school of Confucianism is built on the concept of training government officials. Buddha looked on all men equally. He treated kings in the same manner as he treated a beggar or any other outcast. Likewise, Confucius did not care what walk of life his students came from. He would take anything for payment of tuition, no matter what its value. Where you came from did not matter, as much as where you were going. Entering his school was like entering Harvard Law School. You do not enter Harvard Law School to become a medical doctor, you enter to become a lawyer. When a person entered his school, they were either going to become teachers or civil servants. These were not civil servants as we visualize them today in America. Certainly they might assume posts like this, but this was only their beginning. They were trained to govern a society. By the time of Jesus, the Confucian school had been officially recognized by the government.

The teachings of Confucius, and his five classics, became the foundation of the Chinese government. To be appointed to any government post the individual had to take a rigorous test on the works of Confucius. This tradition filled every post in the Chinese government, except for the Emperor, until the 1912 Revolution. No ideology has governed a nation this long. Nor has any ideology been used to govern so many people. The population of China has been as much as one-third the world's population. It is definite that to Confucius right livelihood is serving the people through right actions in government. We see, "Great Man is concerned about System, not about poverty" (XV, 32). Confucius never held an important office himself. After his death he ruled China single handedly for over two-thousand years. His legacy still lives. He is not forgotten in China. In countries like Singapore, Korea, and Japan, Confucius is still in direct control. This is amazing, and deserves respect and attention. If there is a compelling reason to study Confucianism, this is it. Something must be right if it worked for so many, so long, transcending time and geography (political boundaries).

Right understanding: The life of any philosophy is dependent on education. If the individual does not learn the philosophy then they cannot employ it correctly. This does not mean book learning. Learning can be through experience, as in the case of Zen. Confucius was very interested in formal education. One disciple said, "Great Man uses the books to bring together friends, and through friendships he bolsters up Manhood-at-its-best" (Analects, XII, 24). He opened a school and proceeded to teach his philosophy. Though he held no significant government positions himself, his students eventually would. When they did, Confucius attained a higher rank than any title could give him. Confucius occupied thousands of important government offices for over two thousand years, through his students.

Being a student and going to class is not enough. Though you may hear a lecture and take good notes, this does not mean you will learn what is being taught. What is required is right comprehension, right understanding. Confucius refers to this as learning.

"Learning without thought brings ensnarement. Thought without learning totters" (II, 15).

We can read textbooks and references all day. Though we may look academic, if we do not understand what we are reading we are wasting our time. We can also sit around and theorize about the secrets of the universe. We cannot make a living off of these theories unless we can prove them with known facts. Without knowledge, theorizing is also a waste of time. There are many people who try to look smart by coming up with theories and showing them off. When one of these people approaches someone with knowledge, a conflict arises as the theorist loses face. But what is knowledge?

"(Knowledge) is to know both what one knows and what one does not know" (II, 17).

This again brings us back right understanding. We must recognize the areas that we do not have knowledge in, and compromise for these weaknesses. To create a theory based on knowledge you do not have is also a waste of time. You can create limitations for your theory so that they apply to what you do know. If you still wish to cover the areas that you do not know, you recognize the limitation and know what you need to look for. Let us make a simple example. If you are familiar with aviation, you know that propellers force air over the top of the wing. You know that birds exist and that they fly, but have never seen a bird, so you do not know how they force air over their wings. If you wanted to theorize about this you would not give birds propellers. You would find and study birds, then you could create your theory from that knowledge.

If you do not understand, then you do not know. In English we have a series of questions we believe lead us to knowledge. These questions are: who, how, what, where, when, and why. For right understanding we must know why. If we know why, then we know the answers to all the other questions because we have transcended them. This is knowledge and right understanding.

Right effort: this ties in strongly with right action. Right effort also requires right intention. Right effort also requires applying right knowledge and understanding. Though we may have a noble war to fight, Confucius reminds us that:

"Leading an uninstructed people to war is to throw them away" (XIII, 30).

If we were to hand monkeys guns and send them to war without first teaching them, the monkeys will surely die. We know monkeys do not know how to use guns. Monkeys also have no understanding of why the war is being fought or how. They would play with the guns, hurt themselves and each other, and be easy targets for the enemy. Using untrained monkeys for war is not right effort. You may have the right intention, to protect human lives, but your intention does not also protect monkeys. You have the right understanding that monkeys can be used, but have not taken this understanding far enough to see their limited use. Without right effort we cannot succeed at anything.

Right effort is also not an extreme. To take an extremist and send them to war is also to throw them away. Confucius noted:

"I would not take along one who, like a raving tiger or raging torrent, would recklessly throw away his life. What is required is someone keenly conscious of responsibility, someone fond of accomplishment through orderly planning" (VII, 11).

Radicals will throw their lives away meaninglessly. They will seek martyrdom. This same kind of person would not be good at taking orders, and would act on his or her own. This not only jeopardizes the individual, but the rest of the military unit. Military units require order and teamwork. If one individual does not act as a member of the team, then the team will be incomplete. The number of persons in a team is not what makes a team. Team effort makes a team. In a team, team effort is right effort. Even if the team does not win, the team has put forth right effort. Thus right effort does not always ensure victory. Right effort unifies forces to work together in harmony. When the right forces are united in harmony, then right effort is possible.

You do not take a calculator in place of a ball to a ball game. You do not take a ball to a math test in place of a calculator. This is an example of not directing the right energies for right effort. When we feel emotionally moved to do something, we tend to devote all our energy into that something. There are even instances where we become too radical, and apply too much energy. Things do not happen alone. Things will also not happen right if they are forced or hurried. Often when we try to force things we end up with undesirable effects. An example of this is Christianity. Some Christians have tried so hard to force their religion on others, that the oppressed people revolt or cling even harder to their own traditions. If a religion really will work for a people, then it only needs to be available to be adopted. Sometimes the right effort does not require much energy. This is certainly true in the area of personal beliefs.

Right mindfulness: Shunryu Suzuki noted that right mindfulness is soft thinking. This is where we are prepared to think, so that there is no need to exert effort in thinking. You may say this is a state where thought is ready to focus its full capacity. We like to think of mindfulness as being prepared to take a situation and apply right thinking to generate an ethical solution. You are mindful of the needs of your loved ones; you are mindful of the safety of others. In Zen we are mindful of reality. We are always prepared for reality, for the changes of reality, to recognize them, accept them and move on.

We see Confucius looking at mindfulness in much the same way as we do in the West, when he says, " . . . Great man does everything possible to help the poor but nothing to enrich the rich" (VI, 4). If the government is not mindful to the needs of the people, then there needs to be a new government. When asked how to make people submissive, Confucius said, "If you employ upright officials in the place of crooked ones, the people will be submissive" (II, 19). Thomas Jefferson once said, "A little rebellion now and then . . . is a medicine necessary for the sound health of government." This is not unlike Jean Jacques Rousseau's social contract theory. This philosophy is also quite natural for the Chinese, who have exercised this in terms of the "Will of Heaven" since before the time of Confucius. This theory is certainly not the creation of Confucius, but he agreed with it. He also applies it to the daily interactions between individuals, as we have already seen. His idea of filial piety certainly applies to this. Later we will discuss "ren" (also transliterated as jen), which applies particularly to mindfulness.

Right concentration: Previously we saw this illustrated with regard to right comprehension. Right comprehension requires focus. There is a big difference between hearing and listening. Listening requires comprehension, where hearing does not. If we are to concentrate, then we must concentrate on certain things. Confucius tells us that we must listen to and be mindful of the needs of others and the needs of the society. This principle is true throughout the world. The social contract theory, developed by Rousseau, agrees with this. The only way a government can maintain power is by maintaining its contract with the people. To maintain the contract with the people, the people cannot be mistreated and their needs must be satisfied. This sounds easy. If we look at recent American history we can see how hard this is to sustain.

After John F. Kennedy's death the American people became divided. President Johnson made this worse by magnifying the American involvement in Vietnam. The result was a virtual revolution. Nixon took office in a country torn by unjustified violence issued by the government on the Vietnamese and the American people, and tensions mounting with the Soviet Union and China. Nixon corrected most of the conflict by ending the Vietnam War, and re-establishing relations with China. With his resignation the American people felt raped, as they saw their culture hero, Nixon, through a different eye. This remained virtually uncorrected until President Bush was fired from his office by the voters. Historians and political scientists look on this with the same opinion. We saw nothing short of a revolution, showing social unrest.

No Western country is immune to this. We have seen the last blows of Glasnost, the tearing down of the Iron Curtain. We have seen countries like Yugoslavia crushed by their own people, dissatisfied with the maintenance of their social contracts. In China the social contract is integral to the society. The Chinese are used to revoking the contract, and re-establishing it under a new dynasty. This is what Confucius warns us about. If we do not concentrate on our duties, then we deserve to be ejected from our offices. We must concentrate on our duties, both ethical and formal responsibilities. This is both rule utilitarian and act utilitarian in perspective.

We have seen that each of the elements of the Eightfold Path of Buddhism are also covered by Confucius. These do not always agree with each other, but they do not have to. They do not have to agree because they address different problems for different questions. What is important here is that these ethical values were the driving force of the Asian cultures in China, Japan, Korea, and Southeast Asia long before Buddhism or Zen were introduced. Though they are not specifically Buddhist thought, they are still reflected in the mannerisms of the people. It becomes difficult to discern whether some of the similarities were actually adopted by Zen, or whether they belong to another part of the culture. One of the difficulties is that Zen is not written down, and often even escapes oral instruction. Without these we have to accept all the cultural values that are shared as important elements.

### Compassion (Ren)

With one voice, all mystics and Eastern philosophers emphasize the same value: compassion.  In Taoism the word te often represents compassion.  In Confucianism both ren and te are used, though ren is the focus of Confucian compassion. As usual compassion is not as simple as the dictionary definition.  To Mo Tse, compassion was universal love.  Mo said, "It is to regard the state of others as one's own, the houses of others as one's own, the persons of others as one's self" (Mei, Vol. II, p. 82). Universal love is what Mo attributes to the cause of most events, especially the cause of violence (Mei, Vol. I, pp. 81-82; Mei, Vol. II, pp. 78-97; Chan, pp. 211 and 213).  Universal love is a wonderful concept.  The problem with Mo's approach was that he said it had to be unconditional, and it had to be equally given to everyone.

Confucius did not try to pretend that people could do this.  Instead of equal and unconditional universal love, Confucius suggested a prioritized universal love.  Through this we find Confucius' concept of a social structure that would be adopted by the Chinese and other societies.  His structure was a grid.  On that grid you loved each person differently, in accordance to their relationship to you.  Your father you loved the most, and your youngest sister the least, within your family.  English is one of the few languages, that I am aware of, that has only one word for love.  Most cultures recognize that your love for your parents is different from your love for your children, is different from your love for your spouse.

Love is not the only issue brought out by compassion.  Compassion also requires caring for others, at least enough not to harm them.  As has been noted previously, compassion is essential to the social contract.  In government it is essential to be compassionate, a process which requires the government official to not be self seeking.  Again we are looking at right action.  No action is right if we are doing it for the purpose of personal gain, even if the desire for such gain is very small.  Any desire for personal gain provide for action that is not right.  The action must be dutiful, and altruistic. It is ironic that Mo Tse was in opposition to this.  To Mo anything that was good had to be profitable.   Mo Tse's influence was short lived in comparison to all the other philosophies in the world.  Mo Tse's idea of universal love was one of the reasons why Moism failed.  I have even found myself criticizing Mo Tse because of his obviously antagonistic style, and pseudo-philosophy/religion.  Mo Tse stands alone in his views of compassion and profit.  Though we should be examining similarities, there are exceptions.  Mo Tse cannot be neglected because his teachings are unique.   His teachings have nothing in common with the other philosophies.  Mo's teachings were obviously formulated as a protest to Confucianism and the other philosophies in China, even in protest of the traditional Chinese religious beliefs.

In all the Eastern philosophies and religions we find love and compassion are essential.  This is somewhat related to the Western cliche,

"Do unto others as you would have them do unto you." In Taoism we see indifference, though compassion is still necessary. Te (power) also means virtue, compassion. We cannot ignore the correlation. Confucianism and Taoism seem to agree on humaneness, at least to a point. Those with power must express compassion and humaneness. Failing to do this will result in the loss of power. Humaneness is essential to power. Though Confucianism and Taoism address completely different aspects of life, they are still comparable. This follows the principles of Rousseau also. From the perspective of Zen the "ren" and "te," as both power and virtue (compassion), relationship is reality.

# CHAPTER VII—
# Meditation

### Introduction

Phillip Kapleau acknowledges a number of problems with texts on Zen. He notes that Alan Watts is dissatisfied with the literature, because there is not enough historical or cultural background provided. Taoism and Indian Buddhism are not emphasized enough, if at all. Kapleau retorted to this, that academia is misleading, futile, and "downright hazardous." Kapleau continues to say that zazen is not emphasized enough. Kapleau states that, "The heart of Zen discipline is zazen. Remove the heart and a mere corpse remains" (p. 90). I agree with both Kapleau and Watts. That is the reason this chapter follows all the historical and cultural background. I cannot give you zazen, nor can I teach it to you. Like anything that is Zen, zazen must be learned without a teacher, and experienced. The title of this chapter is misleading, because what is really being emphasized is zazen. Without zazen you are only studying a corpse. So this is where you must learn to discard all the academic knowledge you have acquired in this book.

Discarding this knowledge is essential to your Zen practice. Otherwise, as Kapleau said, it will be hazardous to the "earnest seeker aspiring to enlightenment" (p. 89). I admit that there is not enough emphasis placed on zazen in this book. Even in this chapter, meditation is discussed more than zazen. What is important though, is that meditation prepares the student for zazen. We cannot expect any reader to be able to seriously practice zazen during the course of reading this book. Every student has different needs, and requires a different amount of time for preparation. Meditation teaches us the initial discipline necessary to practice zazen. When we are finally able to perform zazen, then we discard the meditation as we discard everything else. In true Zen practice nothing is clung to, not even Zen. We allow everything to flow through us freely. We remove all barriers. Instead of opening the gates and leaving screen doors, we open all the doors. Let all the insects, wind, water, knowledge, and everything to flow freely. This is zazen.

In the first sections of this chapter I will introduce you to meditation for beginners. This is only an outline, because you must determine your own best methods. This cannot be taught, it must be learned. You will continue to see this statement throughout this chapter. You must practice on your own, and learn your own technique. When you reach the section on zazen, look on this as your goal in meditation. That goal is samadhi without support, and sunyata. Zazen is emptying, erasing, becoming ichi nen (one mind) and harmonious. To help you to reach this point, koans are discussed. Do not believe that you will find the answers to koans in this book or any other. The function here is to provide an understanding of what koans are, and how they are used in teaching and learning. Most importantly koans are not so much a teaching tool, they are a learning tool. These are tools for guiding the student from meditation to zazen. Again this is not intended to be academic, this is meant to be applied according to its spirit. Anything can be read into words, but nothing can be read into the spirit of a subject.

### Nutrition in Zen

Of the numerous fallacies associated with Zen is that of diet. When most people think of a Zen monk, Buddha, or a bodhisattva they think of a person who fasts. Fasting is an ascetic technique used for cleansing the body. It is not intended for regular use, or for creating a clear mind. On the contrary fasting creates disharmonious thought. It is the period after recovery from fasting that thought becomes clear, because the body has been cleansed and is being well nourished. There are safer methods of cleansing the body that have been clinically tested. As with many subjects Zen cannot take a particular stand and say, "This is a general rule which will work for everyone." Zen never takes this perspective. Zen assumes the perspective that every individual is unique, and as a result every individual must be treated differently. Again this becomes a matter of personal guidance, as it is believed that individuals are more capable of discovering their needs than anyone else.

If we must create a general rule, then good nutrition, a balanced diet, is recommended. Taisen Deshimaru also recommends that a person's diet should have variety. If you go to a good doctor the doctor will tell you to watch your own diet and be your own judge. If a particular food does not agree with you, then discontinue eating it. This may seem simple, and you may wonder why diet would be brought up in a book on Zen. Self-mortification is an important topic in Buddhism. Buddhism does not encourage self-mortification, which helps to distinguish Buddhism from other faiths with ascetic practices of self-mortification, such as Yoga. The issue here is more than just having a good diet so that your mind and body will work well. We can see in numerous texts and articles that good nutrition is important. If we examine the history of Buddhism we find that Buddha Gautama also recognized this, and denounced asceticism for its poor diet. In The Teaching of Buddha we see:

To those who choose the path that leads to Enlightenment, there are two extremes that should be carefully avoided. First, there is the extreme of indulgence in the desires of the body. Second, there is the opposite extreme that comes naturally to one who wants to renounce this life and to go to an extreme of ascetic discipline and to torture one's body and mind unreasonably.

The Noble Path, that transcends these two extremes and leads to Enlightenment and wisdom and peace of mind, may be called the Middle Way. (p. 112).

After having been in the mountains with the yogis for several years Buddha realized that asceticism was not working. While he was with the yogis he had fasted several times, and had almost died on a few occasions. After he left a wealthy woman gave him food and massages daily, and he found that he was able to think clearly. With a full stomach you can concentrate on meditation and attain nirvana. With an empty stomach you will be concentrating on your stomach. While he sat under the Bodhi tree the woman continued to bring him food, and would massage him with oils. Comfort is essential to right meditation.

## Meditation and Nutrition

Meditation is a technique used to develop concentration, in order to purify. As a beginner you are supposed to concentrate entirely on your breathing. This means that you should have no distractions, either internally or externally. In terms of nutrition, you should begin meditating after you have eaten and the food has settled. In other words, you should not be hungry, and nor should your most recent meal weigh heavy in your gut. The amount of food you eat will have an impact on your ability to concentrate. Let us examine an extreme case dealing with food: Thanksgiving. Many people will skip two or three meals before the Thanksgiving feast. This means that the individual has not eaten since at least the night before. In a situation like this, what were you thinking about the hour before the feast? Unless you only eat one meal a day anyway, you most likely were thinking about food and filling your empty stomach. After you have eaten at the Thanksgiving feast you are full. This is not a good full. For hours after you have eaten all you can concentrate on is the pain in your gut from overeating. You have taken your body on a nutritional roller coaster ride, and your mind has faithfully followed.

Buddha said, "The lazy glutton, eating large meals and rolling in sleep, is like a pig that is fed in a pen. . . . " (Dhammapada, # 325). He also said, "those who overcome their selfish cravings will have sorrows fall away like drops of water from a lotus flower" (Dhammapada, # 336). Buddha did not speak kindly of indulgences. The easy way always seems the most pleasurable, but in the long run these pleasures will have negative consequences. It is important not to over indulge. You must guard against attachment to anything, including the passions for good food. Eat until you are satisfied. If you want to taste everything, eat less of everything. If you want to eat more of everything, then spread it out.

In Zen the body is the mind and the mind is the body. We think with our whole being. Doctors have agreed that the condition of the body affects the brain's ability to work well. Particularly of importance to the function of nerves, are the minerals potassium and sodium. Both of these are deadly poisons alone. Both are essential to the function of nerves though. These two elements are used to charge neurons (the nerve cells). When a neuron receives a message, that message is transmitted electronically. In order for this electrical impulse to travel along the neuron, the potassium and sodium must be positioned for the correct polarity. Otherwise these elements carry a neutral charge when the neuron is not activated. Without potassium and sodium, neurons cannot function properly. Other vitamins and minerals are also credited with improving memory and other neural functions. In order for the neurons to be most efficient, a regular and well-rounded diet is necessary. Some of these vitamins and minerals, like potassium, are relatively rare.

For meditation it is wise to eat only enough to be satisfied. Soyen Shaku seems to contradict this with one of his rules of conduct, which he practiced when he came to America. His rule was, "Eat with moderation, and never to the point of satisfaction" (Reps & Senzaki, p. 26). Let us clarify the meaning of what is being said here. You should eat until you are neither full nor still hungry. The suggested approach is to eat until you are no longer hungry, then stop. If you eat quickly you will find that you will go from hungry to full without knowing it. If you eat very slowly you will spend the entire day eating. You must find the speed, which works best for you, so that you can tell when you are no longer hungry. Remember that the stomach is slow to tell the brain that it has received something. You must allow for this communication gap. There is also the matter that some foods weigh heavier than others. Heavy foods do not always carry such a heavy weight of nutrition. An example of this is the potato. Heavy foods like potatoes are good in moderation, but they fill too quickly. Foods like chicken, fish, and vegetables are very light. Again you must be cautious not to eat too much. Your body still needs other foods. A very important food is grain. Whole grains help the digestion, and help to prevent constipation. Constipation will also distract concentration. Examine your diet and be sure you are eating properly.

A good way to understand eating is to go to a buffet. A buffet is comparable to Buddha's analogy with pigs. When many people go to a buffet they have one thing in mind, eating as much as they can. You will notice at buffets that the heavy foods, which are less expensive, are provided in abundance. Light foods, like fish and chicken, are served in small amounts. If beef or ham are present, then there will be a server to limit the amount taken. If you really want to "do them damage" do you start your meal eating potatoes? No. You might start with the salad, but you will most likely start with the meat. Between servings of meat you might have salad, vegetables, or Jello. Why? They are not filling, and they provide the time for the meat to settle. If you did this every day, and you had bowel problems, you will find your problems getting worse. If you had no bowel problems, after doing this for a while you will. From this example you can see how you can eat more nutritious food with a balanced diet. What is missing is the grain.

Deshimaru also has mentioned a problem that exists between people who over and under indulge. Zen and Buddhism both discourage any form of indulgence. If you eat too much, then you should reduce your diet. If you eat too little, then you should increase your diet. Zen is the middle path in every respect. If we exist at extremes then we cannot be pure in our thoughts. If our diet exists at an extreme, then our bodies will be unhealthy and our thoughts will not be pure. Find a diet that works well with you. No one can tell you exactly what will work best for you. You have spent every day of your life with yourself. No one else can say that. Your mind has a record of every event in your life. No other record is so thorough. Only you can find your own middle path. Eating is like breathing. Breathing too heavily or lightly will cause you to faint. Being unconscious is not the right state of mind for effective contemplation.

**Posture**
No book can instruct meditation that will work for everyone. No teacher can teach meditation that will work for everyone in the class. Though these are true you will find many books and many classes on meditation. The good classes will encourage an individual approach, and provide personal guidance by the instructor. There are books that discuss the thousands of methods and positions of meditation. None of these may work for you. There are other books that avoid positions entirely and attempt to guide you to your own system. The important word in all this is individual. You must find your own way, no one can give it to you.

In Zen there are few rules. The reason is that we always find exceptions to the rules. It is difficult to get either schools or Zen masters to agree on issues. If there is one thing all zennists can agree on, is that they disagree. Something that most agree on is the importance of posture in meditation. During meditation you are supposed to sit comfortably with a straight posture, so that your blood can flow easily and there are no other distractions. You do not sit so comfortably that you sleep though. I disagree with those who believe that this is the only true form of meditation. This is important to beginning students, but the conditions become less necessary as one becomes more adept at concentration and having meditation permeates throughout all activities.

Comfort is certainly an issue to the beginner. Though I suggest having a good diet and relieving your body in every respect, there will still be discomfort. To help my wife with a skin irritation I took her hand and struck it. She asked me why I did this, and I responded, "What hurts?" She answered, "My hand." In turn I told her, "Your hand does not hurt, it is your brain that hurts. Pain and itching are creations of the mind. The body is filled with nerves, so the entire body thinks. Since pain and itching are creations of the mind, the mind can turn these feelings off." In this, one of my objectives was to distract her from the itching so she would think of something else. In meditation you must accept discomfort. You should never completely ignore or turn off an irritation. Irritations are your body's way of telling you something is wrong. Acknowledge the discomfort. Tell that part of the body it is okay, and that you will tend to the problem when you are finished meditating. Then refocus your attention on your meditation. For example, you are carrying a large box of glassware that requires both hands to hold and your nose itches. Do you drop the box to scratch? No. You wait until the box is safe before you scratch. When the box is safe though, your nose no longer needs scratching. In this respect the parts of the body sometimes act like children, every part wants attention.

When sitting in the lotus position you are supposed to rest one hand inside the other with your thumbs touching. Taisen Deshimaru states that the left hand should be in the right hand. This positioning of the hands is the standard position that is widely recognized. I disagree with this position only partly, because I feel it is inadequate for the needs of all students and all situations. The right handed student should start with their left hand in their right hand. This is a natural position for a right handed person. A left handed person should start with their right hand in their left hand. After having meditated like this many times the student should switch hands. The purpose of this exercise is to get both sides of the brain working. By limiting oneself to one position you are limiting your mind. For this reason you should alternate the position of your hands during meditation.

There are other positions your hands can be in. Like everything else, you should find the form that is comfortable for you. No matter what position you choose, be sure you are allowing your blood and ch'i to flow without hindrance. If your hand or foot falls asleep, then you should adjust your position so this does not happen. Two other positions you can assume with your hands are equally recommended. The first, with your hands in the same place as the previous position, fold your hands so that the second joint on your fingers is bent. Then place your hands together so that the second joints of your fingers are touching, as well as the tips of your thumbs. This should be done without effort, so that you are not forcefully pressing your hands together. You should not be limp either. A second alternative is to place your hands, palms up, on your knees. Your hands will assume a natural cupped position, as if your subconscious is expecting something to be placed in your hands. Both of these positions are good.

Some students have already learned how to meditate, and will have learned different ways to hold their hands. If the position you are used to is comfortable then keep it. What all meditation positions have in common is the posture. The posture should always be straight so that the energy flowing through the body and the spine to the organs and appendages is not restricted.  The correct posture also does not obstruct the flow of blood.  Your posture should never be so relaxing as to put you to sleep, nor should your posture be so rigorous as to distract you.  The purpose of all this is to allow your whole body to work together, for your body to be one with the mind.  This is often called ichi nen, which is Japanese for one mind.

Deshimaru has also mentioned a problem with the thumbs.  The thumbs should not be pressed tightly together, and nor should they be limp.  The thumbs must support themselves comfortably.  If they are too relaxed then the student is too relaxed.  If the thumbs are too tight, then the ki (spirit) and te (power) cannot flow, because the mind is not relaxed.  The student should neither over-concentrate nor relax to the point of slumber.  Neither of these is productive.  In China we see the concept of ch'i, which I mentioned earlier.  The ch'i is the life energy, not unlike ki and te.  Ch'i flow is what acupuncture and acupressure are supposed to manipulate, according to Taoist tradition.  Ch'i finds its origins in Taoism, much as Chinese herbal medicines.  The early Taoists were famous for sticking everything in their mouths, and experimenting with numerous medical techniques.  They learned from this, and the resulting information was naturally absorbed into Zen.

### Concentration and Breathing

The next problem is what you should concentrate on during meditation.  For the beginner this is simple, concentrate on breathing.  Specifically you should concentrate on breathing out.  Other items that are common targets for concentration include that which is being done.  For example, concentrating on walking.  When we walk we should be aware of our walking.  When we work we should be aware of our work.  When we breathe we should be aware of our breathing.  Since we always breathe, breathing is central to concentration.  It is thus important for students to learn to concentrate on their breath.  When the student begins to do other activities, then the student must maintain the awareness of breathing, as well as the awareness of the other activities.  Breathing is not something that is taught, it is something you must learn.  The key to breathing is to breathe out deeply through your nose, using your diaphragm to push out.  By using the diaphragm you will massage the intestines, which will help you to relax.  By breathing out deeply you will encourage your body to breathe in deeply.  When breathing in deeply use your chest, not your diaphragm, and breathe in through your mouth.  Your breathing should be silent.

There are many benefits to breathing like this.  You will notice your body relaxing, and you will think clearly.  This will supply your brain with the needed oxygen.  The brain uses most of the oxygen that you take in.  By starving your brain for oxygen you hinder your brain's capacity to function.  Breathing deeply will nourish your brain with the oxygen it needs.  Finally, why do you breathe in through the mouth and out through the nose? If you sleep with your mouth open you will wake up with a dry mouth. If you breathe out through the mouth you will expel the moisture in your mouth. Breathing out through the nose is soothing and only moisture from the lungs and nasal cavity is lost. Breathing in through the nose encourages nasal irritation. Breathing in through the mouth and out through the nose also reduces the urge to sneeze. Concentrating on breathing is not just for beginners. You must never surrender this technique. Many have gone as far as to concentrate on breathing out a specific nostril, and switching between the nostrils. There is also no reason you should not breathe entirely through your nose or your mouth. You must breath in a way that works for you. This is why breathing is not taught. You will find that your mouth dries faster breathing only through your mouth. There are times that the nose is so clogged that you find you cannot breath through it. Try breathing out your nose. If you force it to work it will. Plus, breathing out your nose will dry out the mucous membranes, which will help you to clear your sinuses.

You will find while you are concentrating that your mind might wander. It is difficult to focus your attention on one thing for even five minutes. As with discomfort accept the wanderings of your mind, and let them go. There are numerous analogies made for describing the wandering of the mind. The wandering mind has been compared to the wind and the weather in the Mahabharata. Certainly the wind and weather are more predictable and stable than the mind. When I let my mind run free it is filled with all kinds of thoughts. These thoughts are seldom related, and the different topics switch very quickly. I let my mind run its course once a day, just before I go to sleep. In this way I let my mind empty itself of all the nonsense it may have clung to during the day. There is a story that is related to this in Buddhist tradition.

One day, Tanzan and Ekido were walking along a muddy road and came upon an intersection. A young beautiful woman arrived, who was nicely dressed, and was not able to cross the intersection without damaging her silk kimono. Tanzan picked up the girl and carried her across the intersection. Then Tanzan and Ekido continued their journey, not speaking again until they had reached a temple that night. Ekido was bothered by the actions of Tanzan. Finally he asked Tanzan why he had carried the woman across the puddle when they, as monks, were not supposed to have contact with females, "especially not young and lovely ones." To this Tanzan replied, "I left the girl there. Are you still carrying her?" (Reps & Senzaki, p. 18).

There is another story in The Teaching of Buddha, that is similar. It is:

Once there was a man on a long journey who came to a river. He said to himself: "This side of the river is very difficult and dangerous to walk on, and the other side seems easier and safer, but how shall I get across?" So he built himself a raft out of branches and reeds and safely crossed the river. Then he thought to himself: "This raft has been very useful to me in crossing the river; I will not abandon it to rot on a bank, but will carry it along with me." And thus he voluntarily assumed an unnecessary burden. Can this man be called a wise man? (pp. 105-106).

It is important to put down those stray thoughts. Leave those thoughts behind, just as the first monk left the woman behind, and just as the wise man would have left the boat behind. Carrying stray thoughts is burdensome. Stray thoughts take up space that is much needed for new materials. When you cross each puddle or muddy intersection, put down the woman you were carrying, let her carry herself. If you had a small cart filled with items that would be damaged going through a puddle, you would carry the cart across a puddle. When you finished crossing the puddle would you put the cart down, or continue to carry it? Obviously you would put the cart down. There is no need to overburden yourself when you can put something down. If your only task was to get the cart across the water, you would leave the cart on the appropriate shore. You would not continue to carry it. This is the way with thoughts. Carry your thoughts as long as you have to, then put them down and walk away, without a backward glance. There is another story, in which a master asked a monk whether a boulder was in his mind or out of his mind. The monk, thinking he was being smart, responded that the boulder was in his mind. To this the master said, "Your head must be very heavy with such a burden!" Thus concentration is not putting something in your mind. Concentration is taking everything out of your mind, releasing the burden.

A somewhat cruel but effective way of teaching concentration is through a bit of contradiction that is really not contradiction. As the student is meditating and concentrating on breathing the master may see the student is concentrating too hard. The master has two options. First the master may strike the student between the neck and shoulder, and tell him or her to concentrate. This is done with a long stick, usually flattened on one end, called a kyusaku, or "waking stick." It is used to encourage or to keep awake. It is not meant to be used for punishment or any other form of aggression. Second, the master may say to the student, "Do not concentrate on your breathing! Concentrate on your breathing!" This presents a koan to the student. The student will stop concentrating on his or her breathing and will concentrate on what he or she should be doing instead. The student is not intended to understand this intellectually or rationally, and be able to respond. The perplexity of the master's instruction will create a new focus, and breathing will flow naturally. You may find yourself focusing too much on your posture and breathing. You must not do this. You will become tense and uncomfortable.

I introduce meditation in basically the same way with all my students. For example, when I introduced my wife to meditation, I suggested starting with her eyes closed, sitting comfortably, but not so comfortably as to put her to sleep. Then I told her to focus her thought on each of her senses individually and to "turn them off". When she had done this, she was directed to focus on a blank screen, to become the blank screen and then to open her eyes. By doing this she was able to disembody herself, and to let her mind fill the screen, not the outer world. During meditation you are supposed to be looking inward, not outward. By concentrating too heavily on a function like breathing you are concentrating on something that is outside your mind. After her experience, my wife exclaimed "Why use drugs when you can meditate?" It is interesting to note that many faiths, especially tribal religions, rely on drugs for making contact with the spirits, or seeing reality. For example, Aldous Huxley exclaimed while under the influence of mescaline (the main hallucinogenic drug in peyote), and upon witnessing the "is-ness" of his trousers, his bookshelf, and the legs of a chair, "This is how one ought to see, how things really are" (Goode, p. 211). Peyote is commonly used by shaman in the South West of the United States, for contacting the world of spirits.

No one claims that Zen is easy to do or comprehend. It requires work. Though we spend every moment of our lives with ourselves we often do not know ourselves as well as we think we know the world around us. By understanding ourselves we will understand the rest of the world much better. The only way to understand oneself is by looking inside. You will not see yourself reflected in someone else. When looking in a mirror we see our physical self, but we cannot see within. In meditation you are creating a mirror within your mind, so you can look at your inner self in the same way that you look at your physical self in a normal mirror.

Most people are familiar with their outer appearance. Most animals are also familiar with their outer appearance, which is evidenced by the fact that animals tend to prefer companions of similar appearance. To rise above the animals we must look inside. What man has that animals do not have is a cognitive ability. Our body is that of an animal, but the mind is able to think ahead and to improve itself through logic, creativity, and introspection. By looking in we come in touch with ourselves and solve our own problems first. Confucius once said, when questioned about death, "You do not understand even life. How can you understand death?" If you do not understand yourself, how can you understand anything else?

## **Zazen**

True meditation practice in Zen is zazen, not meditation. As has been said earlier in this text, zazen is not the same as meditation. Meditation implies concentration on something. In meditation we "empty our cup." In zazen we not only empty the cup, we erase the existence of the cup. Zazen is thoughtless thought, concentration without concentration, emptiness. Again we are discussing emptiness in terms of Zen, not in terms of the void. Scientifically speaking, there is no such thing as a complete void. Even the "void" of space is not completely empty. We cannot make a vacuum that is even close to as empty as space. There is always something there. We can also recognize the theoretical perspective, where there is an absolute zero, an absolute void. This theoretical perspective is not reality though. Even when we reach the absolute void there is still something there. What is there? The absolute void is occupied by the absolute void. Thus the void is filled with the void. In this way we can see that the void is not truly empty in the common sense. The void is empty in the Zen sense of being full with itself. We can see this syllogistically in mathematics. If we examine the two equations:

$ax + b = 0$
$cy + d = 0$

We see that these two equations are equalities. Thus we can place them together so that:

$ax + b = cy + d$

In the first two equations we had two functions equal to a zero, a void. The zero represents the absence of what is being measured. In the third equation we see that there is something there, it is not just a void. The only problem with mathematics is that it is easy to prove anything if you are ambitious enough. Mathematics is not reality, and nor is it representative of reality. Mathematics is only representative of the abstractions we are trying to evaluate. Abstractions are derived from what we believe is reality, not what is actually reality.

In the Dhammapada, Buddha tells us to "Leave the past, future, and present behind" (# 348). These abstractions are what we use to describe time relationships. Time is a continuum, and to focus on one point, or a select number of points, is to neglect the rest of the continuum. It is the goal in zazen to overcome these limitations, so that reality can be seen on a complete continuum. Reality transcends time and space. Reality transcends all forms of measure. By trying to measure we are only creating more limitations. Thus, in zazen, we find the infinite in the emptiness. This is the abstract concept called sunyata. Sunyata is emptiness existing in the unempty. Sunyata is not a state where there is nothing, but it is a state of no-thing. It exists without existing. The cup has been emptied, and then the cup has been erased. When the cup has been erased, the cup cannot be filled. The cup exists in a state of ultimate emptiness, no matter how much tea is added. The presence of tea does not determine emptiness, rather the presence of the cup measures the degree of emptiness. The emptiness allows the Tao to flow through us without hindrance, creating harmony.

Part of the essence of zazen is the absence of the teacher. Meditation is a very personal exercise. Meditating in groups is no different from meditating alone. In meditation we focus on what is inside of us, not what is outside. The same basically holds true with zazen, except the focus is not inside of us either. In Yoga we referred to this in terms of samadhi without support. The mind is focused on no-thing. The result is samadhi or a degree of enlightenment. When you are not practicing zazen, then your thoughts are peaceful, because all things, both good and bad, just flow through you. Buddha said, "Those who enjoy peaceful thoughts, consider the sorrows of pleasure, and remember the light of life, see the end of craving and break the chains of samsara" (Dhammapada, # 350). Buddha also supported the concept of not having a teacher. Again in the Dhammapada we find: "Only a man himself can be the master of himself... " (# 160); and "He who can be alone and rest alone and is never weary of his great work, he can live in joy, when master of himself, by the edge of the forest of desires" (# 305). Not only does Buddha tell us to meditate formally, but to apply that meditation to our daily lives. By doing this, we can escape from the universal suffering (the first noble truth). Thus sunyata is central to zazen, and a common tool used to attain sunyata is the koan.

## Koans

In the next chapter examples are provided of mondos. A mondo is a discussion between a master and a student, a sort of question and answer situation. Most koans are developed from actual mondos. Some have been developed hypothetically, or based on a story. An example of a story koan is the story about the monkey and Buddha. What happens in this story is that the Buddha was holding a monkey in his hand, and made a bet with the monkey that the monkey could not jump out of his hand. The monkey jumped so far as to reach the ends of the Earth. He lost the bet though, because Buddha's hand extended even farther, although it appeared to only be eight inches wide.

Little stories like this are not uncommon within any religion or culture. Zen is not any different. To amplify the teachings of Zen, many koans have been written. Not only are these koans good for introducing outsiders to Zen, they also serve as teaching instruments for the practice of Zen. The koan is best described as an instrument for learning. The koan is a paradoxical puzzle for which there is no intellectual, rational, or creative solution. The only solution to a koan is an intuitive experience. It is the experience, not any number of words that in itself is the understanding and enlightenment of a koan. Having the insight into a koan is having a piece of enlightenment. Eventually enough of these pieces are captured as to reach a state of non-enlightenment.

This state of non-enlightenment may be called nirvana, and it may also be called sunyata. Sunyata is a term meaning the non-empty emptiness. We see in The Teaching of Buddha that "Enlightenment exists solely because of delusion and ignorance; if they disappear, so will Enlightenment" (p. 116). Thus in the completely enlightened state, there is neither enlightenment, delusion, nor ignorance. These all dissolve into the cosmic ocean, the Brahman. The function of the koan is thus to act as a catalyst, to help in the fermentation of sunyata. Sunyata is not nirvana though. To ferment sunyata is like growing wine grapes. It takes work and patience, and when you pick the grapes you still do not have wine.

## An Introduction to Zen Thought

Without the grapes you cannot make the wine. If we were to continue with this analogy, nirvana would be the finished product, the wine. But is this situation really complete? No. What is the point in making wine that is not to be consumed? The consumption of the wine would be para-nirvana, because the wine has been consumed and is forever gone.

No single koan can raise an individual to this state of ultimate enlightenment. Circumstances combined with the right koan may however result in nirvana, but the koan is not acting alone. Koans are not essential to Zen practice. Masters are also not essential to Zen practice. In the Dhammapada, Buddha tells us that the best teacher is ourselves, lest we follow a fool instead of a true master. Thus koans are only one of many tools. Koans are most apparent because many have been written, making them a "formal" tool. Being a formal tool is only a mask though that we give to koans because we have attached something to them, and that something is words. It is common in Western society, with the existence of bureaucracy, to be misled to believing that words are actions. Bureaucrats are credited with talking so much about something that they believe it was actually done. This cannot be the case with koans.

Student: What is the meaning of Nirvana?

Master: Winter, summer, autumn, and spring. The moon is silent.

You will find that an answer to the question posed here seems to have nothing to do with the response. The student asks the master about nirvana, and is instead given what appears to be something else. This is not intended to confuse, but rather to get the student to quit being concerned with nirvana, to drop attachments, and think about something else. That something else is the koan. By intuitively understanding the koan the student is that much closer to nirvana, without being blinded by the light of enlightenment, and missing the target. Thus the goal is not nirvana, nor is it enlightenment. Solving the koan is not a goal either. These are just things that are done and that happen. If you strive for them you will never attain them.

Student: In which direction is the path that leads from samsara
to enlightenment/nirvana/satori?

Master:    The head of the bed
faces west
The foot of the bed
faces west
The head of the occupant
faces satori.

The student is asking for directions, and the master faithfully responds. Which direction is the master suggesting? Though west appears in the response twice the master is really pointing in another direction. That direction is certainly not given in Cartesian or cardinal coordinates. In essence the master has thrown the question back into the face of the student. This is not uncommon. It is called parroting.

Many koans have been documented. Numerous texts cite the more famous of these documented koans such as, "What is the sound of one hand clapping?" Another famous koan is the "Mu" koan of Joshu. A monk asked Joshu if a dog had Buddha-nature. Joshu responded "Mu!" Mu is equivalent to "non" in English. It is a negative prefix; that is, it is not a complete word, but it does bear a negative connotation. The negative connotation was not the bearer of the answer though. The way the original question was worded provided for a yes or no answer, not a non. Does a dog have Buddha-nature or not? Joshu's response tells us that a dog neither does nor does not have Buddha-nature. Also the question is of little importance, warranting a small answer. The answer itself is not an answer, but it is really another question. This is typical of koans. Joshu is attempting to distract the monk from his dualistic thoughts. Does he really succeed? I do not think so, at least not for Western audiences. He could have chosen a more neutral prefix, although prefixes are generally not neutral. For the Eastern audience this may have meant more, because mu (Japanese) is equivalent to wu (Chinese). As such, the audience already understood the concept of wei wu wei (action non-action), which in itself is a koan.

To answer a koan with another koan is very common within the dialogue of a koan. Frequently we can find numerous koans within a single koan. Philip Kapleau's book, Yasutani-Roshi breaks down the Mu koan to illustrate its various parts. First, the monk who is asking the question is asking "in all seriousness." This question was not asked to throw Joshu off, or to make fun, it was asked after careful deliberation and contemplation. Second, the question posed by the monk can be broken into many questions. Some of these may be: What is Buddha-nature?; Is a dog a sentient being?; Is being sentient requisite of having Buddha-nature?; Does consciousness have anything to do with sentience or Buddha-nature?; What is Buddha-nature?; and so on. We can see that the monk's question has a great deal of breadth and depth. Third, the answer of Joshu poses numerous questions, as was already noted. The potential of a koan is limitless.

The earlier koan that I posed, where the student asks, "What is the meaning of Nirvana?," also has limitless potential. Some of the questions embodied here include: What is nirvana?; What is the word nirvana?; How do we interpret the word nirvana?; How do we interpret the experience that is labeled nirvana?; How do we accomplish nirvana?; and so on. The master replies, "Winter, summer, autumn, and spring. The Moon is silent." This response also poses numerous questions. Is nirvana season specific? Is nirvana transcendental? What is the relationship between nirvana and our conceptions of time? Does nirvana transcend words? Is the meaning of nirvana mu? Has the Moon attained nirvana? Is the Moon nirvana? Is silence nirvana? Does the moon know? The Moon must know, because its silent response seems to be the most accurate. The Moon remains silent throughout the seasons. The Moon is also oblivious to the Earthly seasons. What does all this tell us?

As usual, the question and the response both pose many questions. Each of these questions is a koan in itself. Each of these questions is a step in an endless stair case. We can answer this infinite array of koans, or we can transcend them. The koan represents the limitless potential of words. The koan also represents the continuums upon which these words lay. It is the continuums we examine in koan study, not the words. The infinite complexity of a koan makes it impossible to rationally or intellectually interpret and respond. Applying creativity to a koan will only complicate it further, as we have already seen. When we examine a koan creatively, then we will expand the question endlessly. In koan study we do not expand on a question, we reduce it. For example, the monk in the Mu koan had reduced numerous questions down to a simple question: Does a dog have Buddha-nature or not? He could have asked a series of questions, a series that could have filled numerous volumes.

Reducing a question is very important. To answer a koan we reduce the koan until it no longer exists. We turn every koan into sunyata, emptiness. Again we are erasing the teacup. Why would we want to erase the question? The question is composed of words. One master was famous for answering every question by holding up one finger. This particular master was doing his students a favor. By not answering with words, the students had fewer words to erase. Every word is a limitation. Take the koan: "When many are reduced to one, to what is one reduced?" into consideration. This koan is telling you what to do: reduce. Every word becomes a link in the chain that is tying us to samsara, the cycle of reincarnation. That chain is also tying us to ignorance and illusion (maya). In Buddhism we are supposed to overcome ignorance and illusion, thus we must overcome the words that are holding us back.

The koan then serves as a tool for meditation. Meditation for Zen is the equivalent of samadhi with support in Yoga. The more we reduce the koan, the closer to samadhi without support we are. When we have reduced the koan to mu, we are but a short step away from samadhi without support. When the koan has been reduced to the state of sunyata, without the name sunyata attached to it, then we have achieved samadhi without support. At this point we intuitively understand the koan, and it is not uncommon for this state to bring laughter. The enlightenment brings the realization of the simplicity of the koan. It is common for us to try to complicate a problem, especially when we try to solve it intellectually. When we reflect on our vein efforts of intellectualizing we find humor.

**Other Forms of Contemplation**

Buddha said, "Better than a hundred years lived in ignorance, without contemplation, is one single day of life lived in wisdom and contemplation" (Dhammapada, # 111). Buddha is not saying that we are supposed to sit down and let the whole world go by.  Inactivity is not the way of either Buddhism or Zen.  When Buddhism was suppressed in China during the ninth century, Zen and the Pure Land sect were left alone.  Why?  Because they were productive.  Many schools of Buddhism, especially in mainstream Theravada and Mahayana Buddhism, are unproductive. Films portray monks, such as Theravada monks in Ceylon (Sri Lanka), as recluses that spend all their time meditating and performing rituals.  The most these monks seem to do beyond formal meditation and rituals is walking meditation, called kinhin.

Kinhin is walking contemplation.  Many monks use kinhin between periods of zazen.  This is not its only function.  To live a day in contemplation is to live a day in awareness.  Kinhin is the awareness of walking while you are walking.  In Zen you must be aware of what you are doing in every moment.  In one film a monk is shown doing kinhin.  This monk was taking very slow steps with his head slightly bent.  Why this monk was chosen I am not certain.  This monk had poor practicing techniques.  Obviously the photographer and researchers were not well versed in Buddhism and meditation.  This monk, when performing sitting meditation, appeared to be asleep.  He had poor posture while he was sitting, and poor posture while he was walking.  His slow steps and unsure posture showed his insecurity.  This monk was concentrating too hard on his kinhin, and too little on emptiness and just being (is-ness).

In this same film another monk was asked several questions.  This monk reported that sometimes he missed the luxuries of regular life.  As a form of meditation, living is also contemplation.  We must be aware of our activities and ourselves.  We must avoid attachments.  This monk was fooling himself.  Deep inside he was not happy, and did not belong in the monastery.  His efforts were self-defeating, and his awareness was buried in illusion.  If he was truly aware, truly concentrating, he would have recognized this problem.  If the master of his monastery was aware, the master would have told this monk to leave until he was ready to return.  These portrayals would not be allowed in a Zen monastery.  If you are not happy in living contemplation, then you do not belong.  If you contemplate what you are doing too much, instead of just being aware, then you are bound to get hit with a kyosaku (awakening stick).  Living in contemplation is not equivalent to being dead.  For this reason, in Zen, we also have working meditation.  Working meditation is called samu.  Samu can be done either in or out of doors. Samu is physical labor.

Everything we do must be done with awareness.  So long as we contemplate and are aware, we are practicing Zen.  We practice everyday Zen, every-hour Zen, every-minute Zen, every-moment Zen.  We cannot step into a room and say, now I will practice Zen.  Zen practice is not putting on another set of clothes.  In the Dhammapada we see: "If a man speaks but a few holy words and yet he lives the life of those words, free from passion and hate and illusion-with right vision and a mind free, craving for nothing both now and hereafter-the life of this man is a life of holiness" (# 20); and also: "Many wear the yellow robe whose life is not pure, who do not have self control" (# 207). Just because you put on the yellow robes of a monk does not make you a monk.

Zen is not something you can change like you can change your clothes. Zen is not a mask that is put on when you enter the zendo, and taken off when you leave. Zen is within, and is part of everything you do. If Zen is not in everything you do, then you are only fooling yourself. That is the life of maya, illusion. The life of awareness is the life of joy, the life of contemplation. The life of awareness is the life of Zen. The one who professes to practice Zen but does not do, is the fool. He may speak a thousand words that are not worth one word spoken in earnestness. He may do a thousand deeds, building temples, ordaining monks, and translating scriptures, and have not accomplished anything. The man who spends one day in contemplation has achieved more than a thousand who have spent their lives doing good deeds. The man who spends every day in contemplation, what he accomplishes can never be overshadowed, and is second to none. Contemplation enables us to be aware of the reality, and to manage that reality in the most effective way. Thus everything we do, we do as Zen practice. There are no limitations to the forms of Zen practice.

# CHAPTER VIII—
# Schools and Teaching Zen

In the study of law there are many popular terms. One of these is the term prima facie. If you did not understand Latin or the definition for this word you might guess its meaning as "prime face." You would not be far from the truth. Prima facie means on the surface it appears to be so. A prima facie argument is a one sided argument that stands by itself, before there is a counter argument. When the counter argument is posed we have dialectic, and in the courtroom this is supposed to educate the court so the court can make a decision. In essence prima facie is the face of an issue, the prime or center point. In a sense it is the prime face. In Zen there is no prima facie for any issue. Arguments can be made, but they are nothing but empty words. Even dialectic is not acceptable. The reason is that dialectic suggests a duality, for which Zen poses no support.

Zen neither denies nor admits to an issue. Zen will acknowledge the presence of an issue, if that issue is real. You must also remember that in Zen there is no such thing as real and unreal. These are viewed as one and the same. The same holds true with an issue. With every issue there are opposing sides. Sometimes there are two sides, and sometimes there are more sides than can be counted. Zen only takes the real side, which encompasses all sides and others that are unknown. This puts Zen in the middle. Zen does not make a judgment, and nor does it mediate. Though Zen is in the middle, it does not participate in the conflict. Zen has no interest in conflict, and will avoid conflict. This is not to say that schools of Zen thought do not have their conflicts. A good master though will not get involved in a conflict. An example would be a major difference between the Soto and Rinzai schools. In the Soto school the monks meditate facing the walls of the dojo. In the Rinzai school the monks meditate facing the center of the room, away from the wall. Most masters will not condemn or condone the acts of the other schools. This has been a problem of controversy between students though.

There is no absolute correct way to practice Zen. For each person the correct way is different. Dogen—the founder of the Rinzai School—traveled to many monasteries before he was enlightened. He practiced in the methods of each school. With each he was dissatisfied. In the last school he attended he achieved enlightenment. Whether his enlightenment was the result of the teachings of that school or his life is not made clear. The latter is the most likely. The teachings of any particular school are not guaranteed to work for anyone.

What generally defines the schools is their techniques. At heart they are all Zen; they are all Buddhism. Zen equally recognizes the three other major branches of Buddhism as well. The four major branches each began as a school. Each of these schools became very influential, and other schools developed from their teachings. A school develops from the teachings of an individual. The individual did not necessarily attain mastery or enlightenment before they opened their school. Mastery and enlightenment are important though to get followers.

The predominant schools were developed from the teachings of masters who had attained enlightenment. The reason the schools have different techniques is that they follow the teachings of their founder. A typical technique of teaching is experiential. Thus whatever techniques the founding master found effective on him or her self were emphasized in that school. The development of Zen in the United States has given rise to new schools. This has happened to meet the demands of the American culture, and as a result new masters have found different paths. Religion and philosophy are business. Zen is not different. To meet the needs of my own students I have adjusted my sessions to meet their needs. This is not a wrong technique. There is strong emphasis throughout Zen and Buddhism to individualize teaching. My students come from varying cultural backgrounds. For my Chinese and other Eastern students my sessions are quite different. For these students I provide deeper discussions that are much more philosophical and less wordy. I also emphasize the denouncement of materialism. For my Western students, I have to tease them with concrete responses.

Western audiences are less receptive to anything that does not appear to give them something. Westerners want something they can touch. If they do not see how they can apply the teaching, they are dissatisfied. These are materialistic problems. Materialism is a dominant theme in the West. We want things. It does not matter what they are; we want them anyway. There is another side to this, and that is that Americans are also more willing to surrender their material objects, easier to part with money, because materials are fluid to them. These are a part of Western culture that Zen has to deal with. For this reason my sessions for Western are designed to gradually take care of these problems. Materialism and want are discouraged in Zen training.

Eastern students are much less materialistic in some senses. They are more likely to be frugal with their money. If the Chinese are materialistic, their desire is for money. This is in part because China does not provide the system necessary for capitalistic gains. Other material gains are not very available either. We can understand their frame of thought when we remember Abraham Maslow's Hierarchy of Needs. According to his model, food and other items for survival are the first thing we think of. With the extremely limited supply of everything in China, we can see why the Chinese cling to their money, and where they spend it. They spend their money on food. The difference between the two cultures is extreme. This creates a cultural shock for the Eastern students. It is like taking someone from the Great Depression and throwing them back into the 1920's. There was almost no money during the Depression, forcing people to have to be frugal in order to survive. Thrown into the prosperous twenty's, these people would be misers, terrified of spending their money because something could go wrong. The Chinese also do not want to surrender their native culture, but they do want to fit into ours. These are needs that I have to fulfill with them. Their needs require more accurate responses, with a carefully tailored slant.

My sessions are not usual in that I do not have the students meditate during the session. My sessions are limited to questions and responses. With so many students, each with a tight schedule, my students do not have the time for long sessions. The Eastern students usually already know how to meditate. For students who do not know how, I show them. If they need help with meditation I handle them by appointment. Questions and responses are important to a session. This is the interactive aspect of Zen training. New students to my sessions are informed of the content of the interactions. In the process I tell them that they bring their own answers, because I do not give answers, only responses. To give an answer is to give concrete information. A response is not an answer. A response is generally in the form of a metaphor. The purpose is to get the student to release the answer within him or her self. Responses must be tailored to the needs and abilities of the individual student. This is one of the reasons my sessions are divided according to cultural upbringing.

To discuss this is easy. To understand this concept is not. Let us look at some examples of popular questions, and appropriate answers according to cultural background. I will use an asterisk (*) to indicate a response that is without sound or reaction by the person responding to the student.

Eastern Cultural Background:
Student: What is Zen?
Master: *. Next. . . .
Student: You did not answer my question!
Master: Yes, I did. Next?
Student: I do not understand.
Master: Then let me explain a little better. *. *. Next?
Student: Do you mean silence is the answer?
Master: Silence is as important to Zen as any other word.

(The master is illustrating a very strong point here, that is easy for the student to overlook).

Western Cultural Background:
Student: What is Zen?
Master: Zen is a Japanese word derived from the Chinese word Ch'an. Zen is usually translated as meditation or contemplation. It is also sitting. These are fundamental to the school of Zen. This is why this school of Buddhism has adopted the name of Zen or Ch'an. Zen is meditation, and meditation is what we do in Zen.

# An Introduction to Zen Thought

(This is quite a different response, compared to the Eastern Cultural Background. It does not really answer the question. This is certain to be followed by a train of questions. Eventually the master will have to get the student to stand down, so that other students may ask their questions).

Eastern Cultural Background:
Student: What is Nirvana?
Master: You tell me. (or: "Mu!"; or "Is.")
Western Cultural Background:
Student: What is Nirvana?
Master: Nirvana is a state of being that can only be experienced. Nirvana is generally attained through meditation. Nirvana is not the goal of meditation though.

Eastern Cultural Background:
Student: Why do we meditate?
Master: We meditate for the sake of meditating.
Western Cultural Background:
Student: Why do we meditate?
Master: You will find that meditation will improve you both physically and mentally. Meditation teaches us control of ourselves. During meditation we are controlling both our physical and mental being. This is also good for our spiritual being, because we understand ourselves better.

It is fairly obvious from these examples that responses can vastly differ. These are not the only possible responses. The answers provided for the Eastern cultural background are not limited to Easterners. These are responses for slightly advanced students. Eastern students are not necessarily advanced in any way. Western students are not necessarily novices either. Again the responses must be tailored for the needs of the student, so the master must understand the student's environment, attitude, and understanding.

### Students and Masters:

I have been misleading you with the use of master and student. This is a dualistic situation, and as usual Zen frowns on such a situation. For our purposes here, the student is a traveler. This traveler has chosen one or more schools to attend in order to better understand the path he or she is traveling. The teacher is more of a travel guide. The purpose of the master is to keep the student from getting lost. The master does not provide a map or describe details. There are two main purposes of the master. The first major purpose is to tell the traveler when the traveler has reached his or her destination. The second—and more important purpose—is to tell the traveler that he or she has not arrived.

The path is never claimed to be simple or easy. Many students have spent ten years or more on the path, before they have reached their destinations. Some have spent their entire lives on various paths, and never reached their destinations. The key to right action is to follow your instincts. If you are not comfortable with a technique, then find another.

This is the obstacle that many have not overcome, and have thus failed. Just because a technique works for many others does not mean it will work for you. The path must be your own path. We cannot find the path anywhere outside ourselves. If we spend our lives looking outside of ourselves for the path, we will have wasted our lives. No school holds nor claims to hold a monopoly on technique.

A good master does not impose technique. The techniques are consistent within a school because the adherents want to follow the path of their master. The master did not tell them to follow. You should notice also that masters have been known to react violently to students who copy their techniques. Masters have dismembered and even killed students for copying them. Buddha set the precedent for this (though not violently) when he told his followers not to follow his path or his teachings. What did they do? They followed. Perhaps in this way Zen often oversteps its very nature. Students and teachers get into a mold, and they follow a specific pattern. Mastery goes beyond the mold.

To be a master one must escape the mold. This is why many masters have risen from strange places. One master was the lowest ranking person in his monastery, when he was chosen to be the dharma heir. Why is this? The master does not adhere to any mold. The master is conceptual. A master will often teach from experience. This is misleading to the students, and is why there are so few masters. A person may be chosen to become a master without being enlightened. A true understanding of Zen may be all that is required. But the student knows that masters are chosen with the requirement that they are enlightened. This paradox makes the student feel inadequate. The student does not understand why he or she was chosen. This provides a koan for the student.

The inadequacy itself is enlightenment. Sometimes the best person for a job is not the one with all the training, and one that fits into a mold. Realizing inadequacy the new master looks deeper into himself (note: most but not all masters have been males. Ananda, Buddha's favorite disciple, set the precedent for Buddhism being not traditionally sexist. Though Ananda was not a woman, he made Buddha realize that men and women could both be recognized equally in the sangha). The master finds himself, and does his best. This is all that can be expected. Mastery does not mean perfection. The only answers the master has are answers to his own questions. These answers he generally cannot put into words. For this reason masters tend to be confusing, and seem to be elusive. The master is not trying to sidestep questions. The problem with the answers is two fold. First, the answers cannot be put into words. Second, even if the answers are put into words, they are misleading and will misdirect the student.

Masters are in a tough position. Perhaps the hardest master to understand is the novice master. The novice is afraid of making a mistake,

## An Introduction to Zen Thought

and by doing so to discredit his office and himself. As the master becomes more practiced he will become comfortable and freer with words in his responses. He will have learned how to moderate himself, and to tailor for the needs of each individual. The master never surrenders from being a student. As the students grow so does the master. The method of "instruction" in Zen is a combination of experience and interaction. In the learning process these are the most influential ways to learn. This is what the master has to nurture.

By saying that interaction and experience are the most influential, I do not create a sufficient argument. To understand this we can all look at ourselves. As small children we learned how to walk. This we learned from watching our parents, siblings, and other people, and from experience. We wanted to copy the actions of our intimate social contacts. Our family also wanted this, and encouraged it. They encouraged it by helping us, and showing us. We learned from this and practice. By learning something like this we cannot forget it. We may suffer a physically debilitating injury, and have to retrain our nerves and muscles to compensate for the changes. We never forget though.

This is the same with Zen. When we practice Zen we become Zen. We apply Zen to everything we do. Zen becomes a normal body function. This normal body function regulates both the mind and the body. It makes our thoughts clear and our actions precise. We gradually build harmony with ourselves. This harmony incorporates into all of our activities. This includes work, walking, sleeping, eating, going to the bathroom, play, religion, research, sex, and everything else. This is why Zen does not provide lessons on information. Information that can be put into words can be forgotten. We can no more describe Zen then we can tell someone else how their body performs a simple task like walking. Certainly scientists can tell us about nerves and synapses. Can we tell this to our small children and actually get a result of their learning to walk? No. The same is true of Zen. Through experience and interaction we learn to live Zen. Once we live Zen we will always live Zen. It is like riding a bicycle: you can never forget how once you have learned.

Another important aspect to Zen study is the perspective of Zen. As I have emphasized so much, Zen does not take sides. To illustrate this point I like to say: Studying differences Little can be learned by. Real progress is made when we study similarities. If we examine the sciences and religions we can easily see their differences. What is truly important is their similarities. If we were to take a group of scientists and theologians and study them, we would find commonalties. Seldom is there an exchange of information between the disciplines. When there is, we see that an individual with diverse interests is the one responsible for the exchange. Usually when people of different disciplines discuss the same subject they tend to quarrel, because they have limited views. Each one is right from their own perspective. Their perspective is narrow, and does not take in the whole situation. What the disciplines agree on is reality. The rest is empty conjecture. This conjecture is what they believe is true from their own perspectives, not what are really the facts.

Zen absorbs these details, where the disciplines agree. In this way Zen maintains its neutrality, and realizes the reality of a situation. It is interesting to find that the philosophies, including Zen, have known for thousands of years what science is only today beginning to realize, and that is interconnectedness. In many areas science still disagrees with the philosophies. No philosophy claims to have all the right answers, but they are seldom far from the facts. Because of this, science will continue to realize, anew for itself, basic philosophical knowledge. You may say science is slowly proving philosophical concepts. Sadly, science does not look to philosophy for answers; instead science turns to philosophy to criticize. Again we find that man is narrowing his views by only looking at the differences. If science looked for the similarities, science would start with philosophy, not end up arriving at it through elaborate research. In this way science is being counterproductive.

In our current society science is very important. We prefer to think empirically. If we cannot detect something, then it does not exist. If we cannot prove something through scientific method, then it is not possible. In Western philosophy we see the Greek philosophers using deductive reasoning to develop theories. In science we see scientists using syllogistic logic. Syllogistic logic entails the use of a formula. Scientists today use the scientific method as their formula. Philosophers have no formula. Einstein's formula was basically the perspective of philosophers. His formula, when confronted with a problem, was to ask himself, "If I was God, how would I do it?" After he developed his theory of relativity he was dissatisfied. He realized that he was missing important information that could only be found in other disciplines. He wished to develop a unified field theory, specifically so that information could easily be exchanged between the disciplines on a common ground. This is what philosophers and mystics have done for thousands of years. Since the mid-sixties, this is what Bohm, Pribram, and others have been attempting to do with the holographic paradigm.

The problem for the student is then to overcome their socialization. Western people have been socialized for a scientific society, which demands scientific thought. We have been socialized to specialize in a field, and to work that field in an empirical and syllogistic manner. Our socialization process has provided us with these limitations, and others. For clear thinking, for right thinking, we must do away with these limitations we have learned throughout our lives. This is not an easy task. We are trying to break the habits of our behavior and thought patterns, which we have learned through experience and interaction. Our socialization is programmed into us as deep as our ability to walk. It is possible to reprogram this through experience and interaction. Most people have reprogrammed their walking skills. First we reprogrammed ourselves to run. Then many of us have reprogrammed ourselves to swim. We still are able to walk after each reprogramming though. The same will hold true with Zen. When you have reprogrammed yourself to live Zen, you will not destroy your socialization skills. Learning to live Zen does not require destruction of any previous information. The previous information is just as important as the new information. If we destroyed it, then we would disappear into the mountains never to be seen again. We would lose our ability to interact with our culture. This is not the purpose of Zen. Zen should enhance your abilities to interact with your culture, just as running enhances your ability to walk. Yes, even swimming enhances your ability to walk and run. For this reason we are finding athletes using swimming to enhance their strength, speed, and agility in their other sports activities. As thinkers we are athletes of the mind. Our mind and body both need exercise, the right exercise. Zen is swimming for the mind.

When students realize this they relax. It is common for a student to try to suppress or push aside previous information. This is counterproductive to the learning process. An example of this would be American History classes in America. Early in school we are taught that Christopher Columbus discovered America. When we get to college we are given numerous other stories. Perhaps the most accurate of these is that the American Indians discovered America. As for Western discovery of America, there are at least two that predate Columbus. When we get to college we have to unlearn a lot of what we were previously taught. This makes college difficult for many people. If we start with the right education in the beginning, then we will not have this problem later. So long as we are not forced to displace other information, we can learn easily.

If we were to look at this from the perspective of the holographic paradigm we can understand this more clearly. Holograms are not perfect representations of the original object. Our memories are very similar. If we used the same holographic plate twice, with two different objects, without changing angles or other variables, our picture would be distorted. Both images will try to project themselves simultaneously. The result of this is the projection of one object that is the combination of the original two. If we double expose a piece of film, the outcome is very difficult to comprehend. Two or more images in the same place create confusion. The end result is no answer. Memory will either turn up blank, or will relate half-truths.

When teaching Zen it is not our purpose to try to write over anything else. In writing over something it becomes difficult to interpret what was originally said, and what was said later. The more often we over write, the less we can decipher. Zen does not seek to compete; it seeks to coexist. Thus when we teach Zen we encourage previous information. We accept the previous information and continue on. We try to give the holographic plate a new angle so that the same space can be shared without distorting the original picture.

**Dokusan**

Dokusan is a period of interaction between a Zen student and a Zen teacher, which is done according to a regular schedule. This is a personal encounter, in which the teacher is able to probe and stimulate the student's understanding, and the student is able to ask questions directly related to practice. Questions during dokusan are supposed to be limited to matters arising specifically from Zen practice. Essentially the questions can be about anything, because if we live Zen, then everything we do is Zen practice. This is exemplified by the following hypothetical interaction during dokusan:

Student: Are you a Zen Master?

Master: What do you believe I am? If you believe I am a master—that is a shame. If you believe I am a student—that is a shame. If you believe I am an imposter—that is a shame. If you believe I am a fraud—that is a shame. If you believe I am what I am—that is a shame. I am what you believe I am.

Student: Why is it a shame?

Master: It is a shame that you attach such meaningless titles to me. By doing this you are barricading yourself. You must overcome this if you wish to live Zen.

Student: How do we live Zen?

Master: You already do. Now you have to let it be.

Student: How do we let it be?

Master: By releasing it from the cage of words and dualisms.

Student: How do we release it?

Master: By meditating.

Student: So we meditate for the sake of releasing our Zen life (Buddha-nature)?

Master: We meditate for the sake of meditating. We meditate for meditation's sake.

We can see the probing in this interaction. A new student often has doubts. Since the student has doubts, the student will ask probing questions. Since the student is new, the master has to probe to know what he is dealing with. The probing of the master is much more subtle. Where the student judges the master by his responses, the master evaluates the student by the student's questions. By listening to the questions the master can understand the needs of the student, and meet those needs. Here is my personal response to this question:

Student: Are you a Zen Master?

The Author: A.

You may have noticed the master's evasive answer in the first example, to the question, "Are you a Zen Master?" That response was tailored to be too wordy, so that you could have a prior understanding. The second example provides a perplexing koan, possibly ranking with Joshu's koan "Mu." "A" is a word, letter, a vowel, and a tone. Which of these is meant? Are any of them meant? What is the question? As with the Mu-koan, you must focus yourself on the response: "A." This cannot be intellectually, rationally, nor creatively solved. I must say though, that my response of "A" is still too wordy. That itself points to the moon and says, "Isn't the silent moon singing loudly?" A true master will neither admit nor deny being a master. What is a master? Master is a word, an empty title. True masters are above titles, and discourage the use of titles. To be called a master is to be looked upon through dualism. If a person can be called a master, another may not be a master. We are all masters in the eyes of Zen. There is no distinction. It is better to refer to the master as a guide, and the student as a traveler. For example:

Student: What is your function?

Master: I am a guide; you are a traveler. Yours is a journeyless journey. My most important function is to tell you when you have not arrived.

Student: Arrived where?

Master: Arrived.

Student: Why is it not your most important function to tell us when we have arrived?

Master: That is my least important function, because it will not be needed.

Student: We will know when we have arrived?

Master: No. You will be.

Student: As a guide, will you show us the way?

Master: I cannot tell you which direction to go. I cannot tell you which path to take, or the name of the path. I cannot tell you anything about the path. You must experience the path. Everything about the path is beyond words.

As usual the master does not claim to have any answers. We cannot master anything until we master ourselves. Then we are an authority on ourselves, not an authority on others. The title master implies that an individual has authority over others. A master cannot give a person Buddha-nature, enlightenment, nor tell them the way. Buddha himself could not do these things. Buddha only told us that there was a path, and that path was inside of us. Any person claiming to be a master is not a master. Any person who denies being a master has other problems. The problem is that they are denying themselves, and is creating a dualism in their minds. By denying mastery a person is admitting to having caged themselves inside words and dualisms. If asked, "Are you a Zen Master?" an individual responds "No," then the cage is very strong. This is a flat out refusal, signifying a very strong barrier. When the response is tied in with reasons, then the individual has found windows in the cage. The reasons act as avenues of escape. They weaken the barrier, though the person is still a prisoner of the barrier. This dualistic thinking has to be abolished before the barrier can be surmounted. Until then this is a very strong barrier, and no progress can be made so long as it is there.

## Dharma Talk

The dharma talk is a lecture on a Buddhist topic. Dharma talk serves its purposes. Since Zen is primarily wordless, dharma talks are much less emphasized than dokusan or meditation. Even samu is emphasized more. Samu is Zen work, either in or out of doors. Samu can be gardening, farming, cooking, dish washing, or any other essential task. The dharma talk is important though, because it provides for formal instruction. Formal instruction serves awkward purposes in Zen. The formal instruction itself is not essential to Zen practice, but it provides food for thought. It provides a foundation for students to meditate on, and later to ask about during dokusan. Another purpose of dharma talk is to provide general information, so that the students are not ignorant. With dharma talks the students are provided with common knowledge, so that they can better understand the conversations during dokusan. This knowledge acts as pre-knowledge. The knowledge itself is not Zen or Buddhism. It provides a purpose and a general understanding.

This book may be considered dharma talk. It is not necessary to discuss the sutras or shastras, the Dharma, or the Dhammapada during dharma talks. Relying on these is limiting. In general the master discusses an issue that the students are being confronted with, or will be confronted with. The dharma talk could be about dharma talk or dokusan. This does not require the use of any text. In general dharma talk is at its best when it does not rely on any text. This book does not rely on any text, though I have used some references. Occasionally I mention other literature and views, but these are only to compliment the dharma talk I am providing, and to verify information.

The dharma talk does not have to be long, and is usually less than an hour. As a lecture it is not uncommon to find no questions being asked during dharma talks. This is not to mean that questions should be forbidden during dharma talk. I prefer to have questions asked during dharma talks. My reason is that I do not want to unnecessarily lose the students. If a student does not understand something, that will cloud the student's mind and make the rest of the lecture empty. If the student does not understand, and no explanation is provided, then the dharma talk has been wasted. Thus it is important to me that students understand what I am saying.

At the same time, dharma talk is not meant to be fully understood during the lecture. In dharma talk, concepts are provided for the students to ponder and apply for themselves. This is something that cannot be provided by the dharma talk. The best questions are clarifications, or requests for examples. Sometimes a word is misunderstood. Without feedback there is no way to be certain of the meaning being conveyed. Sometimes a demonstration or example is useful. An example of this would be meditation. The master may discuss posture and all the other aspects of meditation, but this is not enough. The master should demonstrate, or have someone else demonstrate. If someone else demonstrates the master can show the students what he is talking about better. This provides a model for the students to walk around and see for themselves. The master may even choose to have the students model for themselves. Then the master can provide personal guidance. The problem with this is that the master must be careful not to overcorrect. Learning meditation techniques is a gradual process. No one can be expected to meditate perfectly their first time. To overcorrect can be discouraging. The master is supposed to encourage, not discourage.

**The Zen Sesshin**

A sesshin is a gathering of zennists for a number of days to practice Zen. During this retreat the zennists stay at the zendo. Everything they do is on the grounds of the zendo. Generally their days are long and full, starting at about four in the morning, and ending around ten at night. The purpose of a sesshin is to provide an environment for focused Zen training. This training is fruitless unless the students carry their training into their regular lives. The sesshin is more than focused instruction—it is practice. Everything done in the zendo is Zen practice. The emphasis of Zen practice is intentional. In the daily chores the students are practicing Zen. After they have practiced in the zendo they bring their practice home, and incorporate it in their daily lives. It is a common mistake for the student to feel that they only practice Zen in the zendo. The lesson during a sesshin is that we are always in a zendo, and should thus always practice Zen.

Everything we do is Zen. Zen is in everything we do. So long as we understand this and allow it to be, we can live Zen. Zen is a way of life, not a philosophy or a religion. Zen is the way we think and act. Philosophers try to arrange things in an orderly way, to create order that we can understand. Understanding is thought. When thought is there we cannot capture what is beyond thought. In Zen we go beyond thought. As Bohm said in The Holographic Paradigm and Other Paradoxes, "Thought cannot grasp that which is," (Wilber, 1982, p. 64). This is the purpose of Zen, to grasp that which is, to be aware of reality. Zen does not really grasp reality either, because to grasp it would be to lose it. In the zendo during a sesshin, the student learns this. One sesshin is not enough to fully learn this lesson though. Some have spent many years in Zen monasteries and still have not learned this lesson. It is often difficult to grasp, because the concept is very abstract to dualistic thinking. The sesshin provides another important situation. This situation is exposure to normal life outside the zendo. This is what many monks miss in the monastery, and the reason they have such a hard time embodying this concept.

When a sesshin is over, everyone goes home to their regular lives. Your regular life is quite different from that in the zendo. This provides students with their own koans. This koan forces the student to practice Zen in everything they do, as they ask themselves, "How would I be doing this in the zendo?" Then the student tries to apply their answer to what they are doing. This can easily become misleading to the student. If the student continues meditating and going to the zendo and to sesshins, the student will improve.

**Teisho**
There is one final activity that is important during a sesshin, which is teisho. Teisho is a formal, nondualistic commentary on a koan by the master of the sesshin. The koan should be carefully selected according to the needs of the students. It should apply to the daily lives of the students, so that the students can better understand their practice after the sesshin. It is a commentary, because the interpretation of a koan is very personal and individualistic. The master could take the opportunity to introduce different aspects of the koan, which the students can relate to. Most koans are very old, and the students may not understand how the koan can relate to them. They cannot answer the koan for themselves, if they first do not understand the question. This is a very important part of the sesshin, because it is something the students will take home with them to their regular lives.

You should be aware of the procedures followed for teisho. The master delivering the teisho faces the Buddha on the shrine, as do all the students. The teisho begins with three prostrations toward the shrine, out of respect, and for humility. The master recites, and then begins the commentary, first reading the koan. All of this is done facing the shrine, presenting the teisho not to the students, but to the statue. No questions are asked, and the only person who speaks is the master giving teisho. The reason no questions are asked, is that theoretical questions do not help to provide for experience. The purpose of teisho is not to provide any special insight, but rather to help the students to find their own path, their own experience. When the commentary is done the Four Vows are recited: 1) All beings I vow to liberate, without number or prejudice. 2) I vow to uproot all the endless blind passions. 3) I vow to penetrate every level of truth. 4) I vow to attain the path and way of the Buddha and the Dharma.

You should note that earlier I said that I encourage questions during lectures. I do not encourage idle questions, or questions that ultimately have no answers. These questions do not receive responses. If they are responded to, the response is throwing the question back at the questioner. The only questions I will entertain are questions to clarify,

## An Introduction to Zen Thought

where clarification is possible. You may realize that there is little that can be clarified. As a result my responses often are: "What do you believe?" or: "Why are you asking me this, since you have already decided on an answer?" How do I know they have decided on an answer? I know because they asked the question. An example of this is the "A" koan mentioned above. I am asked if I am a master and I respond "A." Why is this response wordy, as I said it is? Because the questioner has already decided what the answer is. Whatever I say is wrong, according to their preconceived idea. If they had not reached their decision before they asked the question, they would have never asked the question. In most of our questions we are seeking affirmations of what we have already decided are the answers. Sometimes we ask a question and have not decided on the answer. Instead we have a list of possible answers, and try to match our selections with the answer provided. This is why the blind man in Circle of Iron told Cord, "Do not ask a question until such time as I have given you an answer," as the main condition of being Cord's teacher. Be aware, and you do not have to ask questions. If you ask questions, you will receive illusion and lies. When you are aware, the facts will come to you.

# CHAPTER IX—
# The Far Side of Zen

### The Far Side

Gary Larson has become a very popular cartoonist with his little windows of reality. The fantasies he creates in "The Far Side" are little fingers pointing at the absurdities of humanity and society in the real world. The sense of humor Larson draws on is two fold. The relatively uneducated can appreciate his simplistic humor, and at the same time this humor is even more appreciated by the intelligentsia. Why? Because the intelligentsia understands his profound implications and language. The intelligentsia, who are fond of criticizing humanity and society, see the reality he portrays. These comics illustrate a biologist's view of a profane world. They embody humility, iconoclasm, and the fundamentals of effective humor. These are the topics of this chapter.

These three topics seem almost trivial on the surface. You may even wonder why an introductory book would discuss topics like this. In reality, these three topics are of extreme importance to the understanding of Zen. These topics are so important that I originally wanted to give each its own chapter. There were two problems with this. First, there is very little literature on these topics with respect to Zen. Second, these are themes that arise through Zen training, and are numinous. By numinous I mean that they must be experienced in order to be appreciated. This may be why there is so little literature and research done on these topics. What literature is available, covers all three topics together, under the central theme of Zen humor.

If you should choose to assume a life of Zen, then you will become acutely aware of the significant role of humor in Zen. Humor becomes a tool for insight in Zen training. From Taoism, Zen adopted the posture of indifference. This posture is where Zen humor comes from. Does this sound like a contradiction? In the simple terms used, it is a contradiction. However, it is a fact. I begin this chapter intentionally with the topic of humility. Humility is the product of ego. If there is no ego, then there is no humility. When there is no ego, there is indifference. Humiliation is a tool used to pluck out the ego of the student. The student must lose the notions of I, me and mine. The student must also lose the notion of status, which is fundamental to the ego. When indifference has been achieved, then humility becomes a subject of humor.

I end this chapter with a discussion on iconoclasm. Iconoclasm has been used wrong in many cases. In other cases, iconoclasm has been used as a tool for instruction. Where iconoclasm has been non-violent it is both humorous and useful. In iconoclasm we can understand the role of scriptures and the sacred in Zen. What is this role? There is no role. This is the profound lesson of iconoclasm. Students are taught not to have attachments to themselves or materials. In the process of this, the students often redirect their attachments to scriptures and idols. It becomes necessary to destroy this obstacle in order for students to make progress. When the students have been made aware of the profanity of their attachments, there is humor. Once again this humor comes from indifference.

## Humility

Humility is one of the most important elements of Zen. Humility is derived from the value we place on ourselves. If we place no value on ourselves, then we cannot be humiliated. Essentially this is related to the second noble truth, which is that suffering is caused by greed, by desire. If we do not want or have desire, then we will not be disappointed, we can never fail. Let us begin our discussion from a point that Westerners can relate, and that is money. Let us say that a person needs only $10,000 a year to survive, and that person lives 100 years. This person may be said to be worth one million dollars. Some credit cards provide life insurance for the card holder when they are traveling. The credit card may provide your family with $500,000 if you die in an accident. To take this a step lower, there are gangs that will kill a person for a fee as low as a case of beer, and they will kill you publicly. How does this make you feel?

How much would you pay for a pile of dog feces? Nothing is the usual response. We do not value excrements, unless we have a farm to fertilize. In this sense, the value of fences rises above money, because there is no dollar value for it. But feces has many things we do not have. First, feces is pure-it is Buddha nature. It is Buddha nature because it exists without existing. Feces is also in harmony with nature. It provides nourishment, and it complies to all of nature's demands without any personal motivation or will. Not even Buddha Gautama had pure Buddha nature until he was dead. When he died he reached para-nirvana. Alive, even the Buddha was less valuable than fences because he was not in complete harmony with existence. He hungered, he suffered, he had personal thoughts. Feces has none of these limitations. Even a pile of fences is worth more than a human being, because it is priceless. To help make the point, consider this story: A Ch'an master named Sozan was asked what the most valuable thing in the world was. He responded, "The head of a dead cat." When he was asked why, Sozan replied, "Because no one can name its price" (Reps & Senzaki, p. 61).

Are these humiliating to you? If you say no, then you probably have little or no humility left in you. Most people are humiliated at this prospect. This is not bad, but nor is it good. The lesson here is not one of morality. This is not intended to validate acts of violence on the grounds that life is worthless. On the contrary life is also beyond monetary value. We cannot create life from nothing, but we can end it with ease. By placing a value on ourselves we place ourselves below even fences. What is the lesson in regards to the low value of an individual? In Zen we do not recognize our low value in terms of money. We also do not value ourselves in terms of longevity. Living a long life does not mean living a full and happy life. Living a short life does not mean living an unfulfilled and unhappy life. This is a recognition not of our mortality in comparison with other things, but of respect and harmony. Through this we can respect the world around us and live in harmony with the Tao.

I use Tao quite purposefully here. Taoism is a key player in Zen, as has been mentioned earlier in this book. From this perspective we are only the tiniest and seemingly insignificant part in the Universe. If one person dies the effect is immeasurably small upon the Universe. Even if our planet were to be destroyed, the effect on the entire Universe would not be more than the ripples caused by dropping a pebble in the ocean. This recognition and acceptance of our insignificance is important to Zen. By accepting your insignificance you accept humility. By accepting humility you can cleanse yourself of duality. You realize that every good deed creates an equally bad reaction. From this there is no duality, merely reality. By accepting reality without false and misleading labels, you see everything as it is now without misconceptions. This creates harmony, and happiness.

Humility does not just come in the form of monetary value. There are numerous forms of humility, so many that they cannot all be listed. There are important forms that we see referred to throughout religion and civilization. Notably, personal humility and mortal humility are paramount. We see personal humility every day on the news. If we watch the sports news we see teams and individuals winning and losing. The losers feel personally humiliated. Should they be humiliated? No. The winners should be humiliated because they were not beaten. Why? We only learn and get better by being challenged. The ultimate challenge is to face a more powerful opponent. The more powerful opponent will win. From losing we learn.

An example of this is martial arts training. In martial arts training the black belts will spar with the brown belts. The black belts learn nothing. The most the black belts will get is a blown up ego, and practice at their defensive skills and maybe their kata. The brown belts learn to moderate and defend themselves against a more powerful opponent. Even though the brown belts generally lose, they learn more. The most important lesson they learn is humility. When the brown belts win, then the black belts have become too confident. This re-teaches them humility, and breaks down their egos.

Mortal humility is something that religions around the world have tried to come to terms with since the dawn of mankind. Being an animal with foresight man has long since recognized his mortality. "Someday I will die. Then what?" Religions create a sense of immortality for the people, something to believe in. This belief makes accepting death easier because there is a promise of eternal life in a beautiful place where all things are good. Zen looks on this and says, "Get a reality check." Zen does not affirm or deny that there is or may be an afterlife. Zen just points to reality. Zen does not take the view that there is an afterlife, because no one has ever come back. The concern of Zen is not metaphysical; it does not try to answer these questions. Instead it points to the reality of the now.

My wife concerns herself with my seeming indifference to holidays. I respond simply with, "Why can't every day be a holiday?" Why wait for Christmas, Chanukah, or a birthday? Why should we label a particular day as special? Our life in this world is limited. Tomorrow you or I could die. If we enjoy every day as if it were a holiday then we can live a happy life. Why must we only be happy a few days of the year? Life is too short not to appreciate and enjoy every moment. Yes this is humility too. This is similar to a story about a Zen teacher who received the governor of Kyoto. The governor sent a messenger with a note to call upon Keichu, the Zen teacher. The note read: "Kitagaki, Governor of Kyoto." When he saw this, Keichu said, "I have no business with such a fellow. Tell him to get out of here." The messenger returned to Kitagaki with Keichu's message. "That was my error," said Kitagaki, who then scratched out the words "Governor of Kyoto" and sent the messenger back. When Keichu saw the new message he said, "Oh, is that Kitagaki? I want to see that fellow" (Reps & Senzaki, pp. 31-32).

There is another story, where an Emperor of China visited a Zen master. When the Emperor arrived, the master remained seated. The next day the Emperor sent one of his guards to deliver a message. The master arose and met the guard at the gates to the temple. Asked why he did this, the master said that he treats those who demand respect with no respect, and those who do not expect respect with the utmost respect. We can look on these two narratives as illustrative of humility, and a notion of Zen indifference. After reading these two stories, you can understand why everyday is just another day in the eyes of Zen. Then why should every day not be a holiday?

Death is another humiliating concept to those who want to live. In Buddhism, death is viewed as a higher state. The Buddhist does not enter heaven or hell upon death. There is no purgatory or after life. Death is looked forward to as an escape from universal pain, and the achievement of true harmony. If there is an after life, the Buddhist may be disappointed. Why would the Buddhist be disappointed? A comedian once said that when we die we get back everything we ever lost. This included thousands of pens and pencils, hundreds of pairs of sunglasses, and everything you lost and had replaced every time you moved. Do you really want all these things back? Do you really need all these things? Even if there was something you really wanted back, like a picture, finding it in your personal lost and found could take an eternity. There is also the aspect of eternal life. Would you like to live forever? Once you know everything, then what could you do to make life interesting, worth living? Most of you that are reading this book are young. You do not as yet appreciate death. It is probably the furthest from your mind. Have you ever known an old person or a terminally ill person that looked forward to dying? We see stories like this in the movies and on television, and we sympathize. At the same time the people who are sympathizing want to live forever. Why? Because we do not relate to the characters in the stories, we are detached from them.

As we get old we get bored with living. We grow tired of all the suffering. As friends and family die off we begin to grow lonely and feel isolated. As these things happen we begin to look forward to dying. For those of you who live long lives you will experience this first hand. You may not believe it now, but it will happen. As young people we look on the aged and separate ourselves from them. We cannot believe that they were once young and had the same feelings. Yes, the elderly once felt exactly as you do about wanting to live forever, and that they were different from the old people then. To drive this point home we should remember what Plato said about the younger generation of his day. He felt that the younger generation was degenerating morally and that the world was doomed at their hands. This sounds exactly like the older generation of today. This feeling is timeless. This is the reason that the older generation is venerated in the orient, especially by Confucianism. The older generation has experienced all and more that the younger generation has, only in different ways at different times. The places and names are now different and technology has improved vastly, but human nature has not changed. The changes that have occurred were lived through, so the older generation has the advantage of more experience.

Mortality is humiliating. People do not want to believe that they will die and be forgotten. They feel that they have lived and that they are significant. Every person is significant, but at the same time they are insignificant in comparison to the whole universe. The Tao will move on no matter who lives or dies. We have no power over it. Few of us even have power over ourselves. In our mortality we feel small and insignificant. In Zen we do not seek significance. We are significant to ourselves in the here and now. By seeking significance we only create more pain for ourselves. In Zen we are.

**Humor in Zen**

Humor is an integral part of society. Though we like to think of humor as being personal, and thus reserved to private matters, humor is important everywhere. In the West we often think of political and religious offices as being so formal, as to shut out humor. Humor is important for our health, or at least that is what many doctors have said. From this we know that even in the "sacred" places of our civic and theistic religions, humor is not absent.  On the other hand, it is looked down upon, because of Western prejudices on the meanings of humor.

In Zen, humor is essential.  Few texts give this subject any attention, partly out of apprehension for Western responses.  The biggest problem here is the misunderstanding of humor in Zen.  Zen humor is completely different from Western humor, at least in purpose.  Zen humor also is not structured to defame anyone.  When an individual or group is defamed, it is done sarcastically.  In other words, a highly respected group or individual is the "butt of the joke."  In order to understand Zen humor, we must first look at Western humor.  Please remember that none of the examples that will be presented are intended to slight anyone.  These are common jokes, illustrative of patterns of humor.

## **Western Humor**

Western humor is not anything particularly special.  When we mention humor, we often think of jokes.  We also find that every culture has its jokes.  There is also a pattern, as to what constitutes a joke.  By titling this "Western Humor" I do not mean to limit this section geographically.  Contrarily, we find that the humor discussed here is practiced throughout the world.  The more appropriate distinction between this humor and Zen humor would not be insightful or even materialistic humor.  Thus, we are not necessarily focusing on regional humor.  For these reasons we must maintain a sense of neutrality in our observations and reporting method.

There are numerous types of jokes that we are exposed to in our daily lives.  The most common form of humor is egoistic.  This is humor that builds the ego, by defaming another.  The resulting jokes are often prejudiced, either ethnically, religiously, or culturally.  These jokes almost never have any element of truth.  The only thing these jokes tell us is where prejudices exist between groups.  An example of this would be "Polish" jokes in the United States.  We also see regional prejudices such as "Black" jokes in the Southern United States, "Irish" jokes in Scotland, and so on.  Let us look at a couple examples:

"Why is there no ice in ___? Because they lost the recipe."

"How many ___ does it take to screw in a light bulb?  That depends on the size of the house."

"A man was driving along and saw a ___ walking along the side of the road.  He swerved and hit the ___.  Later he saw a minister hitchhiking, and picked up the minister.  As he was driving he saw another ___ along the side of the road.  Rather than offend the minister, the driver swerved to "scare" the ___.  When he did this he went, "Oh my God! I missed him didn't I?"  The minister responded, "Don't worry son, I got him with the door."

A Jewish guide was showing some Americans around Israel one day.  A tourist noticed some tents in a field, and asked about them.  The guide responded, "Oh, those belong to the Arabs.  The Arabs bring their sheep in to keep them warm at night, and to keep the sheep from being poached. Really, the sheep don't mind the smell."

In the West we laugh at jokes like this every day. In reality they are offensive. Every one of these jokes belittles an ethnic group. In the United States if you are not white you are considered a minority. To call an ethnic group a minority is absurd and demeaning. In reality we are all racial minorities. "But I'm white," some might say. No, you are Scottish, Welsh, Dutch, Irish, Norse, German, French, Italian, and so on. These are all racial groups too. The bottom line is that there is no real ethnic majority. There are concentrations of ethnic groups though, and we find prejudices in those communities. We also find that the ethnic prejudices influence humor.

This is egoistic humor, because in it we are fortifying our belief in our "racial superiority" and the "racial inferiority" of another group. We have seen this become state policies throughout our century, and not just in Nazi Germany. Even in the United States the government has suppressed the Native American Indians even to the date this book was written. We see radical groups, like gay bashers, the KKK, and the American Nazi Party attacking innocent people because of their ethnic background, and or sexual or religious preferences. By posing jokes like this we are only one step behind those who believe in "the final solution." We are attacking others to make ourselves feel superior.

An important element to this humor is the environment. If we were in a predominantly Black community, like the Republic of South Africa, we would not find Black racial jokes funny. However, if we were to substitute "White" for "Black" in these "Black" jokes, then the joke would fit the environment. In order for a joke to be effective it needs to be conveyed in understandable language, appropriate language for both the audience and the content of the joke, in the right environment, and to an audience that can understand the absurd twist. If any one of these elements is absent, or not properly accounted for, the joke will not be humorous. These same characteristics are also evident in Zen humor.

Language is very important to the comprehension of a joke. A joke told in Chinese to an American audience would receive no response from the audience. A joke told to a general audience in the appropriate language, but using terms that are too complicated will also not receive a response from the audience. A joke that is too complicated, even if the words are simple, will not receive a response from the audience. Jokes must be simple and in the vernacular. In other words, the joke has to be given in the common language that the people understand and use. The joke must be short, with a simple plot and a simple twist. The twist can be very absurd, and still be simple. The more absurd and true the twist, the funnier the joke. The twist does not even have to be unpredictable. In fact, some of the funniest twists are so true that we already know them before the joke is told. What is funny about these twists is the added twist that we had not seen the twist in the first place. When this happens, the joke is on us.

We do not see much tasteless, egoistic humor watching comedy shows. If an ethnic joke is told, then usually the person telling the joke belongs to that ethnic group. When this happens, we know the comedian wants us to laugh at him or her. Ethically, this is the best way to tell jokes like this. Those who do not abide by this ethical rule tend to find themselves not accepted in comedy shows. Most jokes we see in comedy shows make fun of all of us. Comedians make us look at ourselves, showing us how silly we can be. These same comedians attack our society, government institutions, homemaking, childbirth, child raising, and other common experiences. Those that stay in this realm go the farthest as comedians in Western society.

Materialistic humor is based on pleasure and gain. This humor stems from our desires in a materialistic world. It is natural in our society for humor to have a materialistic quality to it. Comedians exploit this with jokes about buying a new car or house, moving, love making, dating, and countless other topics. How is dating materialistic? "I've been seeking the right man. A man who can be romantic, compassionate and a good father. Above all, I want a man who can bring home a lot of money for me to spend!" Yes, this is a sexist joke. What kind of comedian tells this kind of joke? A woman who makes hundreds of dollars a night, getting up in front of audiences telling jokes like this. Does she have a boyfriend? No, she has a husband. He stays home with the kids, and probably works a basic job. If my wife was making that kind of money I would probably do the same, wouldn't you? That is perhaps the funniest aspect of this particular joke.

In America we even tease our materialism. Why not? When we laugh at ourselves we are recognizing our own faults. The problem with this is that we often forget these faults quickly after the joke is delivered. We forget because we get swamped with jokes, all revealing some absurd aspect of our daily lives. We might remember part of one of these jokes, but we fail to see the serious side of it. The joker has been revealing our true nature throughout recorded history. Take the Fool in Shakespeare's play King Lear. The Fool was constantly haranguing King Lear, a vulture capturing every stray absurd act the King did. The Fool is a very powerful character. This is evidenced by the fact that Lear banishes and punishes others who are less forceful than the Fool. Being the Fool even saved the Fool's life from the wrath of Lear. While all the other characters kowtowed to Lear, the Fool pointed to reality, and got away with it. Shakespeare's plays are riddled with fools like this. These clowns are all powerful. They see reality. No matter what they say or do, they are immune from the usual consequences. They are also often ignored. This is what our society does with its clowns.

You can learn a lot from a clown. In the West we laugh at their jokes and absurd antics. Who is the dummy, the actor, the piece of wood (puppet), or the audience? It must be the audience, because they are failing to take the dummy and the clown seriously. They laugh, but their laughter is only half of the lesson. They are overlooking the phantom moon, the moon the comedian is pointing to and saying, "Now there is reality." In the mind's eye we admit to this phantom moon. We laugh at its absurd nature. At the same time we fail to embody the fact that the phantom moon is us. We are the orbiting body that is following this absurd path. What do we do about it? Nothing, because we aren't taking it seriously.

### **Zen Humor**

One of the biggest fallacies about the orient and Zen is that emotions are suppressed. The perspective on emotion is that there is a time and a place. By completely suppressing emotions we would create emotional and psychological problems. By letting our emotions dominate we will enter into a psychosis of fantasy. Neither of these extremes is desirable. One principle of Zen, which applies to everything, is to seek moderation and control, a middle way. Another principle is to be natural in everything you do. Though it may seem obscure, these two principles are really one principle. They become one because being natural does not mean to exist in extremes. Thus to be natural is to be moderate. Being natural also is not domination or anarchy. To be natural we must have control. You can cup your hands and hold water. If you grab the water you cannot hold it, and the tighter you grab it the quicker it slips through your fingers. By controlling we are not letting the essence of life slip through our fingers.

How does this apply to humor in Zen? There are moments in Zen where humor seems to dominate. Humor is like any other emotion, it is selective according to circumstances. The time when humor assumes its most powerful form in Buddhism is at the time of enlightenment. Researching this is difficult in the West, because few authors ever recognize humor in Zen. It becomes obvious though, as a standard, when we look at Zen art, especially statues and pictures of Buddha, monks, masters, and other bodhisattvas.

Even non-genuine statues of the Buddha depict him smiling. Sometimes the smile is very slight, but it is still there. There is also the famous laughing Buddha. This Buddha is depicted as a heavy set man, often shown playing with children and laughing. This is not Buddha Gautama, it is Hotei (Pu-tai), one of the Zen masters and a Buddha. Hotei is one of the key players in humor. He was a very profound character. He wore rain clothes during good weather, and good weather clothes during bad weather. A famous portrayal of Hotei shows him walking and laughing, as he is pointing and looking up. If there is anything that shows him as a Buddha, this does. Many people wonder what he is pointing at, and then wonder what he is laughing at. There are two possibilities for what he is pointing at. First, he may be pointing to Heaven (T'ien). Second, and more likely, he is pointing to the Moon. He may also be pointing at both. Why is he laughing? You cannot walk to either the Moon or Heaven. Neither Heaven nor the Moon has the answers, but people strive for them with the vein hope that they do have all the answers. He is laughing because he sees that he is in both places, and neither, and it was simpler than walking. He laughs at himself and everyone else.

Hotei is also frequently portrayed as playing with children. In the Orient, Hotei is one of several "Santa Claus" figures. It is ironic that he is not alone, as Saint Nicholas and Santa Claus are in the West. The common misconception that the Orient suppresses emotion is thrown out the window when we take this into consideration. With only one Santa Claus figure in the West, we are really the ones that are too serious. Hotei was a living Santa Claus. He played with children in the streets, gave them fruits and sweetmeats, and was the epitome of clown figures. Of all people, Hotei took the lesson of returning to childhood to attain original nature very seriously. In him we see that the clown can be the most serious individual in society.

In the West we see many arguments pertaining to the original nature of people. Some argue that we are inherently evil, where others argue that we are inherently good. Both of these schools neglect the fact that the new born mind is empty. It is a blank page for the world to write upon. Thus what is our true nature? Our true nature is indifferent, neither good nor evil. In the beginning children get into mischief because they are curious, and do not know better. Then we teach them what is right and wrong. Once children have learned this, they have been damaged for life. Their curiosity has been suppressed, and they have learned to categorize and prejudge. Their minds become filled with the categories we teach them, and they no longer have the blank mind for the world to write upon. A new born child does not recognize limitations. When new born baby squeezes your finger you will find it has a lot of strength. That is the true strength, not the strength we believe we have. As we learn our limitations we prejudge, limiting both our mental and physical strengths. This is why we seem to get weaker as we grow up. Then as we get older we continue with this notion, and keep limiting ourselves more. "I'm too old to do this." "I am getting old and weak." Not Hotei. Hotei continued to get younger as he got older.

Have you ever noticed that children seem not to care about puddles, the weather, or much of anything else? Child nature is very much egoistic though. Children are very possessive of parents and objects. "Me, me, me; mine, mine, mine!" These roll out of their mouths shortly after they learn to speak. Where do they get this from? The parents. Children learn directly from their parents. If a child is never taught the concept of ownership, then the child will never be materialistic. Few cultures have ever been successful with this. Sadly, these same cultures are almost completely destroyed by White man's materialism.

Does a new born baby care about what blanket you put on it? No, it only cares that it is comfortable. Does a new born care about the decorations you put in its room? No, it does not even notice them. You can change anything in a newborn's environment, so long as it is still comfortable, it will not care. This fresh little mind is truly a Buddha. Nothing bothers it. It's only instinct is to remain comfortable, which is only intended to keep it alive. The new born wants nothing more than to live, and even that it does not want, it only does. The will to live is not conscious, leaving the mind pure. By returning to this state, we find that children are the closest to sunyata. The older we get, mentally, the further from sunyata we are. So we must return to the unrestrained merriment of youthfulness, in order to find sunyata (emptiness).

Laughter is usually associated with enlightenment. Have you ever had a pen in your hand and looked all over trying to find it? Have you ever had a pair of glasses on top of your head that you could not find? When you found these items in their obvious places you most likely laughed at yourself. You would laugh harder if the glasses were on your face. This is what Buddhists experience when they reach enlightenment. The glasses were on their face the whole time! This is also why it is said that Buddha nature is in everything and everyone. If you search for the glasses that are on your face, you will not find them. They will not be anywhere that you look. If you just let them be, you will discover them with effortless effort. This is the way of Zen. We already have enlightenment. By looking for enlightenment, especially outside ourselves, we will not find it. In meditation we allow Buddha nature to surface, not by looking for it, but by letting it be. Then it is as obvious as the glasses on our face.

When enlightenment is reached, it is funny. It is not uncommon for the enlightened person to laugh for several days, if not for the rest of his or her life. When Buddha Gautama held up the flower, and his disciple smiled this was the first transmission. The disciple smiled because he was enlightened by seeing the presence of Buddha nature in everything. Like all the others he had sought enlightenment in words and everywhere else, when it was always with him. This revelation was funny. Buddha had succeeded with his sermon, by not saying a word. This has been the way of Zen. Whether the story is true or not is uncertain. The story is very possible though, and is not the only one of its kind. In Zen we find many such stories, where a student was struck by a master, or by a natural object like a fruit, and has been enlightened. In each case the student laughed, as the student became the master and became the student.

There is a story about a wealthy man who was seeking enlightenment. He searched for a master to teach him, and could not find one. One day he overheard some beggars talking about a great master. He asked them where the master was, and gave them food in return. He then sought out

## An Introduction to Zen Thought

this master, and at every place he went to, the master was not there. One day he came to a village and was directed to an old beggar. Prostrating himself before the beggar he asked to be the master's student. Three days later the master nodded his approval. The student promised to follow the master for twelve years, to live as the master, and do as the master asked him to do. On many occasions the student was hurt. Each time the master reminded him of his obligation. Seven years had passed, when the student was told to go get some food. Having no money, the student tried begging, but was not allowed because of a holiday. He found some soup, stole it and brought it back to his master. The master ate, and for the first time the student saw the master happy and smiling. He was excited. The master asked the student for another bowl, and the student was happy to go get one.

In the town the student was caught stealing the second bowl, and was beaten. A couple days later the master walked by the student, who was still laying in the street, and once again reminded the student of his obligation. In the last month of the twelfth year, the teacher provided one final lesson. The two had stopped to rest, and the master took off one of his shoes and struck the student in the face with it. The student was enlightened.

As with most stories like this in Zen, it is humorous. Humor is not the only important thing in this story. The situation had to exist. In this story, the master, in part, created the situation. In terms of enlightenment, preparing the situation takes a lot of time. With a pair of glasses the situation is usually created in less than an hour, but we laugh at it. This situation took twelve years to create. The student had looked everywhere for enlightenment. When he was slapped in the face, this was symbolic of the simplicity of the problem. The master was slapping him in the face for looking in all the wrong places. Essentially this was not any different than the flower being held up by Buddha. Buddha had created a situation, one that took decades. He had given sermons and taught, but his students had not caught the true spirit, the true teaching. When he held up the flower, without saying a word, only then did one disciple learn.

The story is also a koan. As a koan it poses innumerable questions, and cannot be understood intellectually. Without having lived through this experience we cannot appreciate the entire quality of this koan. Many people go to monasteries and become monks. Like this character, the monk feels like it is all a big game. Buddha admitted that he had this feeling for quite a while after he started. It is like taking an airplane to another country. We will do things we would normally never do. Why not? Nobody is watching. Besides, we can always go home and forget it all. After living in a situation for several years it stops being a game. If we spend our time looking forward to the conclusion, because we have already predetermined it, then we may cage ourselves in with this. Surprisingly this aspect is not dealt with in this particular story. The humorous twist in this story has nothing to do with the predetermined date though. Instead a situation had been developed. All throughout the story, the student does everything the master bids him to do. The student seems more like a servant than a student. The student felt loyalty and companionship with the master. His role seemed obvious, and he permitted himself to be used.

Placing himself in a subservient, yet humane status, the student became comfortable with all the discomforts. Why? Because he was still with this great master. There is also a sense of novelty involved with new situations. For a while, at least, it is easy to be disillusioned in an unusual environment. It seems like a vacation, until you realize it is not. Was the old beggar a great master? This was the unspoken question in the act of hitting the student. The student realized many things. First, he realized that suffering is universal, and that the world is always changing. From this he realized that he was his own master, and would need to continue learning and changing. The slap filled him with questions. With each question was an equally absurd response. The answer to each question was the slap in the face.

In the movie Circle of Iron, Cord is bothered by the actions of the blind man. Many times he threatens to leave, and many times the master responds with a simple goodbye, and keeps walking. Finally Cord cannot take it anymore. The old man has risked their lives to fix a broken wall, has destroyed a kind family's boat, and broken the face of a beautiful boy. Declaring he is no longer the student of the blind man, Cord demands answers. Previously the blind man told Cord that Cord could only ask a question after an answer was given. Then Cord turned the table. "Did you smell the bag of coins (in the wall)?" "Did you hear the horses?" "You didn't feel the boys face. . . . " With each question the blind man shakes his head no, and smiles. Finally Cord realizes the truth, and exclaims, "You've been here before!" To this the blind man slaps Cord on the face and says, "How many times?"

Humor is more than a feature of Zen, it is an essential element. Without emotions we cannot be natural. When we accept our emotions, and let them exist in the now, only then can we be natural. By laughing at enlightenment we are not taking a step back, we are not stepping forward. By laughing we have achieved the now of the situation, and have moved from dualistic thinking to harmony. True enlightenment transcends even itself. The enlightened mind realizes this, and laughs at the absurdity of this thing called enlightenment. Why? Because enlightenment is the opposite of illusion and ignorance. Without ignorance and illusion you cannot have enlightenment. Thus to be truly enlightened, you must surrender illusion, ignorance, and even enlightenment, because they all exist together. When this is intuitively understood it becomes a humorous paradox, where the absurdity and the humorous twist in the plot is the path to enlightenment itself. Nothing is funnier in Zen than Zen and the zennist.

## Iconoclasm

The term iconoclasm is relatively uncommon. Some Western religious groups refuse to acknowledge idols, and disapprove of idol worship. An example of this is the Quakers. The Quakers do not wear jewelry or fancy clothes. They do not adorn their churches with statues nor paintings. This is not iconoclasm, although religious groups like this do suppress the worship of idols. Iconoclasm is an extreme. It is the literal hatred and destruction of idols of worship (also called icons). In Chinese history there are two groups who were famous for their iconoclasm, the followers of Mo Tse and the Taipings. Both of these groups actively sought and destroyed all religious art work, and other symbols of religion. This is not the extreme adopted by Zen.

In Zen, iconoclasm is usually not active in the destructive sense. Zen iconoclasm is also not usually interested in non-Buddhist idols. Idols are not worshipped, but in general art is highly respected. Then why are we discussing iconoclasm in Zen? Zen masters have a long history of destroying, defaming, and denouncing icons. In some cases these acts were violent, where in others they were just a disregard for symbolism. There are many examples of the disregard for symbolism in Zen. One master burned a wooden statue of Buddha to warm himself. A monk criticized his act, and the master responded that he was seeking the spirit of Buddha in the statue. The monk retorted that it wasn't there, so the master suggested burning the rest of the statues in the temple. In this sense the master had not actively sought to destroy an idol, just to warm himself. The statue was nothing but a block of wood, the fact that it had been shaped to resemble something else was not an issue. At the same time his act was a valuable lesson on the meaninglessness of icons. This was not an act of violence.

To declare an act violent we could look at our own legal system for reference. First if we examine laws governing conduct we often find the elements "willingly and knowingly." You must be willing to commit an act, and know that the act is wrong, though ignorance of the law is no excuse. On the side of defense we see excuses, mitigations, and justifications. In the previous example we saw a justifiable excuse-placing life before objects. When there is no viable defense, the actor is committing an act willingly and knowingly. To teach a lesson, or to force your beliefs on another are not viable defenses. Destruction of property is destruction of property. To commit the act with the intent of teaching another a lesson, or forcing another to your beliefs is an act of coercion and violence. The iconoclasm of Mo Tse and the Taipings are an example of violence. There are Zen masters who have also fallen into this category.

The masters that do this violate their own beliefs. By destroying icons the masters are acknowledging them as icons. In this sense iconoclasm becomes an attack on personal fears and beliefs. This is what psychologists are fond of classifying as denial. In denying we are exhibiting our fears, and the lack of faith we have in an ideology. So long as the masters believe an object is a religious icon, then it is. By believing that an object is an icon, the master acknowledges it and endorses it through negative acts. By attacking the icon the master places himself below those who worship the icon. He has become worse because he is not certain what he believes. This is not a Zen master. There is too much ego involved in such an act.

For those masters that practice iconoclasm I give a profound argument. If people worshipped rocks, would the masters smash all the rocks? The sun was a religious icon, and still is to a few people. Will the masters form a bucket brigade to put out the sun? Art based on religious themes are only icons to the believers, and can be enjoyed for their artistic qualities. Zen has its own art. I have never heard of a single master defacing a piece of Zen art.

Zen art is as much an icon as any other art. By displaying iconoclasm the master shows his insecurity, and uncertainty with his own beliefs. Feeling threatened by the beliefs of others he attacks. Not only is this violent, it is unnecessary. Neither violence nor unnecessary acts are the way of Zen, and are universally denounced by Zen masters. These iconoclastic masters are not masters. They have not learned discipline and harmony.

**Profound Icons**

The absurdity of icons can be displayed without the destruction of art work or other objects of a possibly religious nature. Iconoclasm in its extreme form has seen the destruction of tablets with genealogy on them, and even gravestones. This is disrespectful and unnecessary. Mo Tse went as far as to condemn mourning for the dead, ceremonies, and music. He showed just how extreme iconoclasm could be. On the other hand we can look at ancient civilizations like Egypt and see extreme examples of idol worship and abuse of ceremonies and rituals. Zen is called the middle path for a good reason. True Zen never takes an extreme, or settles for a dualistic system. In teaching Zen it is necessary to provide profound lessons, in order to eliminate the sense of dualism in students. Students enter the zendo (a place where the way of Zen is learned) with many preconceived ideas. Candy is good, poison is bad; living is beautiful, dying is ugly; fire hurts, and a massage relieves pain; life is miserable, alcohol relieves misery. These are all dualities which most people will agree to; they are preconceived ideas that need to be gotten rid of. This does not mean that they are to be destroyed or suppressed. Dualities are creations of our minds, and do not represent reality. By holding on to the dualities we overlook reality.

To conquer duality there is a method in which profound icons are used. Most zendos have a shrine, which marks the focal point of the room. It is not uncommon for the shrine to have a statue of Buddha Gautama. At the end of meditation you are supposed to prostrate (bow) yourself before the Buddha nine times. This is not an act of worship. To create a profound situation the master may someday remove the statue and replace it with something else. My favorite choice is manure. The students must still prostrate themselves. The lesson here is that the statue is not an item of worship. The statue is not an icon. It is an object, no more. If that object happens to be something else, it is inconsequential.

Why do we prostrate ourselves nine times? The answer is manifold. You prostrate for humility, and for respect. This is not respect for Buddha Gautama but for Buddha nature itself. Buddha nature is in everything and everyone. When you prostrate yourself you are respecting your own Buddha nature, and the Buddha nature of everyone and everything else. By changing the object in the shrine the master illustrates that Buddha nature is in everything, not just a statue. The statue has no more Buddha nature than a pile of manure, or the individual person. This is a profound lesson. Prostrating is not just for humility and respect though. Prostrating is very personal. The act itself is a koan, because you must ask yourself why you are prostrating. Humility and respect are not the answer. The answer transcends words. Prostrating is done for your own reasons which cannot be put into words.

Above I indicated that prostrating was bowing. In reality prostrating is an extreme bow. When we bow we bend our body only slightly. When we prostrate we get on our knees and bow down to the floor, arms out and hands open facing up. This is a symbol of how small we are, because we are occupying a very small space. The palms of the hands are open and facing up to receive. What are we supposed to receive in our hands? I do not know, you tell me. It is not Buddha nature, because Buddha nature is already within us. Buddha nature is not nirvana nor enlightenment because not even the Buddha could give that. If it is not these things, then what can it be? The position of the hands suggests wanting to receive something physical. The position of the hands is a profound lesson in itself. It is a lesson that also addresses the issues of dualism. The issue addressed is specifically that of material versus non-material; physical versus metaphysical; being versus spirit. We receive, but we do not receive something that is either material or spiritual. You might say we receive the Tao. But the Tao might be considered spiritual. We receive without receiving.

As you can see, icons can have a positive affect on the student of Zen, so long as their use is managed properly. In the end they cease to be icons, and become simple objects. My home is filled with objects like this. I have statues and paintings that could be considered to have religious connotation. I did not get them for their religious connotation. I got them because I liked them. They do not inspire me, nor do they dissuade me. They are merely decorations. They are also useful tools for Zen training. The average American would be confused by my decorations. I have surrealistic prints, some of which contain religious symbols like Christ, the cross, angels, and other quasi biblical themes. I have statues of Krishna, Buddha Gautama, and Hotei (Pu-tai). The average person wonders what I believe, with such a variety of religious themes displayed. I believe, and that is all. The average person sees these items as icons, I see them as objects.

**Iconoclasm of Scriptures**

Nothing is attacked more in Zen then scriptures. This comes from the principal of wordlessness. Many masters have studied the Dharma, sutras, and shastras. Many masters have added to the shastras, and other literature on Zen. When masters have added to the literature (not the shastras) they have done so out of fear for losing the teachings. We must remember the role of a bodhisattva. The bodhisattva wants to enlighten everything. Some have thought that perhaps they can do this through words. This becomes obsolete when another master comes along and burns the books. The question that needs to be answered here is why?

Why would a master, who has studied the scriptures and texts, turn on the materials he learned from? Why would this same master not use these materials to train his or her own students? What we find is that the master starts with studying the scriptures and texts. Finally the master realizes that he or she is missing something, something the texts cannot provide. What is that something? It is the spirit. This is exemplified in a story:

There was a well known Sanskrit scholar named Jiun, during the Tokugawa period in Japan. He would lecture to his brother and to students on Buddhism and Sanskrit. One day his mother heard about what he was doing, and wrote him a letter. She told him that she did not believe he became a Buddhist because he desired to turn into a walking dictionary for others. She reminded him that there is no end to information, commentaries, glory, or honor. She told him to stop lecturing, and to: "Shut yourself up in a little temple in a remote part of the mountain. Devote your time meditation and in this way attain true realization." Jiun became a Shingon master.

Jiun's mother was right. She recognized that he spent all his time preaching and memorizing. This has been a common problem throughout history, despite Buddha's cautions. Seeking the path in written words is empty and without merit. Not only should you not follow scriptures, Buddha tells us: "You are the master of yourself, and your self is your refuge" (Dhammapada, # 380). For these reasons we see masters burning their books, and refusing to be tied down to a monastery.

The master realizes, when he or she experiences the spirit of Zen, that the texts were a lie. This perception can be violent. The immediate action is to destroy the books. This is a sign of detachment, but it is not yet a sign of indifference. When absolute indifference is reached, then there is no violent reaction. The reality of the books on the indifferent mind is not important. For this reason, many masters have not destroyed their books. Others have gone a step further, and rather than destroy they become profane. These masters have been known to carry scrolls of blank paper, that they call sutras. In effect, their blank scrolls are the most accurate sutras. They are the art beyond the art, the artless art. This gesture is actually positive, where the violent outburst is not. The blank scrolls have all the teachings, they are sunyata.

# CHAPTER X—
## Science Encounters Zen

Since the nineteen sixties a new theory of physics and psychology has been taking form. This theory is called the Holographic Universe Theory, or the Holographic Paradigm. It is metaphorical and not intended to be completely representative of reality. This is the most zennist approach to science I have seen in Western civilization. The Holographic Universe Theory was simultaneously developed by Karl Pribram, a neurophysiologist at Stanford University, and David Bohm, a quantum physicist. Both of these men had long since established themselves as leading authorities in their fields when they developed this theory. Why did they develop this theory? Both were dissatisfied with the explanations of science on natural phenomena, and the failure of science to explain other phenomena. Michael Talbot in The Holographic Universe does an excellent job of describing this theory for the layman.

I am a researcher in many fields, especially since traditional philosophy transcends fields of discipline. For years I researched the mathematics of reality. Being more of a philosopher I have always been inclined to ignore the rules and seek the reality of the situation. When I was exposed to this theory I became enthusiastic, because it put into simple terms what I had already determined through research. Like most people I approached the problem by dividing everything. This bothered me from the start, because from a philosophical perspective everything is interconnected in some way. Every time I divided I found myself directed toward a universal wholeness. Rather than go in conflict with this I accepted it and embodied it. My philosophical conclusion is that science is on the verge of establishing proof of the philosophies, especially Tao in Taoism and Zen. Scientifically I established evidence of universal interconnectedness. To draw from this it will be necessary to go over my findings in physics. Since this is not a book on physics or math, I will not bother with elaborate mathematical proofs here in the text, but I will describe the physical properties necessary for our discussion.

### Holograms

Through the 1980s and 90s Western society has been increasingly exposed to holograms. Holograms have been appearing on television, in movies, and even on the cover of magazines. National Geographic has used holograms on at least three of its magazines. One was a hologram of an eagle, another of a skull, and another of a representation of the Earth. These have been poor representations of holograms. Considering the costs, this is understandable. The best holograms are striking images of three dimensional objects. In some cases a holographic plate was rotated while the subject was in motion. By doing this the hologram catches a

## An Introduction to Zen Thought

fourth dimension of time, dependent on motion. In many cases holograms have been done with laser light that cannot be seen in white light. The vast majority of holograms the general public has been exposed to have been white light holograms. White light holograms can be viewed in daylight, and with conventional household lights. White light is a composite of the entire color spectrum, which allows for some coloration in these holograms.

What is so special about the hologram? If we just look at a hologram all we see is a series of circles and waves, not at all representative of the image. When the hologram is exposed to the necessary light source, a three-dimensional image suddenly appears. Another important feature is that a hologram can be broken, and the image is completely contained in each of the fragments. The hologram is created by interference patterns. The mathematics for these interference patterns is found in Fourier Analysis and Transforms. Every part of the hologram is interconnected with the whole. As a whole the hologram is at its clearest. When it is broken the image is retained in each piece, but the image becomes less clear with each break. If it is put back together, the hologram can recover clarity.

With the Holographic Universe Theory we see that one of the faults of science is failing to look at the complete picture. As a result we receive a very unclear image. It is as if we, as human beings, paint over the rest of a hologram, and only see it through a very small window in the paint. We haven't destroyed the hologram, but we have blinded ourselves to most of it.

### Dimensional Physics

I have researched the relationships between various dimensions. At first my goal was to define two and three dimensional objects in space. Along this path I found myself being distracted by one dimensionality, and by the fact that my work still failed to define reality. The equations I developed only defined boundaries in three dimensions, and were meaningless in terms of matter, energy, and time. To solve this problem it was necessary to examine what the universe is composed of mathematically, because everything that is reality has elements of matter, energy, time, and defined spatial boundaries. This was a big stepping stone to a dimensional matrix. The dimensional matrix is not a standard algebraic matrix, as defined in basic algebra and linear algebra. It is a map of reality that is not actually representative of reality. In it are the major categories by which we recognize everything, organized according to mathematical relationships in a hierarchy. The matrix, in a simplified form, appears as:

$$O \qquad \qquad \text{Origin}$$
$$t' \quad t \qquad \qquad \text{Time}$$
$$M \quad m' \quad m \qquad \text{Matter}$$

```
s   X   Y   Z                Space
E   g   e   r   T        Energy
    Transdimensions
```

Each of the fifteen major dimensions listed in this matrix have sub-dimensions. Each of these sub-dimensions has an infinite number of possible dimensions that exist mathematically, passing through each other, sharing the same or similar space, or are interconnected in some other way. From this we see that dimensions exist within dimensions.

One part of this matrix that confuses people is the Origin dimension. As with all mathematical anomalies there exists a common reference point. In the column with the origin dimension is a series of other origins. Each of these origins is relative to the base origin (O). But O is not the true origin. It is used here to signify the origin (point of reference) for the known dimensions that are in the matrix. Logically speaking this would be interconnected with an infinite number of other origins. In all, the absolute origin would be the Holographic Origin.

Origins are tricky. If we look at the row labeled "Space" we see s, X, Y, and Z. Each of these has subdimensions which we do not see, but do exist mathematically. "s" consists of three specific sub-dimensions in this row which are X, Y, and Z. We are used to X, Y, and Z as dimensions of space. With these we have developed units of measure to determine length, width, and height. Combined as axis, each of these dimensions has an infinite number of possible distances. With all three of these infinite distances combined we have elementary space. When we apply limits to these distances, and add other information we can define an object. The most common mistake with this view is that many people neglect its infinite qualities, and visualize it as a sphere or cube. The important part is that we recognize the quality of wholeness involved. Another part of the dimensional matrix that is confusing is the Transdimension. I labeled it this way because I am trying to signify motion (trans) into another series of dimensions. There is an infinite number of possible families of dimensions within the Transdimension. At infinite this is mirrored, and thus the matrix expands into four lobes.

Each of the four lobes represents a different aspect of reality. The first lobe is the reality we exist in, which is mirrored by an anti reality, the anti-verse. Combined, these two lobes are mirrored by a mirror-verse. The anti-verse is, in mathematical terms, inversed reality. When an inversed function comes into contact with the original function, they cancel each other out. We can see this represented graphically. Where the functions interfere with each other we are left with the base line. What separates us from the mirror-verse is a series of dimensions that I label the transdimension. What separates us from the anti-verse is the origins. These origins represent the baselines. According to this definition we can also determine that the mirror-verse is an inverse function of the standard universe and the antiverse. This means there is, in this matrix, two universes and two anti-verses. The reason I combined the transdimensions into one unit is that there is an infinite number of possibilities that exist between these dimensions, and the Transdimension does not represent a baseline.

We are most frequently concerned with the matter and energy dimensions. You will note that I have labeled matter as having five fundamental components, and energy as having five. The definitions, both mathematical and semantic, incorporate the dimensions into a unified field theory. Each component represents a value, whether we can directly measure it or not, that is significant in the make-up of the universe, of reality. Suffice it to say that we are redefining these quantum variables as waves, similar to Fourier Transforms used in analyzing a hologram, and subsequently the Holographic Universe. Mathematicians should note that the partial derivatives within a row or column provide the next dimension to the left. Taking the partial derivative as many times as there are dimensions in a series will return you to the original dimension.

We have a tendency to create dualistic interpretations. We can add something, or take it away. But is this truly representative of reality? This matrix is not attempting to divide everything into a dualistic reality. If anything it is illustrating a possibility of four realities. But this illustration is only on the surface. Remember that each dimension has an infinite number of sub-dimensions. These provide for an infinite number of possible realities. There is no black and white here, only infinite. As I stated before, each of these dimensions is interconnected. Mathematically the definitions for each of these dimensions create an interconnected anomaly. Each dimension is derived from the previous dimension. When we have gone far enough we find that a cycle is formed. An example of this is the function sine. Sine is its own fourth derivative. These dimensions reflect this same property, showing their relativity and interconnectedness. We see another relationship with Zen, beyond the interconnectedness, in sunyata (emptiness). Since these dimensions cancel each other out we can say they both exist and do not exist. They are sunyata.

We can take two waves, like light waves, that have an inverse relationship, and cause them to interfere with each other. We know we have generated these waves, but they cancel each other out, leaving us with nothing but a baseline. This is a prime example for sunyata as emptiness without void. We are also left with an illusion, maya. This illusion is the presupposition that something exists, specifically the two functions. The reality is sunyata, where the illusion is the two functions. If the dimensional matrix is accurate as a mathematical definition of the holographic universe, then it also proves sunyata, maya, and interconnectedness. The illusion (maya) is the matrix. The sunyata (emptiness) of the dimensional matrix is the existence of inversed functions that cause this matrix to have an enfolding and unfolding quality. The matrix unfolds when we create the illusion on paper or in our minds. The matrix enfolds as the Tao, the way of nature that is oblivious to concepts, emotions, creativity, or any form of knowledge. The interconnectedness is found in the baselines, the points of origin. Without these zero points, we can not formulate a measure.

The bottom line becomes the holographic universe. This becomes a reality when we view the dimensional matrix mathematically. We find that each dimension has a wave quality. Holograms are made by the interference of waves with each other. Each dimension can interfere with all the other dimensions, and all interfere with each other at the same time. If we were to combine all the dimensions into the holographic universe, and define the holographic universe as a dimension in and of itself, we would see that the holographic universe interferes with itself. In other words, the holographic universe is self generating, contributing to itself as much as any other of the infinite other dimensions. Combining all the mathematical qualities of the dimensional matrix under the aegis of the Holographic Universe Theory, we discover the enfolding and unfolding quality of the universe. As a hologram composed of functions and their inverses, the universe is in a constant state of change. This change is caused by the interference of dimensions. What is unfolded does not cancel out. What is enfolded is canceled out. The universe is perpetually enfolding and unfolding, as the interference patterns shift. We cannot say that we are either in the enfolded or the unfolded. To theorize about that is to try and place a value judgment. If we do that, then we are bound to eventually prove ourselves wrong.

**Zen**

It may be difficult for you to see a relationship with Zen here. Remember that in Zen we are achieving harmony. To do this we empty ourselves, and allow the Tao to flow through us. We become one with the Tao. The Tao is the holographic universe. The Tao is everything and it is nothing. The holographic universe is also everything and nothing. In Zen there is a concept referred to as ichi nen. This means one-mind. When we are of one mind we are not divided. Many masters assert that this means we think with every part of our body. In reality, though, we are not thinking with our body. To think with your body is to limit yourself to your body. By placing a limit on something we are violating the teachings of Zen. According to what we have just covered, it is necessary to have one mind with the Tao, to be one with the universe, to be one with the holographic universe.

Michael Talbot discusses some individuals who have tapped this great source. Most of the people he discusses have unwittingly achieved this, where others have worked on it. In his book he discusses near death experiences, out of body experiences, re-cognition, precognition, and telepathy. Something he notes is the increased ability in these areas of

# An Introduction to Zen Thought

people who regularly meditate, and the special ability of some individuals, like yogis, to go even further. Although these ESP experiences are often disparaged by the scientific community, they exist in our community with great frequency. According to Talbot, more than one in five people have had a paranormal experience in their life. Many experimenters have logged hundreds and thousands of cases, and investigated them. Only the holographic paradigm has offered any explanation, and has been accepted, in whole or in part, by the investigators as the possible explanation for these paranormal experiences. Without direct experience it is hard for most people to believe in these experiences. What helps to make them believable is the number of renowned people who have had them.

Scientists, mathematicians, and other professionals have had paranormal experiences. Placing their reputations on the line they have admitted their experiences. When people that have something to lose say something, it is good to listen. They are more likely to be honest. They are also more likely to relate what they are certain of. If they had not had the experience they certainly would not place their reputations on the line. As for myself, I am only certain of precognition and out of body experiences. My precognitions have usually been on highly emotional situations, like death. At one point in my life I thought I was going insane. We see many authorities that have the same first reaction. Eventually they all accept their "gift" and work with it. Some have turned to studying their ability, and attempting to improve it. As for me, I emptied it and turned it into sunyata.

It is interesting to note that those who have near death and out of body experiences describe 360 degree vision, and the ability to see with parts of their body other than their eyes. This is a limiting view of sensory perception. From my own experience, the true 360 degree sense has no relation with any of the other senses, and yet it stimulates all of them. It is not uncommon in history that warriors have gained a sixth sense, a hunter's sense. This is the sense that is honest when all other senses deceive us. Michael Talbot begins his book with an example from Star Wars. It is ironic that Star Wars has both holograms and sixth sense examples. In the movie Luke Skywalker is studying the ways of the "force". Kenobi, the old master, senses the death of a planet and dangers along their path. Kenobi is a warrior. He tries to teach Luke how to use this sixth sense on the Millennium Falcon, by putting a helmet on Luke with blinding visor. Luke complains that he cannot see, and Kenobi tells him that his eyes deceive him.

In Zen we see the same thing. Our body is an illusion, and everything our senses tell us are also illusions. With the holographic paradigm and the dimensional matrix, reality as an illusion is reasserted. By rising above this illusion we gain a sense beyond the dimensions. This sense is not blinded by what we think we see, hear, smell, feel, or taste. We can be convinced that a lemon tastes like a sugar cube, or that we see blue when we are actually seeing red. These are easily attained through hypnotic suggestion. What we do not realize is that we are always deceiving ourselves. If we believe something then it is so, but it is not actually reality. This was what bothered Bohm. In quantum physics, particles were believed to only exist as particles when they were being observed. Essentially the quantum physicists were attaching relativity to observation. This is what happens when we watch, they would say. We do not know what happens when we turn our backs. This is similar to the paradoxical question: If a tree fell and nobody heard it, did it make a noise? This perspective is as ridiculous as believing nothing exists until we experience it for ourselves. Bohm solved this problem by first declaring that particles remained particles even when they are not being observed.

For our purposes let us refer to the reality we experience, both illusionary and non-illusionary, and the reality we do not experience normally as the holoverse. We are part of this holoverse. We interact with the rest of this holoverse, and the holoverse interacts with us. These are illusions of the holoverse. In the holoverse distance does not exist. The physical does not exist in the holoverse either. All of these are still illusions. We can control our imaginations. Imagination creates illusions in our minds. When we see something our imagination fills in what we believe is there. This is not reality in the holoverse, although our minds see it as reality.

Our senses do deceive us. For this reason we have to rise above our sensory perceptions to a holographic perception. With all the information we can predict anything. As a general rule science has been examining our reality by dividing it into pieces that seem easier to deal with. By doing this science is left with a lot of unanswered questions. To answer these questions we have theorized. Our theories are only true in that we believe them, they are not factual. This is because we are not allowing all the information in. Since everything is interconnected in the holoverse all the variables must be known in order to understand. When all variables are understood, there is no such thing as chaos.

It is interesting that the most significant advances in science and math were not done by scientists or mathematicians. Our greatest advances were done by philosophers. Why is this? Philosophers do not tie themselves down with rules. Scientists and mathematicians take a narrow view, feeling that they must work within a set of guidelines. We can see this by looking at such figures as Newton, Einstein, and Pythagoras. These great minds were not scientists. Newton was a theologian, devoting most of his life to religious studies. Einstein was a patent clerk. Pythagoras was a musician. Although as a patent clerk Einstein was undoubtedly exposed to science, his education was in law. While he was in school Einstein was told that he would never be any good at math. The next time we criticize someone when we do not understand, we should all think again.

Each of these individuals found solutions to problems outside the rules. We find that Zen and Taoism emphasize this principle. There are no principals in the holoverse, except the holoverse, and that is not always a fact either. By following rules, and by dividing the holoverse, we neglect the whole picture. We can be shown a picture of a patch of brown fur. If we were expert zoologists we might determine what kind of animal the fur belonged to. If we determine the fur belonged to a horse, could we determine the color of the horse? If the horse was spotted the brown could be a spot. We cannot definitely say what kind of horse it was either. For that matter, without analyzing the fur itself we might not be right about the creature being a horse. If instead of looking at a patch of fur we are provided the whole animal, then we can answer more definitely. We still cannot answer all questions though, as we are limited to the information provided.

Instead of seeing a horse we see the holoverse. If we see the holoverse in everything, then we have all the answers. We have all the answers because all the information is available. The problem is then can we see the holoverse? Yes, we can see the holoverse. The holoverse is infinite and finite at the same time. We can see infinite in everything we do. Look at a yard stick, for example. The yard stick is divided into three feet. Each foot is divided into twelve inches. Each inch is divided in half, into fourths, eighths, and often sixteenths. Some measuring instruments divide further into thirty-seconds of an inch. But this is not the smallest we can measure. Some paper is about one-thousandth of an inch thick. We can continue to divide our measuring instrument until we realize the infinite value available. We can take any measure and divide it infinitely. Thus we see infinite in even the smallest things. This observation of infinite is also finite. By defining our measure we outline an abstraction. On a yard stick we have a finite number of feet. There are a finite number of inches in a foot. We do not have to divide our measuring instrument like this. We can divide the yard into any fraction. The yard is finite, where the possible number of points along that yard are infinite. For this reason we see a strong emphasis on significant figures in science. We can only measure as accurately as our instrument will allow. The closer to infinite that the instrument is divided the closer we are to accuracy.

We do not see infinite well with our eyes. If we try to think of infinite and visualize it, we restrain ourselves. We create an illusion that we are literally seeing infinite. By creating this illusion we make it impossible to see infinite. The reason for this is that we have taught ourselves that we have limitations. Our mind is without limitation. When our mind is disillusioned by the body it creates its own limitations. If the mind believes it has a limitation, then there is a limitation. We cannot visualize infinite, but we can experience infinite, and become one with infinite.

Some masters remind us that breaking through the walls we build for ourselves in our minds, we quickly build new ones. Talbot discusses people who have left their bodies to the realm of near death. Some of these people have discussed varying levels of the near death realm, some of which they could not reach. When we compare these to psychics who see energy fields we see a striking correlation. Some psychics see different levels of energy fields, where others only see one. From my experiences with the holoverse I do not see different levels. The reason is that I did not create the levels. By creating the levels we provide ourselves with limitations. It is interesting to note that the more effective psychics that Talbot discusses only see one energy field. Instead of creating limitations they are seeing the whole picture. We humans feel comfortable with limitations. As children our parents disciplined us, telling us what we could and could not do. As adults we live under laws. We are used to living within a tight framework that specifies our limitations. This framework includes science and religion. We are taught that we cannot fall up. In most religions we are taught that worship and good deeds will be rewarded, and that bad deeds will be punished. We are constantly creating limitations. Zen sides with the holographic paradigm on limitations. The only limitations we have are illusions. We believe them so much that they become part of our reality, even though they are not part of the true reality.

The zennist will not see the holoverse as a series of levels. Nor will the zennist believe that there are limitations. This is why Zen emphasizes experience over teaching with words. Words are limiting. We can imagine the holoverse. As a word the holoverse creates an illusion of something with substance and limit. For this reason the holographic paradigm is only a metaphor. It does not actually illustrate the whole picture. The theory itself should not be limited by this though. Instead the theory only begins with this metaphor. The metaphor is not the end or the means. For this reason, you should be careful not to try to hold on to the metaphor. The holographic paradigm is a concept intended to illustrate a point. It is not the point. To discover the actual point we must go beyond the elementary aspect of the metaphor and experience reality for ourselves. We learn this metaphor and discard it as we do all teachings. It is a reference point to begin our thought process. This paradigm is just as what we did in kindergarten is not the reality we grew into. We start with it to create a simplistic foundation and grow from there. Thus the holographic paradigm is a fantasy that we have created.

If we were to look on mankind as we would a normal human life, we can see the evolution of our understanding. As babies we relied on the knowledge of our elders to sustain us. We were simplistic. As we became toddlers we learned to limit ourselves, to follow the guidelines provided for us by others. Sometime during our preschool years we came to enjoy fantasy in the form of stories and cartoons. This is the stage we have reached with the holographic paradigm.  We still need to go through primary and secondary school.  During those years we were taught concepts and specific information.  This was done to create a foundation so that every individual would have certain required skills to survive in our society.  When we graduate from high school we go on to college.  As an undergraduate we become more focused, but our studies are still fairly general.  With a minor and our liberal studies we are still creating a foundation, and are cleaning out the misconceptions we were taught previously.  In graduate college we focus even more.

Most graduate colleges do not require a minor.  They emphasize a focus, and encourage the student to pursue specific knowledge and to specialize.  As professionals we continue to specialize more and more.  Then we reach a stage where specialization does not matter anymore, and many begin to prepare for death.  If we look on our level of understanding as being that of a preschooler, we are opening ourselves up.  The evolution of our understanding has no definite boundaries.  We are at the bottom, and there is only one direction to look.  If we realize our position, then we realize our potential.  As a preschooler we do not realize our potential.  Sometimes we never realize our potential.  Once we do realize our potential, then the other stages become easy and quick to attain.

This does not mean we can graduate from our present understanding to that of the doctor overnight.  In Zen we see two schools.  One school believes in gradual enlightenment.  The other school believes in sudden enlightenment.  Both school are right.  Looking back in history we can see numerous examples to prove both beliefs.  We as individuals can attain the sudden enlightenment.  As a society it will take time for this enlightenment to spread.  As an individual we can easily convince ourselves that we can do anything.  Where we can convince ourselves, we cannot convince another.  We cannot succeed at telling each other what to think.  We are the only ones that really control our own minds.  If we believe we can be suddenly enlightened, we can.  If we believe enlightenment is gradual, then we will not experience sudden enlightenment.  If we do not believe in enlightenment, then we cannot be enlightened.  To those who do not believe, the enlightened will be a freak show.

This is where it is essential to put aside our misunderstandings.  There is nothing mystical about Zen.  Many people see the word enlightenment and think of mysticism.  It is nothing of the sort.  Enlightenment is nothing more than attaining a higher level of thought.  At one point in enlightenment we reach a level where the levels of thought cease to exist.  This is true enlightenment, nirvana, because there are no levels to thought.  Levels are an illusion that we create as humans that believe in limitation.  Thus enlightenment and nirvana are indefinable.  They are only abstract words created to define a something out there.  Initially this is a wrong approach.  This is wrong because it is not something out there, nor is it in here.  It is not even a something.  Many masters have attacked this because the words have no meaning. These are among the words I suggest avoiding around a master.

The holoverse is beyond words. We can only experience it. We can experience it through our senses. This experience is incomplete and inaccurate though. We cannot imagine the holoverse because we also limit our imagination. We must experience it within ourselves. If I were to make a comparison, I would compare the holoverse with Buddha-nature and the Tao. Buddha-nature and the Tao are in everything. The best place to find these is within ourselves. Though a rock has Buddha-nature, we can not dissect the rock and find the Buddha-nature. Buddha-nature is indivisible. When we break a rock, both pieces still have Buddha-nature. There is nothing that does not have Buddha-nature, and nothing can be separated from Buddha-nature. It is easier to find Buddha-nature within ourselves, then in anything else. The same is true with the holoverse. We can find the entire holographic universe in everything, no matter the size. For this reason we each contain the holographic universe within every part of us. We do not need to look outside where our senses deceive us. We must look inside without the influence of our senses or our predetermined beliefs. Predetermined beliefs govern our thoughts. In meditation we shed ourselves of our physical and mental limitations. There is no way to describe true enlightenment, nirvana. The reason is that when we attain nirvana we are no longer limited by our physical or mental being.

### Chaos and Order

In this chapter I related two very simple but important principles. The first principle is that of the holographic paradigm, which is: Everything is interconnected. The second principle is related to this: Prediction requires knowledge of all the variables. This is not limited to the specific properties of what we are examining. This is all the properties of everything. Let us apply this to order and chaos from both the perspective of these principles and of Zen. If everything is interconnected, then everything affects everything else. We also see that everything reacts specifically in accordance with its own properties, and how those properties interact with the properties of everything else. These interactions are stronger or weaker depending on the locality and the varying strengths of everything involved. This holds true for both the microcosmic and the macrocosmic (micro meaning small, and macro meaning big). What does this say? There is no such thing as chaos.

What is chaos? In the beginning everything was chaos. Slowly man began to learn things. When he learned something it became ordered. Eventually he realized that he needed something to put his findings in. He created a box, and labeled it "Order." He continued to forage, picking up pieces of chaos, getting an understanding of those pieces and putting them in the box labeled "Order." As he was foraging man realized that he collected a lot of things he could not explain. For these he built another box and labeled it "Chaos." He continued to forage, and also continued to think about everything he did not understand. Occasionally man has taken something from the chaos box and put it into the order box. He has also taken what he has found and understood, and put that into the order box. Chaos is what we do not understand. Order is what we do understand.

In Zen the boxes have been burned. Why? Do we really understand anything? Everything has known and unknown properties. Just when science thinks it has an answer, nature provides an exception. Science has had the habit of putting it into the order box anyway. Attached to this is a note, stating that science has also put something into the chaos box on the same subject. Chaos is a creation of our imaginations, as is order. I saw a poster once that converted the word chaos to order. On one line was the word chaos. On the next two lines the characters were distorted. On the fourth line the distortions became the word order. Order and chaos are relativistic terms that are abstract and meaningless. We believe there is chaos, when there is not. We believe there is order, when there is not. Zen only believes. "I think therefore I am," becomes "I believe therefore there is."

We can find order in anything if we try hard enough. Chaos is an easy solution, an escape. "This does not follow the rules, it must be chaotic," is the attitude of many scientists. An entire branch of mathematics has developed on chaos. What is being accomplished? Nothing. A mathematician working on chaos will lose his or her work if that mathematician finds order in what is being studied. If it has order then it is not chaos. This is extreme, and it is limiting. By limiting our thoughts on chaos and order we have built a wall around science. We can compare this to the dark ages. It is dark because we did not even bother to put in a window, let alone a door. Science must tear down this wall if it plans to do any progress. You, as an individual, must tear down walls like this, and prevent new ones from being constructed. If a wall must be built, remember to put in doors and windows. You must be able to see out, and to move around freely outside the walls. Any obstructions must be removed. For the clearest sight and interaction with everything, there cannot be any wall. Since you are just beginning, you should worry about the doors and windows first. They are easier to put in. If you devote yourself to the project every moment, then tearing down the walls will also be easy. After the walls are torn down it becomes easier to keep them down, with practice.

# CHAPTER XI—
# The Future of Zen

We know the history of Zen. Zen tradition dates itself back to Buddha and his wordless sermon. Zen as a specific school then came into existence formally with Bodhidharma (about 470-543 C.E.) when he brought Ch'an to China. From there Zen spread throughout East Asia and Japan. From Japan it has been brought to Europe and America. Westerners have not accepted Zen with open arms. A few Westerners have adopted Zen, but many more have not. Westerners generally have a view that Zen is mystical; that it will interfere with their own religion. What these people do not realize is that Buddhism does not conflict with other religions. Buddhists are encouraged to study other religions and philosophies. This is not to compare Buddhism with other religions and philosophies; it is to understand oneself and others better. This is also done so that the individuals can find their own paths.

You will find books by masters who make specific references to Christianity. These masters are not comparing Zen to Christianity. They are showing that much of the same philosophy co-exists, and that there is no conflict. Zen and Buddhism are independent of religion. This allows for a harmonious existence between the philosophy and whatever religion the individual has. Buddhism is scientific. It is not unusual to find a commentary where a Buddhist is talking about the advancement of science with scientists, and relating these discoveries to the Buddhist teachings. Buddha said that pain is universal. Buddha also said that life means change, thus change is also universal. Judaism, Islam, and especially Christianity are less inclined toward change. The Buddhist looks forward to change, and always remains the student in order to maintain harmony. From this philosophy Western religion can and will grow. To fight change is to fight the Tao. The Tao will win.

In the last century Christians have seen a revolution in Christian thought. When Charles Darwin came up with the theory of evolution the Church turned its back. Buddhism accepts this theory with open arms. Since Darwin the controversy has settled. Now there are few creationists who have a problem with Darwin's theory. Necessity is the mother of invention. Discovery is the father of invention. With Darwin's discovery, and the needs of medical science, twentieth century medical science has been revolutionary. The only way to use Darwin's theories for technological advancement was through liberal acceptance.

Zen can provide Westerners with the patience, and the openness necessary to accept change. Western religion will not be alone in being changed. Zen is always changing, and will be changed by Western religion and philosophy, history and technology. The entire setting is different in the West, and Zen will accommodate. Unlike Western religion,

## An Introduction to Zen Thought

Zen will easily accept other cultures. It is true that Islam has a long history of religious toleration, but none of the Western civilizations are innocent of atrocities. Christians have a history of being very intolerant, such as the crusades and the Inquisition. It is not uncommon for Christians to argue this, pointing to their present state of quasi tolerance, in a separate and somewhat unequal world. How are Christians intolerant? If you are a Catholic you do not go to a Baptist Church. If you are Mormon you do not go to a Christian Scientist Church. The tendency is to try to convert others first to Christianity, then to a particular denomination. Zen makes no effort to convert, nor does it tell you what to read, where to go, or how to conduct rituals like funerals and baptisms. The school of Zen you belong to is not important. Zen is Zen. Zen is Buddhism.

So how will Zen change? Zen has already begun to change. We can see through martial arts a significant difference between the Orient and the West. In the Orient martial arts is taught traditionally over a very long time. The martial artist spends their life on their art. In the West, people go in to learn how to fight and defend themselves. When a Western student goes to the dojo they expect to learn something new. In the Orient, the student expects nothing. I agree with Nicol's master-if you want a black belt, go buy one, it is much quicker. Some students stay in training long enough to become interested in Zen. Often the student does not know what Zen has to offer, but they think it will provide an extra edge, an even higher status. For Western people gain is very important. Traditionally Zen offers nothing. This may have to change. When this change occurs it will only happen with words. Western people relish words, so Zen will give them words. The words will mean nothing to anyone except the student. As a student you can go through many levels. Finally there is a point where levels become meaningless. This will also happen in Zen. When levels become meaningless, that is when the real learning begins, because the ego is no longer in control. We may think that Zen has changed, but it really has not. Zen will have adapted itself.

Zen will also acquire the stories and philosophies of the West. As was mentioned earlier, Buddhism encourages the study of other religions and philosophies. Zen has already begun to adopt Western philosophy and religion, digging deep into Western thought and bringing forth the essence of these ideologies. This does not contradict these ideologies, it gives them credit. At the same time Western thought will give credit to Zen. Again there is no contradiction. In the West Zen will be accepted more, as the people become more aware of it. This book is only a beginning. Many other books have been written, that have helped to introduce Zen to the West. Most of these books have had limited audiences. In the last fifty years, since D.T. Suzuki, the West has seen a growing audience to Zen. With this book I hope to have brought this acceptance to yet another level of our Western Civilization. Even this book will have a limited audience though.

With this book college students will be formally introduced to Zen, either to fulfill a liberal studies requirement, or to compliment a degree in philosophy. This brings Zen a step down from the independent researchers to more practical people. In the future we will see this expand, until Zen has become an integral part of our society. This may not happen in our life times, or for centuries. Zen is patient. We must remember that Zen has had fifteen hundred years to be integrated into the Orient. I doubt it will take that long. In a thousand years Zen will be as much an element of our culture as it is in the Orient.

What about religion though? What is the fate of religion? Man enjoys thoughts of the supernatural and metaphysical. We have seen a decline in religion in the last two millennia, and especially since the eighteenth century. Agnostics and atheists have been growing rapidly in number, and are becoming more accepted. With the revolution of technology religion has taken a serious blow. The scientific method, derived from the Greek philosophers, and scientific research have eroded religion in the same way water erodes rock. Science has proved to be like water. It is soft, but persistent. Science is not to blame though, human nature is. It is human nature to be curious. Not only are we curious, we are constantly seeking to improve our lives. The way we do this is through science.

Science will never prove that God does not exist. Faith will be lost as science progresses though. What will be left are the stories told by our religions. Moses, Jesus, David and Goliath, and Samson will all outlive Christianity and Judaism. From these stories the underlying philosophies will rise above deism. In Islam, the philosophy will also rise. Worship will become a piece of history. People will no more believe the gods of the Koran, Bible, or Talmud than they believe in the gods of Classical Mythology. They will be forced to believe in themselves and reality.

This is a sad fate for religion. Most of you that are reading this are religious, and it is difficult to believe that religion could be phased out. What do you get from your religion? Most religions provide comfort. They give us something to live for, an explanation for the unknown, incentive to do good deeds, and a sense of direction after death. Most religions also provide a sort of social structure, with rituals. Today we see fewer religious rituals, and more de facto (of the fact) rituals. Most children do not receive a ritual that declares their adulthood from their Church. Today the rite of passage has become the driver's license. When we die the only ritual we are guaranteed is the paperwork; especially the death certificate and the coroner's report. None of these are very ceremonious. Unfortunately we see them growing in our society. One of the many things that contributed to the decline of Moism was Mo's condemnation of rituals. Ritual is necessary for public faith, for religion. This includes civic religion.

Confucius noted that rituals were very important. Even though Chinese are not religious in the same way as Westerners, ritual is still an element of their culture. Rituals may take a different form, but they will have to stay.  They are important for any society, and for the emotional well being of the individuals.  If something outlives our religions, it will be ritual.  When ritual dies, the individuals will lose their self identity and faith.  When self identity is lost we become ants.  At that point neither religion nor philosophy are needed, and are discarded.

Humans are too emotional for this.  Humans want guidance, a feeling of belonging, and a feeling that they are going somewhere.  These are important for you as a leader.  These are what religion today tries to fulfill, and what philosophy will take over when religion ceases to be significant.  We will not see our world free of religion in the near future.  Nor should we try to make it happen.  Religion is alive.  So long as there are believers, there is religion.  There is nothing inherently wrong with any religion.  Every religion means well, and serves its purpose.  If you take up a life of Zen, do not neglect your faith to your religion.  If you give up your religion, do not do it because you think it is the way of Zen.  Only give up your religion for one that suits you better.  Never allow a philosophy or religion to be imposed on you.  If you do, you will not be happy.

If there is something Zen gives us is faith.  I often preach that we should have faith in ourselves first, and then if we have faith to spare, have faith in our fellow people.  If we still have faith to spare, have faith in nature, the Tao.  If we still have faith left, we should give that faith to our religion.  If you are not religious, then help other people to have faith in themselves, by having faith in them.  What is faith?  Faith is a belief.  If we attach anything else to this definition we limit it needlessly.  By limiting the definition of faith we limit ourselves, and leave no opening for change.  Faith in God is wonderful.  With religious faith we believe we will have a beautiful life after death, something to look forward to.  In Zen no empty promises are made.  In fact, there are no promises made.  The emphasis is on the self, so faith must be in the self.

By having faith in yourself first you will serve God better.  You may feel that this goes against your religious belief, but it does not.  How can you love someone if you do not first love yourself?  The same holds true for faith.  If you have faith with yourself, you will be able to have faith in someone or something else.  If you do not have faith in yourself, then you will not have the faith to follow your religious beliefs properly.  When you have faith in yourself, following your religious beliefs will flow naturally.  Nourishing faith is what Zen has to offer religions.  Faith is also what Zen and other philosophies will provide after religion has ceased to exist.  Zen makes no effort to make predictions.   What I have said here are possibilities, and scientifically they are very probable.  In your study of Zen do not look to the future.  In this chapter I have outlined a theoretical future.  This is only a fantasy.  There is nothing distinctly definite here.  We cannot make accurate predictions.  In Zen we do not predict.

I have predicted here, because Western people love to dwell in dualities.  This is the past, and this is the future.  Zen stands in the middle, saying this is the present. By looking at this chapter we can see the present. We look into ourselves and see the reality. So long as we look at these predictions as fantasy, we will live in the present. If we try to fulfill these, the tides of the Tao will overpower us. What this chapter has done is relax the minds of those who are afraid of Zen. I have shown a possible future, where Zen and other philosophies still exist. I have shown why religion will fade away, but the essence will continue. I have also provided insight into how Zen and religion can coexist in harmony. So long as we believe in conflict, conflict will exist. Faith in conflict feeds conflict. Man has lived in conflict since the dawn of the most primitive civilizations. Many people believe that conflict is man's nature. When a baby is born it knows nothing about evil or conflict. A small child will walk up to a lion and pet it, not realizing the possible danger. A small child will play with a lion cub, and neither will have any idea of a possible conflict. Conflict is not man's true nature. It is a creation of man.

When we examine the world's religions and philosophies we would see little difference. Despite the similarities, we have seen wars over religion throughout the history of mankind. I have yet to hear of a war over Zen or Buddhism. When the Emperor Asoka learned of Buddhism, he embodied it, and stopped conquering. Buddhism actually stopped violence! Asoka then turned to sending missionaries throughout South Asia. His empire conquered half the world without violence, and may eventually conquer the rest. The fastest growing religion in the world is Islam. Close on the heals of Islam, Buddhism is the second fastest growing religion in the world. Where does Christianity fit into this list? I do not know. Buddhism does not pretend to be the one and only, nor does it pretend to be the solution. Because Buddhism has made no promises, it has made no lies. We must not lie to ourselves, and think our belief is the only right one. By accepting others for what they are, we have made ourselves better Christians, Moslems, Jews, Buddhists, and the list goes on.

Finally, there is a piece of philosophy that we find in every faith, even shared by agnostics and atheists. This philosophy is so simple we think nothing of it. What is this philosophy? Do unto others as you would have them do unto you. When thinking about another person's beliefs, think of this piece of philosophy. Westerner's often forget this, and imagine conflict. When this happens, they have created conflict. Conflict is not harmonious. It brings death and destruction. Let us all remember this philosophy, and live it. If we live this philosophy then we fulfill all the obligations of every religion in the world. We cannot go wrong. This is the Tao, and this is harmony.

# Appendix A—Chronologies

A lot of history is covered throughout the text, very briefly. It is difficult to visualize some of the descriptions provided without a general knowledge of Asian history. Even with a general knowledge, chronology charts are useful for helping to bring things together. For this reason I will provide here, in this appendix, a series of chronology charts. These charts list names and events that are not in this text, as well as those that are listed in this text. These are intended as an outline to help your thought process. You can also use these tables for research. The tables are:

Chronology of Japanese History
Chronology of Chinese History
Chronology of Buddhist History
Chronology of Important Persons
Alphabetical Listing of Important Persons
Table of Religions Based on Vedism Key
Historic Relationships of Eur-Asian Religions and Philosophies

## Japan

### B.C.E.:

ca. 7000 - 250     Jomon culture
ca. 250 - 300 C.E   Yayoi culture

### C.E.:

| | | |
|---|---|---|
| ca. 300 - 645 | Yamato Period | |
| 710 - 784 | Nara Period | |
| 794 - 1185 | Heian Period | |
| 1185 - 1333 | Kamakura Shogunal Period | Note: Japan claims a continuous dynasty, dating back to the mythical first Emperor, Jimmu. Periods primarily indicate changes in power, as the Emperor lost political strength until the Meiji Restoration. (Source: Hall, pp. 358-361) |
| 1338 - 1573 | Ashikaga Shogunal Period | |
| 1568 - 1600 | Shokuho Period (period of civil war) | |
| 1600 - 1868 | Tokugawa Shogunal Period | |
| 1868 - 1912 | Meiji Period (including the Restoration) | |
| 1912 - 1926 | Taisho Period | |
| 1926 – present | Showa Period | |

## China

**B.C.E.:**

| | | |
|---|---|---|
| ca. 2205 – 1766 | Hsia Dynasty |
| ca. 1766 – 1122 | Shang Dynasty |
| ca. 1122 – 771 | Western Chou |
| 770 - 256 | Eastern Chou |
| 722 - 481 | Spring and Autumn Period |
| 403 - 221 | Warring States Period |
| 221 - 207 | Ch'in Dynasty |
| 202 - 9 C.E. | Western Han |

**C.E.:**

| | |
|---|---|
| 9 - 23 | Hsin Dynasty |
| 25 - 220 | Eastern Han Dynasty |
| 220 - 280 | Three Kingdoms Era |
| 266 - 316 | Chin Dynasty |
| 315 - 589 | Era of North-South Division |
| 581 - 618 | Sui Dynasty |
| 618 - 907 | T'ang Dynasty |
| 960 - 1127 | Northern Sung |
| 1127 - 1279 | Southern Sung |
| 1264 - 1368 | Yuan (Mongols) |
| 1368 - 1644 | Ming Dynasty |
| 1644 - 1912 | Ch'ing (Manchu) |
| 1912 - 1949 | Republic of China (moved to Taiwan in 1949) |
| - present | People's Republic of China |

(Source: Hucker, Appendix A).

## Buddhism

**B.C.E.:**

| | |
|---|---|
| ca. 3,000 – 1200 | Invasions of India by the Aryans. |
| 2nd millennia B.C.E. | Aryans broke up and invade Europe and India. |
| ca. 563 – 483 | Gautama Siddhartha |
| ca. 180 | Brahman-led Hindu uprising almost extinguishes Buddhism in India. |

**C.E.:**

| | |
|---|---|
| 62 C.E. | Introduction of Mahayana Buddhism to China. |
| 552 | Introduction of Mahayana Buddhism to Japan (from Korea). |
| 4th century | Pure Land Buddhism (Ching-t'u in China) brought to Japan by Hui-yuan |
| 4th - 6th centuries | Establishment of Ch'an, starting with Tao-sheng and ending with Bodhidharma). |
| 653 | Zen learned by Dosho during visit to China. |
| 805 | Tendai (T'ien-t'ai in China) School brought to Japan by Dengyo Daishi |
| 806 | Shingon (Ch'en Yen in China) School brought to Japan by Kobo Daishi |

Yool—Introduction to Zen Thought

| 841 – 846 | Buddhist Suppression in China. |
| 9th - 12th centuries | Missions from Japan to China. |
| ca. 1187 | Rinzai Zen founded and brought to Japan by Eisai Zenji. |
| 1227 | Soto Zen founded and brought to Japan by Dogen Zenji. |
| 1274 & 1281 | Mongol invasions help popularize Zen in Japan. |
| 1850 – 1864 | Taiping Rebellion in China (20 million people killed; permanently weakened the Ch'ing Dynasty). |
| 1893 | Soen Shaku Introduces Zen to the United States. |

**Important Persons**

*B.C.E:*

| 4th Century | Lao Tse (Supposed Founder of Taoism). |
| 551 – 479 | Confucius (K'ung Fu Tse; Founded Confucianism). |
| ca. 563 – 483 | Buddha Gautama (Founded Buddhism). |
| ca. 470 – 396 | Mo Tse (Founded Moism). |
| 427 – 347 | Plato (Defining Justice in The Republic). |
| 384 – 322 | Aristotle (Dialectic). |
| 372 - 289 | Mencius (Meng Tse; Confucian Philosopher). |
| ca. 340 – 280 | Chuang Tse (Taoist Philosopher). |
| ca. 335 – 275 | Euclid (Greek Philosopher and Mathematician). |
| died 232 | Emperor Asoka Maurya (spread Buddhism throughout India and Southeast Asia). Ruled from ca. 273. |
| 6 B.C.E - 30 or 33 C.E | Jesus Benjoseph (Christ; of Nazareth). |

*C.E.:*

| 121 – 180 | Marcus Aurelius (Roman Emperor and Stoic Philosopher). |
| ca. 337 – 417 | Hui-yuan (Founded Pure Land Buddhism). |
| ca. 360 – 434 | Tao-sheng (Founder of Ch'an). |
| ca. 384 – 414 | Seng-chao (Contemporary Sudden Enlightenment Believer). |
| ca. 470 – 543 | Bodhidharma (Brought the Spirit of the Dharma; credited with founding Ch'an). |
| 570 – 632 | Mohammed (Founded Islam). |
| 628 – 670 | Dosho (Earliest recorded Zen teacher in Japan). |
| 638 – 713 | Hui-neng (Sixth Zen Patriarch). |
| ca. 850 – 916 | Hotei (Pu-tai; the Informal Spirit of Zen). |
| 1225 – 1274 | St. Thomas Aquinas (Just War Theory). |
| 1483 – 1546 | Martin Luther (Founded Lutheranism & translated Bible into German). |
| 1685 – 1753 | George Berkeley (Theory of Reality as an Illusion). |
| 1712 – 1778 | Jean Jacques Rousseau (Social Contract Theory). |

An Introduction to Zen Thought

| | |
|---|---|
| 1724 – 1804 | Immanuel Kant (Ethical Formalism). |
| 1743 – 1826 | President Thomas Jefferson (Believed in the Need for Revolution for Good Government). |
| 1818 – 1883 | Karl Marx (Social Conflict Theory; Communism). |
| 1819 – 1892 | Tanzan (University Professor and Zen Master; portrayed in many contemporary Zen stories). |
| 1870 – 1966 | D.T. Suzuki (Introduced Zen and Mahayana scriptures to the West, beginning in 1897). |
| 1876 – 1958 | Nyogen Senzaki (Important to Modern Western Understanding of Zen). |
| 1883 – 1969 | Morihei Ueshiba (Developed Aikido, and wrote The Art of Peace). |
| 1893 – 1976 | Mao Tse Tung (Formed modern Chinese state orthodoxy). |

# Alphabetical List of Persons

This listing is not done last name first. The names are ordered according to how they appear in the text. Modern Western names are provided both ways for your convenience.

Aquinas, Thomas (Saint) - see St. Thomas Aquinas.
Aristotle (Dialectic). 384 - 322 B.C.E.
Asoka Maurya, Emperor (Ashoka; Spread Buddhism throughout India and Southeast Asia). Ruled from ca. 273, died in 232 B.C.E.
Aurelius, Marcus Antonius - see Marcus Aurelius.
Berkeley, George - see George Berkeley.
Bodhidharma (Brought the Spirit of the Dharma; credited with founding Ch'an). ca. 470 - 543.
Buddha Gautama (Founded Buddhism). ca. 563 - 483 B.C.E.
Chuang Tse (Taoist Philosopher). ca. 340 - 280 B.C.E.
Confucius (K'ung Fu Tse; Founded Confucianism). 551 - 479 B.C.E.
Daisetz T. Suzuki - see D.T. Suzuki.
Dosho (Earliest recorded Zen teacher in Japan). 628 - 670.
D.T. Suzuki (Introduced Zen and Mahayana scriptures to the West, beginning in 1897). 1870 - 1966.
Euclid (Greek Philosopher and Mathematician). ca. 335 - 275 B.C.E.
Gautama - see Buddha Gautama.
George Berkeley (Theory of Reality as an Illusion). 1685 - 1753.
Hotei (Pu-tai; the Informal Spirit of Zen). ca. 850 - 916.
Hui-neng (Sixth Zen Patriarch). 638 - 713.
Hui-yuan (Founded Pure Land Buddhism). ca. 337 - 417.
Immanuel Kant (Ethical Formalism). 1724 - 1804.
Jean Jacques Rousseau (Social Contract Theory). 1712 - 1778.
Jefferson, Thomas - see Thomas Jefferson.
Jesus Benjoseph (Christ; of Nazareth). 6 B.C.E - 30 or 33.
Kant, Immanuel - see Immanuel Kant.
Karl Marx (Social Conflict Theory; Communism). 1818 - 1883.
K'ung Fu Tse - see Confucius.
Lao Tse (Supposed Founder of Taoism, believed to be Li Erh, an elder contemporary of Confucios). ca. 6th Century B.C.E.
Luther, Martin - see Martin Luther.
Mao Tse Tung (Formed modern Chinese state orthodoxy). 1893 - 1976.
Marcus Aurelius (Roman Emperor and Stoic Philosopher). 121 - 180.
Martin Luther (Founded Lutheranism & translated Bible into German). 1483 - 1546.
Marx, Karl - see Karl Marx.
Mencius (Meng Tse; Confucian Philosopher). 372 - 289 B.C.E.
Mohammed (Founded Islam). 570 - 632.
Morihei Ueshiba (Developed Aikido, and wrote The Art of Peace). 1883 - 1969.

An Introduction to Zen Thought

Mo Tse (Founded Moism).  ca. 470 - 396 B.C.E.
Nyogen Senzaki (Important to Modern Western Understanding of Zen). 1876 - 1958.
Plato (Defining Justice in The Republic).  427 - 347 B.C.E.
Pu-tai - see Hotei.
Rousseau, Jean Jacques - see Jean Jacques Rousseau.
St. Thomas Aquinas (Just War Theory).  1225 - 1274.
Seng-chao (Contemporary Sudden Enlightenment Believer).  ca. 384 - 414.
Senzaki, Nyogen - see Nyogen Senzaki.
Suzuki, D.T. (Daisetz T.) - see D.T. Suzuki.
Tanzan (University Professor and Zen Master; portrayed in many contemporary Zen stories).  1819 - 1892.
Tao-sheng (Founder of Ch'an).  ca. 360 - 434.
Thomas Jefferson, President (Believed in the Need for Revolution for Good Government).  1743 - 1826.
Ueshiba, Morihei - see Morihei Ueshiba.

# Table of Religions Based on Vedism Key

The following table illustrates the historical relationships of Eur-Asian religions and philosophies. This table does not include denominations of religions or philosophies, only the mainstream units. Not all mainstream schools of thought, are listed. Please note that the dates for early Aryan history are not certain. The first Aryan invasions of India were about 3,000 B.C.E., and the last was about 1,200 B.C.E. The invasions of Greece and Anatolia also happened during the second millennia B.C.E. The following are some abbreviations used in this table:

U? - Either unknown contributions, or contributions not relevant or relative to this diagram.
p - practiced in the present.
T.C.T - Traditional Chinese Thought
N.E. - Near Eastern Aryan Invasion
Upan. - Upanishadic
Conf. - Confucianism
Zor. - Zoroastrianism
Hindu 1 & 2 are early schools of Hinduism, which are identified historically as being different from modern Hinduism.
* - Moism was virtually extinguished in the second century B.C.E. with the rise of Confucianism to state orthodoxy under the Han Dynasty. Moism would be revived in the late 18th century C.E.

An Introduction to Zen Thought

## Historic Relationships of Eur-Asian Religions and Philosophies

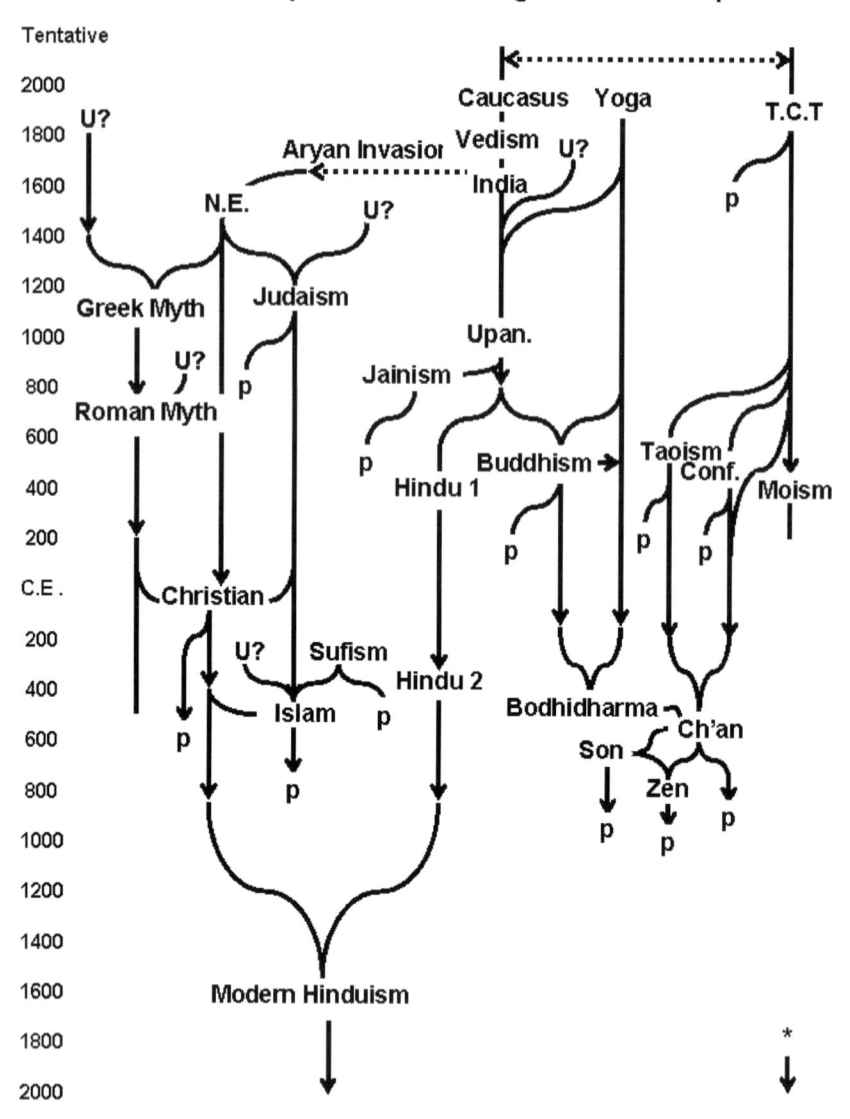

Tentative

```
2000                                    Caucasus   Yoga
         U?                                                        T.C.T
1800              Aryan Invasion  Vedism    U?
1600                                 India
              N.E.                                            p
1400                        U?
1200    Greek Myth   Judaism
1000              U?                    Upan.
 800             p          Jainism
        Roman Myth
 600                                             Taoism
                         p        Buddhism →     Conf.
 400                  Hindu 1                              Moism
 200                              p        p    p
C.E.     Christian
 200          U?   Sufism
 400                       Hindu 2
              Islam   p           Bodhidharma
 600      p                             Son       Ch'an
 800          p                                  Zen
1000                                      p       p    p
1200
1400
1600    Modern Hinduism
1800                                                        *
2000
```

# Appendix B—Meditation

## Purpose
Meditation is a universal concept of focused contemplation, used throughout history to develop concentration, discipline, and spiritual development.  It should be noted that meditation is nothing new to Western thought, though Western views of meditation are only recently beginning to integrate with those of the East.  With the recent integration, spiritual development is now being accepted globally as a method rather than an objective of meditation.  Our goal here is to develop your self-discipline and your ability to concentrate.

## Discipline
Discipline here means control; doing something the same way every time; retaining professional composure in the face of extremity.  As a professional, you must be able to separate your personal feelings from your work.  Here is a story to illustrate.
> A samurai was once commissioned to assassinate an enemy of the Emperor.  The samurai eventually tracked down his target, cornered him, drew his sword and prepared to execute his mission.  Just as he was about to strike, the victim spit in the samurai's face.  The samurai sheathed his sword and walked away without harming the victim.

The action of this samurai was discipline.  When the victim spit in his face, the samurai became enraged, making his next act one of passion rather than that of a professional.  Rather than be dishonored by acting out of passion (e.g. acting unprofessionally by separating his personal self from his work), the samurai had no other choice.

## Concentration
To achieve the discipline to distinguish and separate your professional and personal lives, you must develop your concentration.  The most favored method of learning concentration throughout history is known by its Japanese name as zazen: sitting meditation.  Zazen is composed of several different elements including: ritual (setup), posture (back and neck), position (legs & feet, hands, head), and content (the subject of focus).  We will examine, and when appropriate, diagram these items sequentially.

### The Setup Ritual
While making setup a ritual is optimum, you may not always have the opportunity to perform the ritual as desired.  The purpose of the ritual is

## An Introduction to Zen Thought

twofold: first, rituals require discipline (like the Japanese tea ceremony); second, your setup must meet the needs of the position and posture you wish to use. Since discipline is a matter of consistency, your ritual is whatever step-by-step procedure you want to use to put you into the "mood". Let us examine common elements of the ritual, in their most common order for setup.

1. Wear non-restrictive clothing (loose clothes). Typically you do not wear shoes or socks during meditation, as they tend to apply pressure and restrict blood flow and comfort.
2. Find a quiet place, where you can minimize distractions and relax, with space enough to meditate. This could be a room, a place at the park, the forest, etc.
3. Lay out a mat or towel large enough to stretch your legs out on. This helps define your use of space, keep your clothes clean, prevent chaffing on your legs and feet, and cushion for your knees.
4. Set on one end of the towel a cushion (a semi-hard throw pillow works nicely—$5, or you can buy any number of zafu cushions specifically designed for this purpose—$25+).

If you are indoors you might use candles, incense, soft music (without words if you must), etc. In places where meditation is taught, two wooden blocks are usually clapped to indicate the beginning of meditation, and a gong (most commonly the bowl-shaped variety) is rung three times to mark the end of the meditation. Where meditation is taught at length, a gong or clap could be used to indicate time to shift position (e.g. rearranging the legs).

### *Sitting Posture*

1. Your first step in the actual sitting part of meditation is to sit on the cushion with your legs outstretched (you can bend your knees to be comfortable). The cushion is intended to force you to elevate the buttocks above the knees, thereby arcing the back, as it should be.
2. Straighten yourself up and back, so your shoulders are straight and your shoulder blades are roughly in line with your buttocks.
3. Adjust the position of your legs and feet (below).
4. Adjust the position of your arms and hands (below).
5. Stretch your neck up, so the crown of your head is pushing up into the sky (your chin will be slightly tucked in).
6. Focus your eyes in a gentle gaze at your sternum level about five feet in front of you.
7. Breath through your nose using your diaphragm (belly).
8. Begin your concentration.

### *Leg and Foot Position*

The purpose of position is to assure a good posture that allows ideal blood flow and arrangement of organs and bones. The positioning of your legs and feet is critical to retaining comfort and composure in your posture. Among the following, find the position described and diagrammed that works best for you. In each of the following, normally you begin with positioning the right foot. I recommend trying to start with both, so you can determine which way is most comfortable for you. No matter which position you pick, be sure you do not force the position and restrict circulation.

**Burmese**—Bend the first knee, grasp the first foot with both hands and place the bottom of the foot against the opposite inner thigh. Bend the second knee, grasp the second foot with both hands and place the bottom of the foot against the opposite outer shin. The backs of both feet will be against the cushion, knees pointing down and touching the ground.

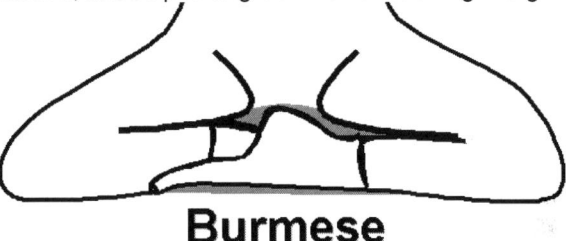

## Burmese

**Half Lotus**—Bend the first knee, grasp the first foot with both hands and place the bottom of the foot against the opposite inner thigh. Bend the second knee, grasp the second foot with both hands and place it on top of the opposite thigh bringing the heel as close to the navel as possible. Both knees should be on the ground, with the back of the first foot against the cushion, and the sole of the second foot pointed upward.

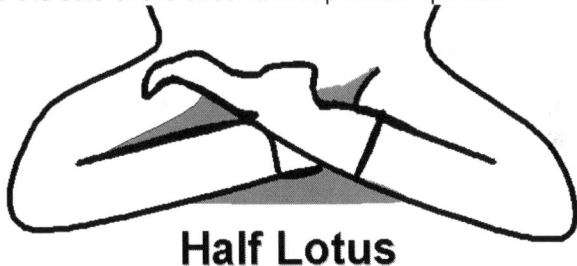

## Half Lotus

**Full Lotus**—Bend the first knee, grasp the first foot with both hands and place it on top of the opposite thigh bringing the heel as close to the navel as possible. Bend the second knee, grasp the second foot with both hands and place it on top of the opposite thigh bringing the heel as close to the navel as possible. Both knees should be on the ground and the soles of the feet are pointed upward.

An Introduction to Zen Thought

**Full Lotus**

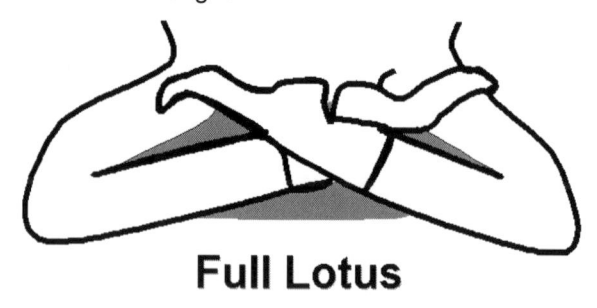

### *Hand and Arm Positions*

As with the legs, your main objective here is to allow circulation to flow freely.

**Palms Down**—For this you merely rest your hands about shoulder-width apart on your thighs, with your arms slightly bowed. This is a good position for starter, because you can move your hands down, push yourself up to straighten, then easily reposition your hands. Do not apply pressure; simply relax the hands and arms.

**Palms Up**—This is a standard Yoga position with two possibilities. In both possibilities, the arms hang loosely at your sides; with the forearms resting on the thighs near the wrists (not on the wrists) with the palms held up and relaxed (they will naturally cup when relaxed). The variation here is in the direction your arms point your hands: point your arms straightforward with the forearms resting about shoulder width apart, or allow them to follow the angles of your legs resting near the joints of the inner thighs.

**Hands Together**—Rest your forearms about shoulder width apart on your thighs, palms up and relaxed. Set one palm in the other and rest the tips of the thumbs against each other. There are numerous variations of this position, which have created innumerable debates. We will leave it simple here.

### Content

You have finally managed to attain your meditation position, putting your body completely to rest. Now that your body is under submission, your mind is free to wander. If you thought getting the body to submit to the meditation was difficult, you are about to discover the greatest difficulty of all: stopping the mind. There are two categories of mental meditation: with object and without object. Since you are just getting started, we will focus exclusively on meditation with object.

When you meditate with object, you focus on some thing, even if that thing is nothing. Now you see why we're putting off meditating without object. Meditating with object is the most common. It usually involves visualizing, like visualizing something simple and pleasant, or focusing on a koan.

## *Visualizing*

Everyone has daydreamed. This is not much different, except that instead of daydreaming scenarios or fantasies, you are daydreaming about a specific thing. Again you are presented with choices: focus on a thing without a setting, or focus on a process. Most people will start with a thing. An easy thing to start with is a blank theater screen. Once you can "see" the screen, put a preferred object on it (e.g. a butterfly, fountain, stream, feather, tree, etc.). As you do in the theater, forget the screen is there, allowing the mind to focus only on your object.

Processes are a little more advanced, but are enormously useful. Process visualization is easily perfected with koan practice, because ultimately you want to become one with the process. Processes can be distinguished as internal or external. For an internal process, say a broken bone or illness, a vivid and appropriate visualization of healing is most effective, particularly when you go to sleep. For example: a broken bone can be healed quickly by visualizing workers using appropriate tools to fix the break. For external processes, focus on successful completion of the process (e.g. endurance exercise).

## *Koan Practice*

A koan is a kind of riddle that cannot be answered intellectually, such as the following:
- What is the sound of one hand clapping?
- What is the taste of blue?
- What is the color of a symphony?
- If a tree fell in the forest and nobody was there, did it make a noise?

In Zen practice with a master, answering or questioning a koan can be extremely problematic (not to mention painful). The difficulty in answering the riddle is that most answers are intellectual. When you ask a question about a koan, then you are necessarily trying to grasp it intellectually. Your goal: TURN OFF the intellect and allow your intuition to flow spontaneously. Actually thinking about the koan results in intellectualizing. To solve a koan, you must "become" the koan—not a part of the koan, the whole thing. Allow the koan to flow like a stream through the channels of your mind. Then visualize your essence as water flowing into the stream. Allow the stream to flow into a bottomless ocean, and then gradually allow the ocean to dissolve into emptiness.

## *Dream Control*

Dreams are creations of the mind; therefore you have control of them. Try this: when you are about to go to sleep, fill your mind with what it is you want to dream about. While you are dreaming, acknowledge that you are dreaming and declare, "This is my dream, and I have control!" Then

**175**

## An Introduction to Zen Thought

explicitly formulate the dream you want to have. For those who are practiced with meditating, many will use this opportunity to dream of meditating. Even if you have only just begun meditating, try dreaming of meditating.

### **Frequently Asked Questions**

Q  Could this violate my religious beliefs?
A  Look up meditation in an electronic encyclopedia and you will find references to all major religions. Meditation enhances spirituality. It is non-sectarian and non-denominational. This is why the number of Buddhists in the world is so hard to count: they often practice another religion because most forms of Buddhism say nothing about belief. Buddha intentionally avoided metaphysical, existential, and cosmogonic topics.

Q  So am I practicing Buddhism?
A  You are practicing meditation. It just so happens that the world religions that have perfected the art of meditation are Zen Buddhism and Yoga. Zen is purposefully unattached to religion, making it a perfect companion to any belief, even non-belief. The choice is yours.

Q  Do I need to use the special equipment?
A  No, but it will help. With practice, you can easily attain correct posture and position without it.

Q  What if I cannot sit in any of the positions listed?
A  You may use a chair, but you may not use the backrest of the chair. If you are using a chair, then ideally you want the chair to be tall enough that the tops of your knees will be in line with the bottom of your buttocks. If the chair is not adjustable, then spread your legs and set them back a little. Ideally, use an adjustable chair so your feet can rest flat on the floor.

Q  I would like to sit in one of these positions, but need to stretch. What do you recommend?
A  The simplest stretching exercise for this is called "bound angle". To do this, sit flat on the floor and put the bottoms of your feet together, pulling them toward your groin with your hands. This alone may be a stretch for you. If it is, then practice this until it becomes comfortable (it may take many practice sessions, so don't expect immediate results). When it is finally comfortable, place your hands on your knees and press down. You ultimately want your knees to be able to lay flat on the floor. Again, this will not happen immediately. Doing this exercise alone may be enough to make any of the positions listed above more comfortable.

Q  How long should I meditate?
A  Fortunately this is not an exercise your doctor will worry about you exerting yourself on, so length is up to you. You should start with at least twenty-minute sessions. Since it is easy to become engulfed in

the meditation, I recommend using an alarm or egg timer to remind you to stop.
Q  Won't I get bored?
A  On the contrary, when you focus on a single thing, you will find that time passes very quickly (hence the alarm above). If you are bored, then you aren't focused.
Q  I can't concentrate.
A  Everyone can. Have you ever watched a three year-old play for hours with the same toy, but otherwise be restless? Concentrating is a matter of motivation. If you want to focus on a thing you will. This is why I recommend visualizing something pleasant.
Q  Where can I find more information, like koans?
A  Go to the Internet or your bookstore. There is an enormous amount of literature available. On the Internet, use a search engine. Type in the word koan, and then follow the results. You will be amazed at how much is free. Do not expect to find a working answer to your own koan this way! If you make the mistake of copying someone else's answer to a Zen master, you are likely to feel the experience an enormous and spontaneous pain for being intellectual.

# Appendix C—Postures

## General Rules
Wear comfortable, non-constricting clothing. Shoes are generally not worn. Knees will always be pressing down for sitting postures, forcing the pelvis to angle, and the back to arch. Sit up straight, if necessary using your hands against your knees to attain straightness. Push the sky up with the crest of your head (your chin will be tucked in slightly). Choose the most comfortable position and get used to it before trying others.

## Bound Angle Pose
Sit on the floor or on a folded blanket on the floor with your legs stretched out straight in front of you. Place one hand on your spine at the back of your waist. If you feel vertebrae poking out, then elevate your sitting bones with an additional blanket. Lift the right leg so that the knee is aimed toward the ceiling and the foot is flat on the floor aimed forward. Keeping a tight fold in the knee and release it out to the right. Repeat with the left leg so that the soles of the feet pressing each other. Clasp the hands around the toes. Keep constant pressure of the heels into each other. Hold onto a strap around the feet if your back or shoulders round. Stretch your knees out laterally, to the sides, not down toward the floor to increase the stretch. Soften the gaze, quiet the hearing. Breathe evenly and comfortably through your nose.

## Burmese
Similar to the Bound Angle Pose. Put bottom of one foot against the opposite inner thigh. Put the bottom of the other foot against the opposite outer shin. The backs of both feet will be against the floor, knees pointing down.

## Lotus Posture (*Padma-asana*) Instruction
Sit on the floor with the legs stretched out straight in front. Bend the right knee and grasp the right foot with both hands and place it on top of the left thigh bringing the heel as close to the navel as possible. Bend the left knee and grasp the left foot with both hands and place it on top of the right thigh bringing the heel as close to the navel as possible. Both knees should be on the ground and the soles of the feet are pointed upward. The spine is held straight but not rigid. The position of the legs may be switched if the posture becomes uncomfortable.

## Comments
The hands should be placed in one of the following three positions:

- Place one hand on top of the other, both palms up, and rest the hands on the heels (this is known as the dhyana-mudra). This variation is recommended for meditation.
- Place the hands on the knees, palms down.
- With palms up, place the hands on the knees, form a circle with the thumb and forefinger and extend the remaining fingers straight ahead (this is known as the chin-mudra). Recommended for pranayama (Yogic breathing).

The padma-asana facilitates relaxation, concentration and ultimately, meditation. The posture creates a natural balance throughout the body/mind. When the knees are stretched enough to remain in the padma-asana without discomfort the posture creates a feeling of effortlessness and ease that will soothe the nervous system, quiet the mind and bring about the condition of one-pointed-ness.

**Duration/Repetitions:**
The length of time to sit in the padma-asana depends on your intention. In the course of a typical asana routine you might hold it for several minutes or until you experience discomfort in the legs. When used as a meditation posture you hold it for the duration of the meditation.

# Glossary of Zen and Buddhism

**A**
Action: The way we express our thought through physical interaction with our environment.
Agura: Sitting cross-legged, where neither foot is placed firmly on the opposite thigh. This is neither the half or full lotus position. It is the common cross-legged position used to sit on the floor in the West.
Ai: Japanese word meaning harmony.
Alaya: That from which consciousness grows and to which it returns. Similar to the concept of Brahman.
Alaya-vijnana: The part of the subconscious that, in response to causes and conditions, sends pieces of illusion from the manas to the five senses and thought. This forms a cycle that is endless, of delusion.
Altruistic Behavior: An act done without any intent for personal gain in any form. Altruism requires that there is no want for material, physical, spiritual, or egoistic gain.
Amitabha: (Amida, Amita) Buddha of eternal light and external life, of the "happy land," the Pure Land.
Ananda: Name of one of Buddha's disciples, joining early during Buddha's second year of teaching; he was one of Buddha's favored disciples, if not his most favored; his name means "joy." He was trusted to teach the doctrines, and to begin sermons. It was Ananda who got women admitted into the Buddhist order.
Anapanasati: The harmonious breathing of correct zazen practice.
Anatolia: Name given to a geographical location in history, that is presently called Turkey. Turkey borders on Europe and the Middle East.
Anatta: Buddhist doctrine that there is no permanent self, no soul (atman). It is the third of the three characteristics of existence. See also dukkha, annica, and ti-lakkhana.
Anicca: Buddhist doctrine of impermanence, change. It is the first of the three characteristics of existence. See also dukkha, anatta, and ti-lakkhana.
Arahat: (Arahant) One who has reached the final stage of spiritual progress, meaning "the worthy." This is a Pali word used in Buddhism, ranking an individual equivalently to the brahmin caste of Hinduism. That means that the arahat is capable of moksha, nirvana, the escape from samsara.
Asana: Third element in the path of classical Yoga, meaning postures.
Ascetic: One who practices self humbling, self mortification, and self humiliation in order to gain spiritual benefit. There are thirteen

practices that monks are supposed to perform as an ascetic. These are: 1) wearing robes made from discarded materials, 2) wearing no more than three robes, 3) begging for food, 4) not discriminating as to where to go for food, 5) only eating one meal a day, 6) eating from only the alms bowl, 7) refusing any more food than can fit in the alms bowl, 8) living in the forest, 9) at the foot of a tree, 10) under the open sky, 11) in a graveyard, 12) being satisfied with one's home, and 13) sleeping in the sitting position. Buddha denounced ascetic practices, though these have been practiced by Buddhist monks.

Atman: Used in Hinduism, it is the self, the soul. "An" means to breath, an association frequently made with soul in religious traditions.

Avidya: In Hinduism this is one of the conditions involved in samsara and reincarnation, meaning ignorance. This is ignorance of spiritual perception, not book knowledge. The origin of tanha (craving) is avidya (ignorance), where tanha is what keeps the living in the cycle of samsara. We can see this reflected in the third noble truth, where the source of greed is illusion, and in order to overcome illusion we must overcome avidya, ignorance.

## B

Bakufu: The samurai "tent government" of Japan, commonly called the Shogunal government. There were three Shogunates, each embraced Zen practice, making it the religion of the samurai, and the civic religion.

B.C.E.: Before the Christian (or Common) Era. Commonly seen as B.C., meaning before Christ, though Christ was actually born in 6 B.C.E. See also C.E.

Bhakti: Form of Yoga emphasizing the control of emotions; the way to god through love.

Bodhgaya: The name of the area Gautama Siddhartha was in when he was enlightened and became the Buddha.

Bodhi: Perfect wisdom and enlightenment. See buddhi.

Bodhidharma: (Daruma in Japanese) In this book he is credited with popularizing Ch'an during the early sixth century C.E. He is also considered, in this book, to be the first eccentric Zen master. Other researchers have credited Bodhidharma with being the founder of Zen. See also Tao-sheng.

Bodhisattva: Gautama used this term to describe himself when he was seeking enlightenment. The Mahayana use this term to identify those who have attained bodhi, but chose not to enter nirvana and become a Buddha. Instead, they vow to provide salvation for every living thing, "every blade of grass."

Bompu: Ordinary Zen, free from philosophical or religious contents, and is practiced for the sole purpose of improving one's physical and mental being.

Bonno: A function of the mind that brings trouble, passion, illusion. Deshimaru states, "Desires are natural; they become bonno when there is attachment" (p. 140).

Bo Tree: Also called the Bodhi Tree. The tree Gautama Siddharta sat under, and when he arose he was the Buddha. According to tradition this was an asvattha tree, though there is no historical evidence to support this belief.

Botsudan: A shrine of the Buddha. This name is used to designate those shrines both in temples and in private homes in Japan.

Brahman: The cosmic ocean, where the soul (atman) is disolved upon death. This ocean is the cosmic soul in Hindu tradition.

Brahmin: The Hindu caste system has four major castes, which in order of rank are: servants, merchants, warriors (ruling caste), and the brahmin. The brahmin is the highest caste, the priestly caste. Members of the brahmin caste may attain moksha, the escape from samsara. Members of the other castes must work their way up in the castes through the cycle of reincarnation, by balancing their karma. The brahmin must maintain a balanced karma in order to attain moksha.

Buddha: The awakened; forever enlightened. Buddha Gautama did not claim to be the first Buddha nor the last. He frequently mentioned previous Buddha's. These have never been proven to historically exist, and were probably made up by Gautama just to make his point. Gautama did not wish to be worshipped.

Buddha-mind: The mind of one who has been awakened to the desire for enlightenment. This is the intent behind the act of releasing Buddha-nature. It is also the inherent wisdom and enlightenment that exists in all sentient beings.

Buddha-nature: The original nature of all people, which is harmonious and non-dualistic. This is always present, whether it is ever realized or not. It is a concrete expression used to signify perfection.

Buddhi: (Bodhi) Enlightenment or awakening; to awake or become conscious; perfect enlightenment or wisdom. Brandon notes three kinds: the disciple of the Buddha, the isolated and independently attained enlightened one, and the universal Buddha who also independently attained enlightenment and proclaims that enlightenment to others.

Buji: "No matter." An attitude acquired toward Zen, in which the individual does not practice because of the rationality that we are all originally buddhas. This is deceiving, as these individuals push themselves further from their Buddha-nature.

Bushi: The samurai, the ruling elite within the Shogunal system of government. Above the bushi were the Daimyo, who were higher ranking bushi. The Daimyo were directly responsible to the Shogunate.

## C

ca.: Abbreviation for circa, a Latin term meaning about, or around. Used to signify dates that we are not exactly certain of.

C.E.: Christian Era or Common Era. A term preferred over A.D. (Anno Domini- the year of the domination or rule of our lord Christ), because it removes the Christian religious element, out of respect for other calendars and religions.

Chakra: (Cakra) The centers of force that are within specific organs of the body. These organs "collect, transform, and distribute the forces flowing through them" (Kapleau, p.15).

Ch'an: Chinese name for Zen.

Ch'i: In Taoism this is the energy of life, somewhat equivalent to ki in Japanese.

Civic Religion: Popular cultural elements and institutions that bring a community together. An example would be democracy, which is a civic religion in Western nations like the United States. The institution of democracy brings the people of the U.S. together, binding them. Zen is a civic religion of Japanese culture.

Confucius: Romanized name of K'ung Fu Tse. His teachings set the social framework for Chinese society. This framework was copied by other countries in East and Southeast Asia.

Consciousness: In Buddhism there are eight classes of consciousness. The first five are the senses (sight, smell, touch, taste, and hearing), the sixth is thought, the seventh is manas, and the eighth is alaya-vinana.

Cravaka: Sanskrit name for the Four Noble Truths.

## D

Daijo: The Mahayana way of Zen, the Great Vehicle. Practitioners must be able to see into their true natures and put forth their beliefs, their way, in their daily lives. Thus they actualize their true nature. This is the form of Zen most emphasized in the Rinzai school.

Daishi: Name used as a title for a great master. See also Zenji.

Dao: A way of transliterating Tao.

Dharana: The sixth element in the path of classical Yoga, meaning concentration.

Dharma (Dhamma): Translated as law. In Buddhism, the Dharma is the canonical texts.

Dharma Dual: A verbal contest of wisdom of the Dharma. Traditionally, wandering monks could stay in a monastery as long as they continued winning Dharma duals.

Dharma Heir: One who is designated as the successor of a master or teacher, one who has apprehended the transmission. Mahakasyapa was the Dharma Heir of Buddha Gautama. See also Transmission.

Dharma-kaya: Kaya means body; this is the body of the law of Buddha, the eternal law. It is one of the three aspects of Buddha, in which everything in the cosmos is one.

Dharma Successor: One who has reached the same level of enlightenment as his or her master, and as such replaces the master when the master dies. This has nothing to do with status within the monastery. Many masters have named the lowest persons in their monastery to be their Dharma successors.

Dharma Talk: A lecture given on the Dharma or any other Buddhist topic. See also teisho.

Dhyana: The seventh element in the path of classical Yoga, meaning meditation. It is equivalent to Zen and Ch'an, which are transliterations of dhyana.

Disciple: One who follows or accepts a teaching or teacher; a pupil; a student of a particular school, religion, master, or teacher.

Do: Translated simply as "the way."

Dogen Zenji: Brought the Soto school to Japan. Lived from ca. 1200 to 1253 C.E.

Dojo: A center of training for Zen.

Dokusan: A period of interaction between a Zen student and a Zen teacher, which is done according to a regular schedule. This is a personal encounter, in which the teacher is able to probe and stimulate the student's understanding, and the student is able to ask questions directly related to practice. Since everything is Zen practice, questions can be asked about anything. This is different from a mondo only slightly, because this involves an individual and a mondo can be done in a group. Mondo is similar enough that it is often used.

Dukkha: Pain, suffering. This is not a pessimistic view of reality, it is actually optimistic, it is an affirmation, a confirmation. Dukkha also represents a fever or illness. It is the first noble truth. It is also the second of the three characteristics of existence. See also anatta, anicca, and ti-lakkhana.

## E

Effort: The energy put into meditation, conduct, and knowledge.

Ego: The individual or self; in Buddhism the ego is an illusion, which helps to perpetuate all illusion.

Eightfold Path: The way Buddha Gautama prescribed to reduce universal suffering. The eight elements are right: understanding, thought, speech, action, livelihood, effort, mindfulness, and concentration. The divisions of the Eightfold Path, with the religious divisions in parentheses, are: knowledge (faith), conduct (morality), and meditation.

Eisai Zenji: Brought the Rinzai school to Japan. Lived ca. 1141 to 1215 C.E.

Ekagrata: One of the purposes of Yoga practice, to attain ekagrata which is the state of single-pointedness.

Enlightenment: A state in which one is aware of one's true nature. This is not necessarily a state of complete awareness, which would be nirvana.

Eternal Now: Living in the moment, the now.

**F**

Fact: That which is real, not necessarily what is believed (truth).

Faith: A belief; in the religious sense, faith is a belief in the supernatural or whatever other force brings the believers together. Faith has nothing to do with fact.

Five Sins: Killing one's father or mother, or an arhat; shedding the blood of Buddha; and destroying the harmony of the sangha.

Four Noble Truths: The central theme of Buddhism, and was first thing Buddha Gautama taught, in his Sermon at Deer Park. The Four Noble Truths are: pain is universal, the cause of pain is greed, the source of greed is illusion (maya), following the Eightfold Path leads to the cessation of pain, greed, and illusion. See also: Dukkha, Tanha, Maya, and Eightfold Path.

Four Signs: The signs that would make Gautama seek enlightenment. These are: old age, sickness, death, and a holy man (an ascetic).

Four Vows: Vows taken by bodhisattvas, that are regularly recited in zendos after zazen. 1) All beings I vow to liberate, without number or prejudice. 2) I vow to uproot all the endless blind passions. 3) I vow to penetrate every level of truth. 4) I vow to attain the path and way of the Buddha and the Dharma.

Fushiryo: Not thinking, as opposed to hishiryo's beyond thought. Not thinking is not a good state of mind, it is a state of non-awareness, where hishiryo has awareness.

**G**

Gassho: Raising the hands, with palms together, in a gesture of respect, humility, or gratitude, or all three.

Gedo: Non-Buddhist Zen; Zen without Buddhist teachings. Often associated with mysticism and super-natural powers, which are usually what is being sought by its practitioners.

Gnostic: Knowledge that is so pure that it cannot be explained or proven wrong, because it is real fact transcending time and space.
Godo: In a Soto zendo, the monk in charge of the zendo, second to the roshi. This is approximately equivalent to the jikijitsu in Rinzai monasteries.

## H
Hanka: Japanese name for the half lotus position of meditation. In this position, one of the two feet is brought up and the back of the foot is pressed against the opposite inner thigh.
Hara: The center of awareness, as well as the center of a person's gravity, energy, and activity; located just below the naval, in the lower abdomen. It is literally the intestines. Zazen and correct practice are supposed to strengthen the hara.
Hatha: Form of Yoga, to which the practice of postures and breathing control belong.
Hinayana: Name given by the Mahayana to the other schools of Buddhism that preceded it. The preferred name for these schools is Theravada.
Hishiryo: Beyond thought; thinking without thought; sunyata of thinking and thought.
Hossen: Japanese word for Dharma dueling.
Hui-yuan: A Buddhist monk, who lived ca. 337-417 C.E. He is credited with founding the Pure Land sect of Buddhism.

## I
Inka: (Inka Shomei) The seal of approval; a formal acknowledgement of a student's completion of Zen training. This does not imply mastery, merely the completion of a program, such as passing a set of prescribed koans. It is a sign, by the master, of being satisfied with the student's level of understanding.
I-shin den-shin: To be transmitted without words; "from my soul to yours."
Is-ness: The immediate state of being; being the now of being, and being.

## J
Jakugo: As part of koan practice, this is a phrase or expression that summarizes or comments on all or part of a koan. It is used to illustrate the student's understanding of the koan. We see something similar in our school system, where children are required to define a word in their own words, so that the teacher knows that the student understands the meaning.
Jen: see ren.
Jihi: Giving happiness by saving all sentient beings from suffering. This is the goal of the bodhisattva.

An Introduction to Zen Thought

Jikijitsu: In a Rinzai zendo, the monk in charge of the zendo, second to the roshi. This is approximately equivalent to the godo in Soto monasteries.
Joriki: The power of samadhi arising from proper zazen practice.
Jnana: In Yoga, jnana is the way to god through knowledge.
Jujukinkai: Japanese name for the ten precepts of the Mahayana school. See also jukai and precepts.
Jukai: Taking the ten precepts of the Mahayana school. See also jujukinkai and precepts.

## K

Kai: (Kairitsu) See precepts.
Karma: In Hindu tradition the karma is the record of all actions from all lives, the consequences for which are determined by the intentions of the act, not the consequences of the act. In Yoga, this is the form of practice that emphasizes work.
Karuna: Japanese term meaning satori wisdom and compassion.
Kasyapa: First to receive the "transmission of the lamp." See Mahakasyapa.
Katsu: (or kwatz; in Chinese it is ho) As with mu, this word has no exact meaning. It is used by masters to help students to overcome dualisms and ego-centric thoughts.
Keiso: A bowl-shaped bronze gong, used during chanting in all the Buddhist sects of Japan. Small keisos are available in curio shops all over the United States. They are commonly called meditation gongs. All keisos are struck on the rim with a padded club. Full-sized keisos are struck with a padded club using both hands.
Kenchuto: The state and condition of absolute naturalness.
Kendo: The way of the sword; the art of fencing and swordsmanship.
Kensho: The first experience of satori, consciousness; an abrupt awakening usually acquired after vigorous stimulation. Many students mistake this for satori, enlightenment, and even Nirvana. Kensho is generally counterproductive, as the student has "tasted" the experience, and subsequently tries to achieve the experience again. Usually used by the Rinzai school. Kensho means literally, "seeing into one's own true nature," and is often used interchangeably with satori.
Kesa: Symbolic robe of the transmission from a master to a disciple. Traditionally, Buddha made his kolomo from sheets used to wrap bodies in for cremation, which he found along the banks of the Ganges River, where the dead were cremated. A kolomo or kesa made this way is a transformation of the lowest of fabrics to the most beautiful and holy.

Ki: The energy of the spirit. This is not the soul or the ego, it is only energy. It is also activity, and the energy of the cosmos and everything within the cosmos, especially in living things.

Kinhin: Walking in contemplation; walking meditation; Zen practice while walking; a focused, quick paced walking zazen. Often done between periods of zazen or meditation.

Knowledge: In Eastern traditions, knowledge is equated with intuition, not just information.

Koan: A Zen riddle, used most notably in the Rinzai School as a tool for transmitting understanding. Any text that claims to have answers to koans is wrong, because the only answer is the experience of understanding.

Kokoro: Japanese word for heart, spirit, soul, and mind. The Japanese believe that the kokoro is in the chest area.

Kolomo: Wide sleeved black monk's robe. Traditionally the kolomo is hand made from the cheapest materials that have been discarded. The kolomo is very personal to a monk, since the monk put all the patches together and died it. See kesa.

Kotsu: A fifteen inch long baton, shaped like the human spine, used by masters when monitoring a meditation session. As with the kyosaku, the master may strike or poke a meditator in order to encourage or awaken.

Ku: Japanese word equivalent to sunyata.

Kundalini: A name used in Yoga for a snake like inner energy that is wrapped around the abdominal region of the body. This is somewhat related to ki, ch'i, and te.

Kung Fu Tse: Chinese name for Confucius.

Kusen: Teaching while in the correct sitting position for zazen.

Kyosaku: An "awakening stick." The kyusaku is a long stick with a flattened end, used by monitros during a meditation session. The monitors use kyosakus to encourage and awaken the meditators, striking them between the neck and shoulder. This is also relaxing if done properly, relieving tension as the area being struck is a pressure point.

## L

Lao Tse: Also Lao Tzu. Supposed founder of Taoism, and author of the Tao Te Ching.

Li: In this text li (pronounced lee-ee) means ritual. There are two other forms that frequently appear. The most frequent is a unit of measure for distance, equivalent to about one-half of kilometer, or one-third of a mile.

Livelihood: The means by which we make a living, support ourselves.

Lotus: Symbol of purity and perfection, Buddha-nature.

Lotus Position: The position that Buddha is depicted in. In meditation, the feet are brought up, and the backs of both feet are pressed against the opposite inner thighs.

## M
Maha: Literally means "greater."

Mahakasyapa: A disciple named Kasyapa was called this after he had understood Buddha Gautama's silent sermon. When Buddha held out a flower in silence, Kasyapa smiled in understanding. Then Buddha gave Kasyapa the flower signifying the first transmission.

Mahamuni: Grand/Great Master, enlightened with cosmic understanding, a living Buddha.

Mahaprajna: Great wisdom; the wisdom of the Buddhas.

Mahayana: The Greater Raft/Vehicle. One of the four main branches of Buddhism, emphasizing salvation for the regular people. The Mahayana school uses the vernacular language to convey its teachings. It was founded some time after Asoka, from his example of spreading Buddhism. It is practiced in China and Japan.

Makyo: Japanese word meaning fantasies and hallucinations.

Manas: The level of consciousness where illusion is generated, it is the subconscious.

Manjusri: The bodhisattva of meditation and supreme wisdom. He is usually depicted riding a lion, carrying the sword of wisdom, which is supposed to cut through illusion. He is frequently the principal figure on the altar of a zendo.

Master: The guide of the traveler (student). Roshi is a better term, if it is used without trying to imply a status.

Maya: Name attributed to Gautama Siddhartha's mother. More importantly, maya is translated as illusion, and is used to describe reality.

Mindfulness: A state of awareness, of oneself and others, as well as nature.

Moksha: In Hindu tradition, the escape from samsara, which can only be attained by a member of the Brahmin caste with a balanced karma.

Mokugyo: An instrument, made of hollowed wood in the shape of a fish. Like the keiso, this is struck with a padded club during sutra chanting in Chinese Buddhist temples. The fish is an important symbol in Zen, since fish never sleep and are forever aware and watchful.

Mondo: Related to the Japanese word mondai, meaning to question, mondo may mean the way of the gate (mon), or to the crest (mon). Each of these connotations fits the purpose of mondo. During mondo the master asks questions quickly, and the student must

respond quickly. This is done to prevent the student from thinking, to allow intuition to control. Used notably in the Rinzai school.
Mo Tse: A philosopher who rebelled against Confucianism, and taught universal love and utilitarianism.
Mu: A negative prefix, somewhat equivalent to "non," "un," or "in." A classical riddle since Master Joshu used it in response to the koan "Does a dog have Buddha nature?" Mu is also a koan used for meditation. Because of its simplicity and that neither intellect nor imagination are fed by it, nor provide a solution for it. It is also used to mean no-thing.
Mujo: The impermanent condition of everything.
Mushin: No mind, spirit, soul, nor intuition.
Mushotoku: The optimum state for Zen practice, in which there is no goal or object, no intention for self gain or profit.

## N
Naisan: An unscheduled and secret visit with a roshi at any time of the day or night, when there are special circumstances to warrant the unscheduled visit.
Nembutsu: "Calling the name." Used by the Pure Land sect, to ritually call the name of Amitabha Buddha, as an assurance of faith that Amitabha will provide a rebirth into the land of the Buddha, the Pure Land.
Nirvana (Nibbana): The ultimate state of awareness, and the penultimate state of harmony. It is second in harmony to para-nirvana.
Niyama: The second element in the path of classical Yoga, meaning disciplines.

## O
Oryoko: The bowls given to a Buddhist upon being ordained, particularly the largest of these bowls that is used for begging and eating. This word means, "that which holds just enough."

## P
Pali: Ancient language used by the Mahayana, because it was the vernacular language.
Paranayama: The fourth element in the path of classical Yoga, meaning breathing control.
Para-nirvana (Pari-nibbana): The ultimate state of harmony within the ultimate state of awareness. Para means death, so this is death while in a state of nirvana, returning the physical being to the cosmos, and escaping samsara.
Patriarch: In Buddhism, the patriarchs are the Dharma heirs, the great masters who have formally received the transmission of Buddha's Dharma. Patriarch is a poor term, since there has also been

female masters, but is commonly used anyway, especially in the West.

Philosophy: The search for and love of wisdom.

Prajna: Essential wisdom. Prajna Paramita is wisdom perfection.

Pratyahara: The fifth element in the path of classical Yoga, meaning the elimination of the outer perceptions.

Pratyekabuddha: Solitary practitioners who attain Buddhahood without a teacher. These are private Buddhas.

Precepts: Teachings regarding personal conduct; rules of conduct, especially for the ordained. Also called kai. In the Mahayana school there are ten precepts that must be avoided: killing, stealing, lying, drinking alcohol or selling alcohol to be drank, speaking badly of others, praising oneself while disparaging others, not willingly giving spiritual or material aid, anger, or disparaging the Three Treasures (Buddha Gautama, the Dharma, and the sangha).

Proselytizing: Actively seeking to convert others to one's own beliefs.

Pure Land: Form of Buddhism that survived the persecution of Buddhism in the ninth century C.E. in China. This school emphasizes meditation to see the Pure Land (the land we go to when we die, a western paradise, purity revealed in enlightenment) and Amitabha Buddha. Founded by Hui-yuan ca. 402 C.E. Oldest and least philosophical school of Mahayana Buddhism in China. Also called: White Lotus sect by Hui Yuan, Ching T'u (in China), and Jodoshu (in Japan).

## **R**

Rahula: Son of Gautama Siddharta and Yasodhara.

Raja: The way to god through psychophysical exercise in Yoga. This is the royal way of Yoga, but not the fastest way to self realization.

Rakusu: A small kolomo/kesa worn during work.

Religion: Derived from the Latin word religio, meaning to bind or bring together. Religion is that which brings people together.

Ren: From Confucianism, ren is the principle of humaneness.

Rinzai: School of Zen emphasizing the use of koans. It is a teacher centered school, where meditation is done facing the center of the room. The Rinzai school was brought to Japan by Eisai.

Roshi: "Venerable teacher." Generally one who presides over a monastery, the master, who gives Zen instruction. This title is best used as a non-title, as the office of Roshi is not one of status, but of being. The roshi can be a layman or laywoman, whose function is to guide disciples, not to dominate, control, or influence the private lives of the disciples.

Ru ja: Chinese name for the school of Confucius (Confucianism).

## S

Saijojo: The form of Zen that emphasizes realization without support, through shikan-taza. This is the form of Zen most emphasized in the Soto school.

Samadhi: A state of higher concentration in meditation. There are three stages in Buddhism (preparation, beginning, and attainment of concentration). Samadhi is the eighth element in the classical path of Yoga, meaning absorption, becoming one with, harmonizing. There are two forms of samadhi in Yoga (with and without support). The greater form of samadhi in Yoga is without support.

Sampai: The prostrating bows performed during practice, where the forehead touches the ground and the hands are held palms up next to the head. The hand gesture is symbolic, according to tradition, of receiving the feet of Buddha. This is a sign of profound respect and reverence, although not necessarily for Buddha or any other thing in particular. It is respect for the self, and a position that teaches humility and impermanence.

Samsara: The endless cycle of reincarnation; transmigration. Literally means to move about continuously.

Samu: Working Zen practice, especially physical labor.

Sangha: A group, who together practice religious Buddhism; a community of Buddhist practitioners. Also used to refer to the Buddhist monastic order.

Sanzen: An interview of a student by a master. Used especially in the Rinzai school.

Satori: A state of consciousness, often associated with enlightenment. Satori is an awareness of Buddha nature, similar to Tao-sheng's concept of enlightenment. In this text satori is placed one step below enlightenment. Satori is essential wisdom (prajna) for the practice of Zen. See also kensho.

Seiza: Traditional Japanese sitting posture, with the buttocks on the heels of the feet, large toes crossed, and a straight posture. This is a typical posture assumed in martial arts dojos.

Shastra: A commentary on a sutra.

Shikan-taza: Meditation without any object, without counting, focus on breathing, nor koans. It is intense sitting, where there is unshakeable conviction that zazen is the actualization, and there is nothing else to gain. At the root, this frame of thought realizes that there is not a struggle involved in the attainment of satori.

Shojo: The Hinayana form of Zen, or Lesser Vehicle. This form, as opposed to the Daijo, is very individualistic, intending to take only the practitioner from maya to nirvana.

Skandha: The five elements that comprise an individual. These are: form (rupam), perception through the senses (vedana), thought (samjna), conformation (samskara), and consciousness (vijnana).

Sodo: A dojo that is used for training monks.

Son: Korean name for Zen.

Sosan: Listening to the general lectures of the roshi, the Dharma talks. This is usually mandatory for beginners, and is done in groups.

Soto: School of Zen emphasizing meditation and formalism. It is a student centered school, where students determine their own koans. Meditation is performed facing the walls of the dojo. This school was brought to Japan by Dogen.

Speech: Any act of communicating a thought, either orally, in writing, by gesticulation, or body language.

Student: In Zen a student is a traveler, one who is practicing Zen under a master or teacher to find self-awareness. The student is really his or her own teacher, though they usually do not know this until they have been enlightened. In this book, student does not mean one who studies Zen academically.

Sunyata: Emptiness or void. Though this sounds negative, sunyata is actually positive, it is an affirmation. Emptiness is not void. Emptiness is not empty. Empty without emptiness.

Sutra (Sutta): Derived from the word to sew, it is a thread of discourse; a discourse given by a master (teacher) to disciples. Literally translated, it is a thread used to string jewels upon. In the Tripitaka the sutras are the portion containing the teachings of Buddha Gautama.

## T

Tada: The state of being absorbed in every moment; is-ness; in the eternal now.

Takuhatsu: The system that is used by Zen monks who are in training, to beg for their food. This is generally done in groups of ten to fifteen. The group goes through the street single-file, chanting "Ho" (meaning Dharma), and sympathizers come down and fill their alms bowls. This is the monks offering of the Dharma and their lives of guardians of the Dharma to the people. According to Zen tradition, the givers should be grateful (Reps & Senzaki, p. 48).

Tan: Wooden platform used for sleeping and meditation, built along the wall of a zendo.

Tanden: See hara.

Tanha: (trishna) The desire for personal fulfillment or gain. Tanha is the second noble truth, the cause of dukkha is tanha (suffering is greed, desire).

Tao: Translated it means the way (Chinese). In the form of the Tao in Taoism, Tao is the way of nature, which is indescribable. For Confucius the Tao is the way of man, society, and government, of

relationships. For Zen, Tao is the way, it is Buddha-nature, Buddha-mind, reality.
Taoism: A philosophy whose origins can be traced back to the seventh century B.C.E.
Tao-sheng: A Buddhist monk, who lived ca. 360-434 C.E. He is credited with founding Ch'an (Zen). See also Bodhidharma.
Tathagata: Name used by Buddha Gautama to refer to himself, meaning "thus come." Some authors feel this is a sign of his enlightened state. I am inclined to recognize this as more like, "This is me, either accept me as I am or not. I do not care." By using this to refer to himself he was humbling his character, and at the same time he was providing a koan.
Te: In Taoism, te is physical power, the power of nature, the cosmos, man, and everything. In Confucianism, te also means compassion (ren). Compassion and power are important together.
Teisho: Orally transmitting the Dharma in the form of a lecture. This is often a formal commentary on a koan, by a master. It is supposed to be non-dualistic, which helps to distinguish it from a Dharma talk.
Theravada: The preferred name for the school sometimes called Hinayana. This is the older school of Buddhism, that emphasizes asceticism; "thera" means elders, thus it is a school reserved for the elders of the faith, whose teachings are presented to future elders committed to asceticism. Prefer to use the Pali language, and adhere closer to Gautama's acts as a bodhisattva.
Thought: The way we process information, both facts and truths.
Three Treasures: (Three Jewels; Tri-ratna) The three central elements or principal features of Buddhism. They are: Buddha Gautama, the Dharma, and the sangha.
Three Worlds: One of Buddhist cosmologies, in which the cosmos is divided into three parts: Desire, Form, and Non-form. The first and last of these three represent attachment to the senses, and are undesirable. Those in the second level have a body but do not cling to the world of illusion and senses. In Zen practice the three worlds are also considered levels or dimensions of consciousness.
T'ien: In Chinese tradition, this is translated as Heaven. T'ien is an important theme in Chinese religion, philosophy, and the Chinese conception of the dynasty and cycle.
Ti-lakkhana: (Tri-laksana) The three aspects or characteristics of existence. These are: anicca, dukkha, and anatta.
Transmission/Transmission of the Lamp: The first Transmission was to Kasyapa, then called Mahakasyapa. The transmission is the receiving of insight. Insight is not given or pursued, it is apprehended.

An Introduction to Zen Thought

Tripitaka: The three baskets, the Buddhist scriptures as one unit. The scriptures are divided into: Vinayapitika-narratives on the establishment and rules of the Sangha; Sutta-pitaka—dialogues of Buddha Gautama; and the Abidhamma-pitaka—where the sutras are reduced and given order by numbers under topic headings.
Truth: That which is believed to be, not necessarily what really is (fact).

## U

Unsui: The novices in a Zen monastery. The word literally means cloud-water. Novices are called this because clouds move about freely, without specific form and unhampered. Water is very powerful, able to wear down even the Earth, but also has a yielding quality. The virtues of clouds and water are desired virtues to the zennist.
Utilitarianism: Belief in the utility of acts; an act must have a benefit in order to be good. Western utilitarianism emphasizes the greatest good for the greatest number of people.

## V

Vajrayana: School of Buddhism practiced in Tibet; in Japan it is practiced as Shingon Buddhism. It is the Diamond Raft/Vehicle/Way. Vajrayana is not discussed in this book. Huston Smith discusses Vajrayana in his book The World's Religions.

## W

Wato: A word, phrase, or other response in answer to a koan.
Wei Wu Wei: Taoist term, literally translated as action inaction, or action non-action.
Wu: Chinese word for mu.

## Y

Yama: The first element of the path of classical Yoga, meaning restraint. In Japanese yama means mountain.
Yasodhara: Wife of Gautama Siddhartha.
Yaza: Zazen done after bedtime in the monastery, which would be after 9 P.M.
Yin and Yang: Principle of polarity in Chinese cosmology, in which the opposite poles eventually blend and become one another in a cosmic connectedness.
Yoga: Tradition that predates Hinduism, and emphasizes meditation for self realization.
Yogi: A practitioner of Yoga.

## Z

Zafu: A cushion used for meditation. The function of the zafu is to raise the buttocks so that the knees are pressed firmly against the ground. During proper meditation the knees should be pushing the Earth down, and the sky (heavens) up. The zafu, in this way, helps to maintain correct posture during meditation, and is also essential to correct posture. Traditionally it is a firm cushion filled with kapok. Any cushion that will raise the buttocks so that the correct posture can be assumed will do, until you can acquire a proper zafu.

Zazen: "sitting practice" to stop thinking; remaining open beyond dualistic, comparative and judgmental thought. Zazen is not an element of the experience of enlightenment, but it is said that zazen is enlightenment. Zazen is done without any goal or object of concentration.

Zazenkai: A one day sesshin, in which the practitioners partake in meditation, listening to Dharma talk and other Zen lectures, and receiving dokusan.

Zen: Literally translated, zen means meditation. Zen is one of four major schools of Buddhism. The other schools are: Mahayana, Theravada, Zen (or Ch'an or Son), and Vajrayana.

Zendo: A place where Zen is practiced. Many formal zendos are only a room. Some may be a building. Others may be a compound. The world is a zendo, as is any place we practice Zen.

Zenji: (Ch'an-shih in Chinese) A highly venerated, greatly respected teacher or master. This is a title usually given after death, though some have had the misfortune of achieving this during life. Yes I do mean misfortune. Titles are not appealing to Zen masters.

# References

Beck, Charlotte Joko. Everyday Zen: love and work. New York: Harper & Row, Publishers, Inc., 1989.

Blakney, R.B. The Way of Life: Lao Tzu. New York: Mentor Books, 1983.

Brandon, S.G.F. Dictionary of Comparative Religion. New York: Charles Scribner's Sons, 1970.

Brinker, Helmut. Zen in the Art of Painting. London: Penguin Books Ltd., 1987.

Bukkyu Dendo Kyokai (Buddhist Promoting Foundation). The Teaching of Buddha. Tokyo, Japan: Kosaido Printing Co. Ltd., 1980.

Chan Wing-tsit. A Source Book in Chinese Philosophy. Princeton: Princeton University Press, 1963.

Cohen, Joan Lebold. Buddha. New York: Delacorte Press, 1970.

Creel, H.G. Chinese Thought: from Confucius to Mao Tse-tung. New York: Mentor Books, 1953.

Deshimaru Taisen. Questions to a Zen Master. New York: Penguin Books USA Inc., 1985.

Doeblin, Alfred. The Living Thoughts of Confucius. Greenwich, Conn.: Fawcett Publications, Inc., 1965.

Dumoulin, Heinrich. Zen Buddhism: A History. Vols. 1 & 2. New York: Macmillan Publishing Company, 1988.

Dunne, Desmond. Yoga: the way to long life and happiness. Funk & Wagnalls, 1967.

Fung Yu-lan. A History of Chinese Philosophy. Vol. 1. Princeton: Princeton University Press, 1959.

Goode, E. Drugs in American Society. New York: McGraw-Hill, Inc., 1993.

Hall, John Whitney. Japan From Prehistory to Modern Times. New York: Delacorte Press, 1970.

Herrigel, Eugen. Zen in the Art of Archery. New York: Vintage Books, 1989.

Hucker, Charles O. China's Imperial Past. Stanford, California: Stanford University Press, 1981.

Hyams, Joe. Zen in the Martial Arts. New York: Bantam, 1982.

Hyers, Conrad. The Laughing Buddha. Wolfeboro, N.H.: Longwood Academic, 1989.

Kapleau, Philip. The Three Pillars of Zen. Garden City, New York: Anchor Press / Doubleday, 1980.

Lao Tzu. Tao Teh Ching. Trans. by John C.H. Wu. Boston: Shambhala, 1990.

Maezumi Hakuyu Taizan and Bernard Tetsugen Glassman. On Zen Practice. Los Angeles: Zen Center of Los Angeles, 1976.

Mascaro, Juan. The Dhammapada. London: Penguin Books, 1973.

Mei Yi-Pao. The Ethical and Political Works of Motse. Vol. II. Westport, Connecticut: Hyperion Press, Inc., 1973.

Mei Yi-Pao. Motse The Neglected Rival of Confucius. Vol. I. Westport, Connecticut: Hyperion Press, Inc., 1973.

Mitchell, Stephen. Tao Te Ching. New York: HarperCollins Publishers, 1988.

Murphey, Rhoads. A History of Asia. New York: HarperCollins Publishers, Inc., 1992.

Nicol, C.W. Moving Zen: Karate as a way to gentleness. New York: Quill, 1982.

Reps, Paul and Nyogen Senzaki. Zen Flesh, Zen Bones: a collection of Zen and pre-Zen writings. Garden City, New York: Anchor Books, 1961.

Ross, Nancy Wilson. Buddhism: a way of life and thought. New York: Vintage Books, 1981.

Ross, Nancy Wilson. The World of Zen. New York: Vintage Books, 1960.

Rottenberg, Annette T. Elements of Argument. 3 ed. Boston: Bedford Books of St. Martin's Press, 1989.

Senzaki Nyogen and Ruth S. McCandless. Buddhism and Zen. San Francisco: North Point Press, 1987.

Smith, Huston. The World's Religions. New York: HarperCollins Publishers, 1991.

Sun Tzu. The Art of War. Trans. by Thomas Cleary. Boston: Shambhala, 1991.

Suzuki Shunryu. Zen Mind, Beginner's Mind. New York: Weatherhill Inc., 1990.

Talbot, Michael. The Holographic Universe. New York: HarperCollins Publishers, 1991.

Trungpa, Chogyam. Meditation in Action. Boston: Shambhala, 1991.

Tseu, Augustus A. The Moral Philosophy of Mo-Tze. Taipei, Taiwan: China Printing, Ltd., 1965.

Ueshiba Moihei. The Art of Peace. Trans. by John Stevens. Boston: Shambhala, 1992.

Waley, Arthur. The Analects of Confucius. New York: Vintage Books, 1989.

Ware, James R. The Sayings of Confucius. New York: Mentor Books, 1955.

Watson, Burton. Basic Writings of Mo Tzu, Hsun Tzu, and Han Fei Tzu. New York: Columbia University Press, 1967.

Watts, Alan W. The Spirit of Zen. New York: Grove Press, 1960.

Wilber, Ken. The Holographic Paradigm and Other Paradoxes. Boston: Shambhala Publications, Inc., 1982.

Zimmerman, J.E. Dictionary of Classical Mythology. New York: Bantam Books, 1971.